Words of Life 2008

Words of Life 2008

Daily Reflections for Your Spirit

Edited by **Caryl Green**

NOVALIS

© 2008 Novalis, Saint Paul University, Ottawa, Canada

Cover design and layout: Audrey Wells
Cover art: Sue Todd (www.suetodd.com)

Business Offices:
Novalis Publishing Inc.
10 Lower Spadina Avenue, Suite 400
Toronto, Ontario, Canada
M5V 2Z2

Novalis Publishing Inc.
4475 Frontenac Street
Montréal, Québec, Canada
H2H 2S2

Phone: 1-800-387-7164
Fax: 1-800-204-4140
E-mail: books@novalis.ca
www.novalis.ca

Cataloguing in Publication data is available from Library and Archives
Canada.

ISBN 978-2-89507-928-6

Printed in Canada.

Today's English Version, © 1966, 1971, 1976, 1979, 1992 by American Bible
Society. All rights reserved. Used by permission.

We acknowledge the financial support of the Government of Canada through
the Book Publishing Industry Development Program (BPIDP) for our publishing
activities.

I would like to welcome you to *Words of Life 2008: Daily Reflections for Your Spirit*. Since its launch in 1998 as a monthly magazine, *Words of Life* has provided readers with readings drawn from Scripture, along with reflections and prayers for every day. This book draws from those reflections and prayers, and is based on the Scripture readings for Year A of the church's lectionary.

Life's stories

The Hebrew and Christian Scriptures tell the stories of individuals and groups searching to recognize and to understand God's presence in their lives. Jean Vanier writes: "Jesus spoke in parables; Hasidic Jews and Sufi teachers tell tales; Hindu scripture is full of stories. Stories seem to awaken energies of love; they tell us great truths in simple personal terms and make us long for light. Stories have a strange power of attraction. When we tell stories, we touch hearts. If we talk about theories or speak about ideas, [people] may assimilate them but the heart remains untouched."*

The reflections in *Words of Life* are based on Scripture *and* on everyday life experiences. They describe how real people continue to seek God in a real way within their lives today and in the world around them. The stories in *Words of Life* describe times when authors have struggled to live according to the teachings of Jesus in matters both large and small. The choice to live with God's Word in their hearts changed not only their own lives, but also the lives of family members, friends and colleagues and the communities in which they live.

---

* Kathryn Spink, *The Miracle, the Message, the Story: Jean Vanier and L'Arche* (Ottawa: Novalis, 2006), 261.

With thanks

I'd like to thank the many people who have contributed their gifts and talents to this publication, especially the authors, editors, proofreaders, photographers and graphic designers. (The names of authors whose reflections appear in this book are listed on page 375.) I'd also like to express my deep appreciation to the many subscribers who, after receiving their final issue of *Words of Life*, wrote to tell me how much they would miss its presence in their lives. You said that you wanted something that would continue to sustain your daily prayer life; it was your feedback and support that made this present book possible. Thank you.

Word Made Flesh

If you are beginning to read this book in January, you will have celebrated the birth of Jesus recently. Many of us struggle to keep alive the spirit of Emmanuel or God-with-us throughout the year. Jesus, as God's Word-Made-Flesh, brings healing to the brokenness we experience within ourselves and in our world. *Words of Life* offers us a still point in our busy lives to be with God's Word on a daily basis. I hope you are able to take a quiet moment with *Words of Life* each day – to centre yourselves in God and to be aware of God working in your lives to transform your burdens into opportunities for change, for growth. And to know the deep peace that God's love brings.

I wish you peace, hope and the knowledge of God's abiding love,

Caryl Green
Editor

We too were slaves of the ruling spirits of the universe before we reached spiritual maturity. But when the right time finally came, God sent his own Son. He came as the son of a human mother and lived under the Jewish Law, to redeem those who were under the Law, so that we might become God's children.

To show that you are his children, God sent the Spirit of his Son into our hearts, the Spirit who cries out, "Father, my Father." So then, you are no longer a slave but a child. And since you are his child, God will give you all that he has for his children.

Galatians 4: 3-7

"...that we might become God's children."

A child's example

When I moved to Toronto a year ago, I was unprepared to cope with the large number of people begging on the streets. It seems that I can't walk a block without encountering people who want a loonie. Sometimes they smell or are drunk; occasionally they're aggressive. After one woman abused me, I began thinking that it was her attitude that led her to the streets.

But then I see the familiar dad and his toddler son. They're approaching a homeless man who's always on the same corner. "There's our friend!" the man tells his son excitedly, and the two give the homeless man food and some coins.

Just as Jesus taught us, this man is teaching his son to love those who seem hard to love.

**God, help me to remember that Jesus loves everyone,
and I am called to do the same.**

The Jewish authorities in Jerusalem sent some priests and Levites to John to ask him, "Who are you?" John did not refuse to answer, but spoke out openly and clearly, saying: "I am not the Messiah...."

"Then tell us who you are," they said. John answered by quoting the prophet Isaiah: "I am 'the voice of someone shouting in the desert: Make a straight path for the Lord to travel!'"

The messengers, who had been sent by the Pharisees, then asked, "If you are not the Messiah nor Elijah nor the Prophet, why do you baptize?" John answered, "I baptize with water, but among you stands the one you do not know. He is coming after me, but I am not good enough even to untie his sandals."

All this happened in Bethany on the east side of the Jordan River, where John was baptizing.   *John 1: 19-28*

> "I am 'the voice of someone shouting in the desert."

Wanted: a desert

Last summer, I had a heavy workload, and our house was overflowing with family and visitors. My sister was visiting from Africa, but we never seemed to get a chance to talk. Finally we rented a canoe and spent an afternoon on the river, and there, in between long bouts of silence, we were able to touch the deep regions of each other's lives.

John describes himself as someone shouting in the desert. If he wanted lots of people to hear his announcement, why didn't he do his shouting on the rooftops or the street corner – or in our kitchen in summertime?

Perhaps I need to go out into the desert, or paddle down the St. Charles River, to prepare my heart for his message.

Lord, teach me to respect my need for the desert.

See how much the Father has loved us! His love is so great that we are called God's children – and so, in fact, we are. This is why the world does not know us: it has not known God. My dear friends, we are now God's children, but it is not yet clear what we shall become. But we know that when Christ appears, we shall be like him, because we shall see him as he really is…. Whoever sins is guilty of breaking God's law, because sin is a breaking of the law. You know that Christ appeared in order to take away sins, and that there is no sin in him. So everyone who lives in union with Christ does not continue to sin.

I John 2: 29; 3: 1-6

"…we are called God's children."

God's child

After my parents died, one of the ways my sorrow and grief revealed itself was through the painful awareness that I was no longer anyone's child. There was no one left who had held me as a baby crying for food, who encouraged me as a child nervously going off to school, who put up with me as an adolescent struggling with the Great Questions of Life, who hoped with me as a young man trying to find his place.

It sounds strange for a middle-aged husband and father to feel like a bereft orphan – but there you have it, strange or not.

So I find John's words comforting and touching. It's reassuring to know that the lonely child, deep inside, is Someone's child.

Your son, Jesus, invited us to call you Abba, Father.
Thank you for your life-giving love.

John was standing with two of his disciples when he saw Jesus walking by. "There is the Lamb of God!" he said. The two disciples heard him say this and went with Jesus. Jesus turned, saw them following him, and asked, "What are you looking for?" They answered, "Where do you live, Rabbi?" (This word means "Teacher.") "Come and see," he answered. So they went with him and saw where he lived, and spent the rest of that day with him.

John 1: 35-42

"...and saw where he lived..."

At home

Jesus invited the curious disciples to see him in his home. How remarkable!

The fact that I am recuperating from surgery made me read this passage differently than I might have otherwise. My illness has forced me see my own home in a different light. No longer is it a place where I welcome other people and make them feel comfortable. Home has become a place where I am my most vulnerable. My hair may not be washed; maybe even the dishes aren't; and a layer of dust is settling over all. To see me at home is inevitably an intimate encounter.

Jesus shared himself in every way with his disciples. He held nothing back: not his thoughts or feelings, not where he lived or who he was.

Dear Jesus, thank you for the gift of yourself.
May I never tire of seeking your company.

The message you heard from the very beginning is this: we must love one another.... This is how we know what love is: Christ gave his life for us. We too, then, ought to give our lives for others! If we are rich and see others in need, yet close our hearts against them, how can we claim that we love God? My children, our love should not be just words and talk; it must be true love, which shows itself in action.

This, then, is how we will know that we belong to the truth.... If our conscience condemns us, we know that God is greater than our conscience and that he knows everything. And so, my dear friends, if our conscience does not condemn us, we have courage in God's presence.

1 John 3: 11-21

> "...which shows itself in action."

Love in action

Several years ago, when my dad retired, he did two extraordinary things. He had already completed thirty years with the company, so his full pension benefit was secured. He set a later retirement date, aiming to pay off an assortment of bills with his remaining paycheques.

Then he learned that Ed, a co-worker (not a friend, just a co-worker), was slated for layoff after twenty-nine-and-a-half years. So my dad did the first extraordinary thing: he bargained with the company to let him retire earlier than he'd planned – in exchange for preserving Ed's job until he, too, had completed thirty years.

Then my dad did the second extraordinary thing: he never spoke of it again. Both what he did – and how quietly he did it – help me understand true love.

**God, let my love move into the world around me,
wherever it is needed.**

Jesus was born in the town of Bethlehem in Judea, during the time when Herod was king. Some men who studied the stars came from the East to Jerusalem and asked, "Where is the baby born to be the king of the Jews? We saw his star, and we have come to worship him...."

Herod called the visitors from the East to a secret meeting and found out from them the exact time the star had appeared. Then he sent them to Bethlehem with these instructions: "Go and make a careful search for the child; and when you find him, let me know, so that I too may go and worship him."

And so they left, and on their way they saw the same star. It went ahead of them until it stopped over the place where the child was.   *Matthew 2: 1-12*

"...when you find·him, let me know..."

Peace in today's world

This story is so familiar, it rolls off my mind like water off a duck's back.

But that metaphor reminds me of watching two mother ducks paddle past each other, each with a brood of ducklings in tow. One unfortunate duckling got confused. It paddled frantically after the wrong mother. She destroyed my notions of the kindliness of nature. She seized the alien in her bill, and held it under water until it drowned.

The same instinct led Herod to see the infant sought by the visitors from the east as a threat to his throne. He wanted them to tell him where to find the baby. And when they didn't, he went on a murderous rampage, slaughtering all the boy children in Bethlehem.

Jesus, I tend to forget that you were born into a world just as troubled as ours. Send us your peace.

Jesus did not stay in Nazareth, but went to live in Capernaum in the territory of Zebulun and Naphtali. This was done to make come true what the prophet Isaiah had said, "Land of Zebulun and land of Naphtali, on the road to the sea, on the other side of the Jordan, Galilee, land of the Gentiles! The people who live in darkness will see a great light. On those who live in the dark land of death the light will shine."

From that time Jesus began to preach his message: "Turn away from your sins, because the kingdom of heaven is near...!"

Jesus went all over Galilee, teaching in the synagogues, preaching the Good News about the kingdom, and healing people who had all kinds of disease and sickness.

Matthew 4: 12-17, 23-25

"...in darkness will see a great light."

True sight

I never met Jane, but I came to know her well through reading her autobiography, which was published after her death at age 49. Although she was blind from her mid-twenties on, she didn't let blindness take over her life. This was a woman who threw great dinner parties, travelled the world, cross-country skied, and even water skied (once!). Oh, and did I mention she was a practising and highly respected physician?

She did all those things and many more without sight. From reading her story, I got the sense that in the midst of her darkness, she could see a great light. I pray for Jane's kind of faith – faith that will help me see the light when darkness falls in my own life.

Lord, sometimes the days and nights are dark.
Let your light shine on me.

When Jesus got out of the boat, he saw this large crowd, and his heart was filled with pity for them.... So he began to teach them many things. When it was getting late, his disciples came to him and said, "Send the people away, and let them go to the nearby farms and villages in order to buy themselves something to eat." "You yourselves give them something to eat," Jesus answered....

Jesus then told his disciples to make all the people divide into groups and sit down.... Then Jesus took the five loaves and the two fish, looked up to heaven, and gave thanks to God. He broke the loaves and gave them to his disciples to distribute to the people. He also divided the two fish among them all. Everyone ate and had enough.

Mark 6: 34-44

"...his heart was filled with pity for them..."

Food for the journey

Jesus and the apostles tried to sneak away to a quiet place to rest, pray and restore themselves. I, too, need to do that on a regular basis! But like the persistent crowds, my family and loved ones can be very creative about pursuing me with their demands and needs. When this happens I may feel angry, resentful and sorry for myself. Like the apostles I may even say, "Go away; take care of yourselves!"

How unlike Jesus! Freely and with compassion he is able to put aside his own needs in order to offer food for both spirits and bodies. He challenges us: "Look within yourselves. Find what you have to offer. Bring it to me. I will bless it, break open its potential and work miracles among you!"

When I have nothing left to give, Lord,
I bring you my emptiness. You know what I need. Feed me!

Jesus made his disciples get into the boat and go ahead of him to Bethsaida…. After saying good-bye to the people, he went away to a hill to pray. When evening came, the boat was in the middle of the lake, while Jesus was alone on land. He saw that his disciples were straining at the oars… so sometime between three and six o'clock in the morning, he came to them, walking on the water. He was going to pass them by, but they saw him walking on the water. "It's a ghost!" they thought, and screamed. They were all terrified when they saw him.

Jesus spoke to them, "Courage! It is I. Don't be afraid!" Then he got into the boat with them, and the wind died down. The disciples were completely amazed.   *Mark 6: 45-52*

"…between three and six o'clock in the morning…"

A lonely time

When I am in turmoil, insomnia hits. Challenges at work, a broken relationship, a desperate friend, a new job prospect – all these can wreak havoc on my precious eight hours of nightly rest. The harder I try to fall asleep, the wider awake I get. By three in the morning I'm frantic, wondering how I'll make it through the next day on so little sleep. It's as if all my insecurities – all the ghosts – descend at the same time, and I am terrified.

Between three and six in the morning is the loneliest time of all: there's no one to call, nothing to do. It's easy to lose hope when this happens, but I know that Jesus is always there, walking toward me, saying, "Courage! It is I."

**Lord, help me find courage
when the world weighs so heavily on my shoulders.**

Jesus went to Nazareth… and on the Sabbath he went as usual to the synagogue. He stood up to read the Scriptures and was handed the book of the prophet Isaiah…. "The Spirit of the Lord is upon me, because he has chosen me to bring good news to the poor. He has sent me to proclaim liberty to the captives and recovery of sight to the blind, to set free the oppressed and announce that the time has come when the Lord will save his people."

All the people in the synagogue had their eyes fixed on him, as he said, "This passage of scripture has come true today, as you heard it being read."

They were all well impressed with him and marvelled at the eloquent words that he spoke.   *Luke 4: 14-22*

> "They marvelled at the eloquent words that he spoke."

True to oneself

School concerts are wonderful events. Excitement fills the gym as the young performers parade their gifts. Each act is warmly received by an appreciative audience.

Now and then, there appears a young soul, so true in voice, dancing or acting, that the entire audience becomes not only attentive, but riveted to the stage. A person's very spirit is being offered; we are privileged to witness that moment. "My gosh, wasn't that Jim and Susan's daughter?" we say as we file out.

Authenticity is a show-stopper in any era. Jesus' spirit rang as true as gold when he spoke among them. No false humility, no pretence. It was stunning to watch. But then again, being completely what God created us to be is always stunning.

God, let me be true to your gift
so that the world may see you in all that I do.

Once Jesus was in a town where there was a man who was suffering from a dreaded skin disease. When he saw Jesus, he threw himself down and begged him, "Sir, if you want to, you can make me clean!"

Jesus reached out and touched him. "I do want to," he answered. "Be clean!" At once the disease left the man. Jesus ordered him, "Don't tell anyone, but go straight to the priest and let him examine you; then to prove to everyone that you are cured, offer the sacrifice as Moses ordered."

But the news about Jesus spread all the more widely, and crowds of people came to hear him and be healed from their diseases. But he would go away to lonely places, where he prayed.   *Luke 5: 12-16*

> "Sir, if you want to, you can make me clean!"

In search of healing

Often when I want something, I pray, "God, I need…" or, "God, if it's your will, please…" But if I'm truly honest, I must admit that it's me wanting God to do my will! How hard it is to let go… of trying to control the outcome of a meeting; of determining how a relationship will develop; of feeling responsible for the choices my children make in life.

The unclean man asks with such trust, "If you want to, you can make me clean!" And Jesus responds, bringing healing through his loving touch.

How I yearn to be healed of the hurts that hold me captive. Their scars have become so familiar they now define me. Can I place myself in God's hands – totally – believing in God's desire to heal, to make all things whole again?

God, help me to turn to you when I feel trapped by my hurts. Help me to believe that your love can set me free.

Some of John's disciples began arguing with a Jew about the matter of ritual washing. So they went to John and told him, "Teacher, you remember the man who was with you on the east side of the Jordan, the one you spoke about? Well, he is baptizing now, and everyone is going to him!"

John answered, "No one can have anything unless God gives it. You yourselves are my witnesses that I said, 'I am not the Messiah, but I have been sent ahead of him.' The bridegroom is the one to whom the bride belongs; but the bridegroom's friend, who stands by and listens, is glad when he hears the bridegroom's voice. This is how my own happiness is made complete. He must become more important while I become less important."   *John 3: 22-30*

> "...while I become less important."

A team player

I guess we all like to grab the limelight. At least some of us do. All right, I do.

And here is John – with the limelight and the followers, the adoring fans – and he willingly gives it all away. Surely he must have been tempted to hold onto some of it.

I remember my good coaches. They taught us what all wise coaches teach: that individual glory, individual goals must not interfere with team goals. Some never learn this lesson; not everyone is like John the Baptist.

The people I most admire know this. The good that they do, they do for others, and not simply to show others how good they are. Sometimes it's hard for me to stand aside, to think of others first. That's when I need to try to follow John's example.

Dear Lord, let me accept my place in the grand scheme of things, and to step aside to let you in.

A t that time Jesus arrived from Galilee and came to John at the Jordan to be baptized by him. But John tried to make him change his mind. "I ought to be baptized by you," John said, "and yet you have come to me!" But Jesus answered him, "Let it be so for now. For in this way we shall do all that God requires." So John agreed.

As soon as Jesus was baptized, he came up out of the water. Then heaven was opened to him, and he saw the Spirit of God coming down like a dove and lighting on him. Then a voice said from heaven, "This is my own dear Son, with whom I am pleased."

Matthew 3: 13-17

"This is my own dear Son, with whom I am pleased."

My own, dear child

I have a son now, and a daughter, too! When I read, "This is my own dear Son...," something happens inside me. A small, joyful pain shakes me – just for a second.

A friend, a Sikh, shows this same emotion when I ask about his grandchildren; and Arnaituk, an Inuk, as he looks at his pregnant wife; and Jamal from Libya, as he speaks wistfully of his beloved daughter, Zeinab, and his wife who lost her life bringing Zeinab into the world: "Incha Allah," or "As God wills."

We all are united by this interior spark. In my life, when things grow dark, this spark lights the way for me. For I know it is the love of God that is still glowing in this troubled world.

**God, may I always be thankful for the gift of love
that I have received.**

Jesus went to Galilee and preached the Good News from God. "The right time has come," he said, "and the kingdom of God is near! Turn away from your sins and believe the Good News!"

As Jesus walked along the shore of Lake Galilee, he saw two fishermen, Simon and his brother Andrew, catching fish with a net. Jesus said to them, "Come with me, and I will teach you to catch people." At once they left their nets and went with him.

He went a little farther on and saw two other brothers, James and John, the sons of Zebedee. They were in their boat getting their nets ready. As soon as Jesus saw them, he called them; they left their father Zebedee in the boat with the hired men and went with Jesus.

Mark 1: 14-20

"At once they left their nets and went with him."

Follow me!

I've never dropped everything to follow God. I like to think I could, but would I really walk away from my family, my home and all the things that make my life comfortable?

I've had some hints of God's call to follow him. I've stayed up all night to comfort my child when she had a frightening nightmare. I've given my time and energy to protest injustices happening in my community. But there's always a point where I seem to draw the line and say, "That's as far as I go. That's enough!"

But perhaps I don't need to leave everything behind. Perhaps I am to follow Jesus in my everyday tasks: caring for my children at home, and being attentive to others at work and in my community.

God, you are the one that I want to follow.
Help me do this at home, at work and at play.

The people who heard Jesus were amazed at the way he taught, for he wasn't like the teachers of the Law; instead, he taught with authority.

Just then a man with an evil spirit came into the synagogue and screamed, "What do you want with us, Jesus of Nazareth? Are you here to destroy us? I know who you are – you are God's holy messenger!" Jesus ordered the spirit, "Be quiet, and come out of the man!"

The evil spirit shook the man hard, gave a loud scream, and came out of him. The people were all so amazed that they started saying to one another, "What is this? Is it some kind of new teaching? This man has authority to give orders to the evil spirits, and they obey him!"

Mark 1: 21-28

"…he taught with authority."

Loving authority

A young boy was very confused. His feelings about his father's death were messing up his life. When he felt scared, he'd lash out in anger; when he felt sad or alone, he'd push away those who loved him most. His mother turned to the medical professionals for help.

Various doctors agreed that the young boy should be medicated, even hospitalized for "behaviour modification," in order to silence the "evil spirit" that seemed to possess him at times. But his mother questioned the wisdom of the doctors' advice.

One day the young boy met with a psychologist who listened, truly listened, to him. As the young boy talked, all the fears and sadness and anger, kept inside for so long, were released. Experience and authority, combined with compassion and caring, helped to heal that young boy.

Thank you, Lord, for those who speak with loving authority, bringing healing to our many hurts.

One night Eli, who was now almost blind, was sleeping in his own room; Samuel was sleeping in the sanctuary. Before dawn, the Lord called Samuel. He answered, "Yes, sir!" and ran to Eli and said, "You called me, and here I am." But Eli answered, "I didn't call you; go back to bed." So Samuel went back to bed.

The Lord called Samuel again… [and then] a third time. He got up, went to Eli, and said, "You called me, and here I am." Then Eli realized that it was the Lord who was calling the boy, so he said to him, "Go back to bed; and if he calls you again, say, 'Speak, Lord, your servant is listening.'"

The Lord came and stood there, and called as he had before, "Samuel! Samuel!" Samuel answered, "Speak; your servant is listening."

1 Samuel 3: 1-10, 19-20

"Speak, Lord, your servant is listening."

God in the silence

I've never been confused by a voice calling to me in the night. Rather, I was called by a silence that refused to speak. Filled with a hunger for God's presence, I tasted only God's absence. And, like Samuel, I was at a loss for how to respond.

Father McGonigle was my Eli. On the first day of class he said that Christian spirituality involved reflecting on the experience of God's presence – or the experience of God's absence. And finally, to this silent hunger that was consuming me, I said, "Speak, Lord, your servant is listening."

The silence has not lessened, but because Father McGonigle invited me to address this silence with hope, it has become for me a silence that is holy.

God, your call comes in so many ways!
Give me ears, and a heart, to hear your call.

Come to our aid! Because of your constant love, save us!
But now you have rejected us and let us be defeated;
you no longer march out with our armies.
You made us run from our enemies,
and they took for themselves what was ours.
Our neighbours see what you did to us,
and they mock us and laugh at us.
You have made us a joke among the nations;
they shake their heads at us in scorn.
Wake up, Lord! Why are you asleep?
Rouse yourself! Don't reject us forever!
Why are you hiding from us?
Don't forget our suffering and trouble!

Psalm 44: 9-10, 13-14, 23-24

"Don't forget our suffering and trouble!"

Hope amidst despair

My life often reads like a series of bad luck stories! Last year, in the space of one month, thieves broke into my house, one of my children had a near-drowning experience and another dislocated his knee cap, and then, to top it all, my house was hit by lightning! At times it seemed more than I could bear.

But then my neighbour offered to help repair the damage caused by the lightning. A camp counsellor spent extra time to help my child overcome his fear of water. A co-worker offered to drive my other child to his physiotherapy appointments.

In the midst of my despair, I am lifted up by these signs of love and compassion. Truly, God's constant love is there to save me!

**Lord, in my moments of despair, help me turn to you –
knowing your love will carry me through the dark times.**

25

Jesus went back to Capernaum…. So many people came together that there was no room left, not even out in front of the door. Jesus was preaching the message to them when four men arrived, carrying a paralyzed man to Jesus. Because of the crowd, however, they could not get the man to him. So they made a hole in the roof right above the place where Jesus was. When they had made an opening, they let the man down, lying on his mat. Seeing how much faith they had, Jesus said to the paralyzed man, "My son, your sins are forgiven…. I tell you, get up, pick up your mat, and go home!"

While they all watched, the man got up, picked up his mat, and hurried away. They were all completely amazed and praised God.   *Mark 2: 1-12*

"…four men arrived, carrying a paralyzed man to Jesus."

Friends!

Would the paralyzed man have made it to Jesus without four friends to carry him? What friends they are! Strong enough to share carrying burdens that paralyze, without seeing their friend as the burden; determined enough to find a way when the going gets tough; with unwavering faith in the healer and in their friend's desire to be healed. They understand that their part is to help their friend before the face of Jesus and then surrender him to the healing voice. They would never jealously think "How dare he?" as the gifts of forgiveness and healing liberate their friend. I imagine these friends dancing in the streets, waiting to receive and rejoice with the one healed.

Oh, to have and to be such a friend!

God, help me to be a true friend to those with whom I share my life. May we together rejoice in your love.

A crowd came to Jesus, and he started teaching them. As he walked along, he saw a tax collector, Levi son of Alphaeus, sitting in his office. Jesus said to him, "Follow me." Levi got up and followed him.

Later on Jesus was having a meal in Levi's house. A large number of tax collectors and other outcasts was following Jesus, and many of them joined him and his disciples at the table. Some teachers of the Law, who were Pharisees, saw that Jesus was eating with these out-casts and tax collectors, so they asked his disciples, "Why does he eat with such people?"

Jesus heard them and answered, "People who are well do not need a doctor, but only those who are sick. I have not come to call respectable people, but outcasts."

Mark 2: 13-17

"I have not come to call respectable people, but outcasts."

Beyond appearances

In a world that is so complex and so unclear, how we want structures to tell us who we are and what we should do!

The law told the Pharisees who they were and what they were to do. And here is Jesus challenging, questioning, breaking the mold… again. Making it difficult and confusing. Making it real. And today, I am faced with the "outsiders," the ones who don't fit in. How easy it is to close myself off, to protect my little world. Maybe the great challenge in a pluralistic society is to live by my chosen values, but not divide the world into "us and them." To accept the unfamiliar and even the unsettling ways of others. To see beyond the external. To see the person.

God, help me live Jesus' challenge to reach out to those in need, rather than to stand in judgment.

J ohn said, "There is the Lamb of God, who takes away the sin of the world! This is the one I was talking about when I said, 'A man is coming after me, but he is greater than I am, because he existed before I was born.' I did not know who he would be, but I came baptizing with water in order to make him known to the people of Israel."

And John gave this testimony: "I saw the Spirit come down like a dove from heaven and stay on him. I still did not know that he was the one, but God, who sent me to baptize with water, had said to me, 'You will see the Spirit come down and stay on a man; he is the one who baptizes with the Holy Spirit.'"

John 1: 29-34

"I did not know who he would be..."

A follower of Jesus

I don't think I have much faith. I call myself a Christian, all right, but I'm plagued by questions and doubts, and often wonder what the point is. Sometimes the whole thing seems downright embarrassing.

I usually think that those who knew Jesus weren't faced with my "modern" situation. Being a follower was pretty clearcut then. After all, there he was. People could make up their minds based on what they heard and saw right before their eyes.

But not John. He spent his life baptizing people, living in the desert, and eating locusts, for heaven's sake. And all for someone who not only wasn't there, but for someone he didn't even know. Hmmm. This "leap of faith" idea may not be such a modern concept after all.

**Lord, give me the courage of John,
who saw in you God's promise.**

On one occasion the followers of John the Baptist and the Pharisees were fasting. Some people came to Jesus and asked him, "Why is it that the disciples of John the Baptist and the disciples of the Pharisees fast, but yours do not?"

Jesus answered, "Do you expect the guests at a wedding party to go without food? Of course not! As long as the bridegroom is with them, they will not do that. But the day will come when the bridegroom will be taken away from them, and then they will fast.

"No one uses a piece of new cloth to patch up an old coat, because the new patch will shrink and tear off some of the old cloth, making an even bigger hole. Nor does anyone pour new wine into used wineskins, because the wine will burst the skins, and both the wine and the skins will be ruined. Instead, new wine must be poured into fresh wineskins."

Mark 2: 18-22

"Do you expect the guests... to go without food?"

Celebrate God's love

Last summer I worked hard all day, and would come home to find the rest of my family relaxing, horsing around, enjoying each other's company – as families should do when they get the chance to be together. But instead I got resentful. Why should I be off working hard, and on my own, while they could relax and have fun together?

Jesus knew that people lived by strict religious laws before he came, and that they would probably make a whole bunch more laws after he left. It seems to be a strong human impulse, if not a necessity.

Jesus gently reminds me that there comes a moment when I am called to relax the rigours of self-discipline, and fully celebrate the reality of God's intimacy with me.

**Lord, give me speed and grace
when switching gears from work to play.**

T he Lord said to Samuel, "How long will you go on grieving over Saul? I have rejected him as king of Israel. But now get some olive oil and go to Bethlehem, to a man named Jesse, because I have chosen one of his sons to be king...." Samuel did what the Lord told him to do....

Jesse brought seven of his sons to Samuel. And Samuel said to him, "Do you have any more sons?" Jesse answered, "There is still the youngest, but he is out taking care of the sheep."

"Tell him to come here," Samuel said. "We won't offer the sacrifice until he comes." So Jesse sent for him. He was a handsome, healthy young man, and his eyes sparkled. The Lord said to Samuel, "This is the one – anoint him!" Samuel took the olive oil and anointed David in front of his brothers.   *1 Samuel 16: 1-13*

> "...and anointed David in front of his brothers."

Marked for life

There's something a little embarrassing about being singled out. Especially when you're a teenager, desperately trying to belong to the group.

Through most of my younger years, I was a teacher's pet. If I got singled out, it was usually for some kind of commendation. Occasionally, I got disciplined. The cause of this special attention didn't really matter. Good or bad, the effect was the same – to isolate me from my peers.

By all accounts, young David was quite self-confident. But I wonder, sometimes, how he felt about being singled out in front of his brothers. Did he, like Joseph, want to lord it over them? Did he sense that they resented his favoured status? Did he retreat to his fields in relief?

I don't want to live in the limelight, Lord.
Please let me serve you in the comfortable shadows.

David took his shepherd's stick and then picked up five smooth stones and put them in his bag. With his sling ready, he went out to meet Goliath....

When Goliath got a good look at David, he was filled with scorn for him because he was just a nice, good-looking boy. He said, "What's that stick for? Do you think I'm a dog?" ... David answered, "You are coming against me with sword, spear and javelin, but I come against you in the name of the Lord Almighty, the God of the Israelite armies...."

David reached into his bag and took out a stone, which he slung at Goliath. It hit him on the forehead and broke his skull, and Goliath fell face downward on the ground. And so, without a sword, David defeated and killed Goliath with a sling and a stone!

I Samuel 17: 32-33, 37, 40-51

> "...without a sword, David defeated and killed Goliath..."

Strength in weakness

"How foolish and idealistic," my friend commented, after watching a movie set in Soweto, South Africa, featuring black schoolchildren attempting to revolt against the apartheid regime. "Those children didn't stand a chance against the ones with all the power."

I wasn't so sure. I noted the children's strong spirit and insatiable desire for freedom for their people. They drew inspiration and strength from their hero Nelson Mandela who endured more than twenty-five years of imprisonment while his spirit remained free.

Eventually South Africa's black people were able to mobilize the few strengths they possessed – solidarity with one another, faith and endurance – and to sling these like rocks into the forehead of the monster called "apartheid." The rest is history, and the world rejoiced.

**Lord, when I fight powers that seem stronger than I am,
give me the wisdom and courage that you gave to David.**

A large crowd followed Jesus…. They had come from Galilee, from Judea, from Jerusalem, from the territory of Idumea, from the territory on the east side of the Jordan, and from the region around the cities of Tyre and Sidon. All these people came to Jesus because they had heard of the things he was doing. The crowd was so large that Jesus told his disciples to get a boat ready for him, so that the people would not crush him. He had healed many people, and all the sick kept pushing their way to him in order to touch him. And whenever the people who had evil spirits in them saw him, they would fall down before him and scream, "You are the Son of God!" Jesus sternly ordered the evil spirits not to tell anyone who he was.

Mark 3: 7-12

"…all the sick kept pushing their way to him…"

So many needs

The press of the crowds, the noise, the pushing. Everyone needing something from Jesus: to be near him, to touch, to be healed…. How it must have weighed on him at times. How alone he must have felt: no one understanding what he understood; no one really knowing who he was, what his life held.

Sometimes I feel weighed down with responsibility, with the needs of others. Often it's hardest when the demands are so real, so legitimate. And I have only so much and have to say "no."

How can I do it all? I am so small and the needs I experience are so great. One of the challenges is to take life "day by day…." Another challenge is to do what is possible and to accept help when it is offered by those who care.

Dear God, let me do what I can and be content.
Send me friends to replenish me when I need it.

L ast of all, Jesus appeared to the eleven disciples as they were eating. He scolded them, because they did not have faith and because they were too stubborn to believe those who had seen him alive. He said to them, "Go throughout the whole world and preach the gospel to all people. Whoever believes and is baptized will be saved; whoever does not believe will be condemned. Believers will be given the power to perform miracles: they will drive out demons in my name; they will speak in strange tongues; if they pick up snakes or drink any poison, they will not be harmed; they will place their hands on sick people, and these will get well."

Mark 16: 14-18

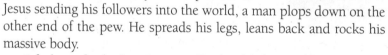

"Go… and preach the gospel to all people."

Go to all people

Rainbow colours filter through the stained glass window. As I study the depiction of Jesus sending his followers into the world, a man plops down on the other end of the pew. He spreads his legs, leans back and rocks his massive body.

I feel repulsed when I notice that he drools. Our eyes meet, he grins, ducks his head, and glances away. Does he sense rejection? I think of Jon, my grandson with special needs. This man could be the adult version of Jon someday, precious in his own way.

"Good morning. Nice to see you," I say. I lean over to shake his outstretched hand and notice his eyes are brown, just like Jesus' eyes in the window above. "Hello," he responds. "Beautiful day, isn't it?"

**Father, forgive. You say to reach out to everyone
and I hesitate before I touch the person next to me.**

I give thanks to God, whom I serve with a clear conscience…. I thank him as I remember you always in my prayers night and day. I remember your tears, and I want to see you very much, so that I may be filled with joy. I remember the sincere faith you have, the kind of faith that your grandmother Lois and your mother Eunice also had. I am sure that you have it also. For this reason I remind you to keep alive the gift that God gave you when I laid my hands on you. For the Spirit that God has given us does not make us timid; instead, his Spirit fills us with power, love, and self-control…. Take your part in suffering for the Good News, as God gives you the strength for it.

2 Timothy 1: 1-8

"…I remember you always in my prayers night and day."

Prayer

A group of us, all men in our sixties, sat around a campfire discussing our lives. John had had a stroke that left him with no feeling in his right side. Initially, it was paralyzed, but gradually he regained movement. "It really made a difference, knowing that all those people out there were praying for me," he said. "And the effect carried on, even after they stopped actually praying for me."

Numerous studies support his claim. Prayer works, even if we don't know how. I like that – it means that my good wishes can actively help those I care about.

But the other side is also true. If I have negative thoughts, they may have a harmful effect on someone else.

**Lord, if I desire only the best for each person,
then all my life can become a prayer.**

A s Jesus walked along the shore of Lake Galilee, he saw two brothers who were fishermen, Simon (called Peter) and his brother Andrew, catching fish in the lake with a net. Jesus said to them, "Come with me, and I will teach you to catch people." At once they left their nets and went with him.

He went on and saw two other brothers, James and John, the sons of Zebedee. They were in their boat with their father Zebedee, getting their nets ready. Jesus called them, and at once they left the boat and their father, and went with him.

Jesus went all over Galilee, teaching in the synagogues, preaching the Good News about the kingdom and healing people who had all kinds of disease and sickness.

Matthew 4: 12-23

"Come with me, and I will teach you to catch people."

Life with Jesus

Were Simon and Andrew eager to leave their nets – and those long hours of back-breaking work that brought so little return? Did Jesus' offer seem an escape from the hard life they knew?

Life with Jesus, however, must have had its own share of challenges. The "catch" they would bring aboard – the flotsam and jetsam found along the roads and in villages – couldn't be tossed back.

At times I'd like the chance to leave the drudgery of my life. Another line of work or a new relationship seem to offer a chance to try something different and exciting. Yet my work – whether it be editing manuscripts or teaching my children life skills – is my opportunity to make God's love visible in my little corner of the world.

God, help me to recognize my daily opportunities to experience your love and to reveal your loving presence to others.

I n a vision long ago you said
to your faithful servants,
"I have given help
to a famous soldier;
I have given the throne to one
I chose from the people.
I have made my servant
David king
by anointing him with holy oil.
My strength will always be
with him,
my power will make him
strong.

His enemies will never succeed
against him;
the wicked will not defeat him.
I will crush his foes
and kill everyone
who hates him.
I will love him
and be loyal to him;
I will make him
always victorious.
I will extend his kingdom
from the Mediterranean
to the Euphrates River."

Psalm 89: 19-25

"I will crush his foes…"

God on our side?

Does history bear out this belief – that God will side with the good
and crush the evil? Or does it say more about us – about how we like
to think we are the "good guys," and that God is on our side?

I remember the first time this concept struck me as odd. A football game: both teams asking the same God to help them win the
game. And now, at this time in our world's history: two sides both believing that God is on their side; both sides asking God to help them
massacre the other, to give them the power to crush their foes.

But Jesus goes meekly to his ignominious criminal's death. No
cries to God for power. I wonder, God, what do these cries for power
have to do with you?

**Dear God, may I never think that I own you,
and can turn you against my enemies.**

Then Jesus' mother and brothers arrived. They stood outside the house and sent in a message, asking for him. A crowd was sitting around Jesus, and they said to him, "Look, your mother and your brothers and sisters are outside, and they want you."

Jesus answered, "Who is my mother? Who are my brothers?" He looked at the people sitting around him and said, "Look! Here are my mother and my brothers! Whoever does what God wants is my brother, my sister, my mother."

Mark 3: 31-35

"Here are my mother and my brothers!"

Frank, my brother

When we opened our family restaurant, my husband and I were warned about Frank: "Don't let him in. He's a nuisance, and he'll drive away customers." Frank was well known in town: always on the street; hitch-hiking just for something to do, just to have someone listen to him. But we welcomed Frank, the way we welcomed everyone else.

I soon learned Frank's story as he sat drinking his coffee and drawing pictures on any scrap of paper he could find. Frank spent hours in our restaurant and, over the years, became our friend.

When my husband died, Frank came and sat at the funeral home all afternoon and drew me a picture of a rose. Frank helped me to look beyond the surface, to find the gem hidden within people. I consider Frank my brother.

Lord, teach me to take the time to listen to others, to discover your presence in them.

Jesus used parables to teach them many things, saying to them: "Listen! Once there was a man who went out to sow grain. As he scattered the seed in the field, some of it fell along the path, and the birds came and ate it up. Some of it fell on rocky ground, where there was little soil. The seeds soon sprouted, because the soil wasn't deep. Then, when the sun came up, it burned the young plants; and because the roots had not grown deep enough, the plants soon dried up. Some of the seed fell among thorn bushes, which grew up and choked the plants, and they didn't bear grain. But some seeds fell in good soil, and the plants sprouted, grew, and bore grain: some had thirty grains, others sixty, and others one hundred." *Mark 4: 1-20*

"Once there was a man who went out to sow grain."

God's grace

"Farmers understand seeding," a preacher once told me. "That's why the 'Parable of the Sower' is so meaningful to them."

I can't accept that. What kind of farmer, having protected next year's seed from rats and mice all winter, scatters it among the rocks and thorns and on paths? Farmers treasure their seed. No farmer would waste seed on the Trans Canada Highway. Or toss it into a ditch. Or fling it over the bare bluffs of the Rockies, on the chance that some seed might take root, and grow. Only a child would scatter seed so wildly, so exuberantly.

And that, I believe, is what the parable is really about. It's not about seeds or soil or results at all. It's about grace. God's grace. God's exuberant, uncalculating grace, scattered wildly for anyone and everyone.

Dear God, thank you for letting some of your seed fall on me, unworthy as I am.

King David went into the Tent of the Lord's presence, sat down and prayed, "Sovereign Lord, I am not worthy of what you have already done for me, nor is my family. Yet now you are doing even more, Sovereign Lord; you have made promises about my descendants in the years to come. And you let a man see this, Sovereign Lord! What more can I say to you! You know me, your servant. It was your will and purpose to do this; you have done all these great things in order to instruct me. How great you are, Sovereign Lord! There is none like you; we have always known that you alone are God. There is no other nation on earth like Israel, whom you rescued from slavery to make them your own people."

2 Samuel 7: 18-29

"I am not worthy…"

A merciful love

David was the best of men, and the worst of men. To me, he is most likeable in this passage where he humbly acknowledges that he is unworthy of everything God has done for him.

In his youth, David seduced Bathsheba and then arranged for the death of her husband so he could marry her. His excesses were legendary. Yet God designated him and his descendants as the chosen line from whom which Jesus would come.

I once read that God is closer to sinners than to saints because he holds each person by a string. When a person sins, the string breaks and God has to retie it, making a knot and bringing that person a little bit closer to him. So it must have been with David.

Have mercy on me, Lord, for I too am a sinner.
Draw me ever closer to your love.

One day, David got up from his nap and went to the palace roof. As he walked around up there, he saw a woman taking a bath in her house. She was very beautiful. So he sent a messenger to find out who she was, and learned that she was Bathsheba, the daughter of Eliam and the wife of Uriah the Hittite. David sent messengers to get her; they brought her to him and he made love to her.... Afterward she discovered that she was pregnant....

David wrote a letter to Joab and sent it by Uriah. He wrote: "Put Uriah in the front line, where the fighting is heaviest, then retreat and let him be killed." So while Joab was besieging the city, he sent Uriah to a place where he knew the enemy was strong. The enemy troops came out of the city and fought Joab's forces; some of David's officers were killed, and so was Uriah.   *2 Samuel 11: 1-17*

> "David sent messengers to get her..."

How long?

King David gets the wife of one of his soldiers pregnant, orders that soldier to the front lines where he will be killed, and then takes her as his own wife. David, who has the capacity to act as ruthlessly as any contemporary warlord, then repents and is forgiven, although it costs him an infant son. His stolen bride, however, is still little more than property. Nobody even bothers to ask her how she feels about the situation.

Three thousand years later, women continue to have their problems among God's people. Today's church is largely supported by women who are working for the good of a church that still denies them complete equality. How much longer must women wait?

**Lord, we pray that you inspire our leaders
to remove the last vestiges of discrimination against women.**

The Holy Spirit was with [Simeon] and had assured him that he would not die before he had seen the Lord's promised Messiah. Led by the Spirit, Simeon went into the Temple. When the parents brought the child Jesus into the Temple to do for him what the Law required, Simeon took the child in his arms and gave thanks to God: "Now, Lord, you have kept your promise, and you may let your servant go in peace. With my own eyes I have seen your salvation, which you have prepared in the presence of all peoples...."

There was a very old prophet, a widow named Anna.... She never left the Temple; day and night she worshipped God, fasting and praying. That very same hour she arrived and gave thanks to God and spoke about the child to all who were waiting for God to set Jerusalem free.   *Luke 2: 22-40*

"...and you may let your servant go in peace."

Go in peace

Old Simeon saw Jesus, and felt his life was now complete. To skeptical minds like mine, the timing seems too pat, too coincidental. But I remember visiting Mrs. Powell in hospital. She was so ill she couldn't speak. I wasn't even sure she knew I was there. I held her hand, muttered a few words, and fled, feeling utterly helpless and useless.

But she refused to die. Until her daughter's wedding. Then, and only then, she let go of life, and slipped away.

The human spirit is remarkably tenacious. If Mrs. Powell could stay alive by sheer force of will until her daughter was married, I see no reason why Simeon couldn't hang on until he saw the promised Messiah.

**I'm a little jealous of Simeon, Anna and Mrs. Powell.
I wish I knew what would make my life complete.**

Now remember what you were, my friends, when God called you. From the human point of view few of you were wise or powerful or of high social standing. God purposely chose what the world considers nonsense in order to shame the wise, and he chose what the world considers weak in order to shame the powerful. He chose what the world looks down on and despises and thinks is nothing, in order to destroy what the world thinks is important.... But God has brought you into union with Christ Jesus, and God has made Christ to be our wisdom. By him we are put right with God; we become God's holy people and are set free. So then, as the scripture says, "Whoever wants to boast must boast of what the Lord has done."   *I Corinthians I: 26-31*

> "God chose what the world considers weak…"

God's chosen one

We just celebrated my mother-in-law's eightieth birthday. People came from all corners of the country. They weren't asked to come; when they heard, they asked if they could come. There was singing and laughter into the wee hours.

My mother-in-law is not rich or powerful. Never was. Not highly educated, in the formal sense. She is not of high social standing. But, how many eighty-year-olds have people coming thousands of miles – or teenaged grandsons missing the year's first football game – to come to their birthday?

Why? She is humble, accepts people as they are, and puts others first. She finds joy in little things. She doesn't seek what the world says she should, but is thankful for what she has.

Dear God, help me be more like my mother-in-law.

I am not afraid of the thousands of enemies
who surround me on every side.
I have so many enemies, Lord, so many who turn against me!
They talk about me and say, "God will not help him."
But you, O Lord, are always my shield from danger;
you give me victory and restore my courage.
I call to the Lord for help, and from his sacred hill he answers me.
I lie down and sleep, and all night long the Lord protects me.

Psalm 3: 1-6

"...all night long the Lord protects me."

Alone in God

As a child, I needed a light left on in my room or else I couldn't fall
asleep. Growing up, I came to feel confident that I could deal with
any "demons" the darkness brought my way. As I've grown older, the
darkness has begun, once again, to gather some of its old strength
and disturb my sleep.

But now, rather than leave a light on in my room, I have learned
to give the darkness over to God. The times that I do lie awake
– wrestling with the darkness in my life – are when I remind myself
that I am never alone.

This prayer-thought has brought me a wonderful peace and many
restful nights that truly refresh me in body and in spirit.

**Lord, let the light of your presence shine
in all my dark corners, and bring me peace.**

There was a woman who had suffered terribly from severe bleeding for twelve years.... She had heard about Jesus, so she came in the crowd behind him, saying to herself, "If I just touch his clothes, I will get well."

She touched his cloak, and her bleeding stopped at once; and she had the feeling inside herself that she was healed of her trouble. At once Jesus knew that power had gone out of him, so he turned around in the crowd and asked, "Who touched my clothes?" ... The woman realized what had happened to her, so she came, trembling with fear, knelt at his feet, and told him the whole truth. Jesus said to her, "My daughter, your faith has made you well. Go in peace, and be healed of your trouble." *Mark 5: 21-43*

> "...she was healed of her trouble."

A love that heals

When I try to imagine how the woman with the hemorrhage felt as Jesus turned and spoke to her, I remember my time in Nepal. The villagers considered me too thin (a sign of poverty), and my hair an ugly brown (a sign of malnutrition). Some wouldn't invite me to their house because I would ritually defile it. I was unlucky enough to be childless (therefore useless); I didn't know how to plant rice seedlings, carry a water jar on my head, or weave a straw mat.

But I experienced love, and felt it all the more deeply because I was stripped of cultural privilege. Like Jesus' love for this woman – who had lost all wealth and social standing – it was a love that changed my insides forever.

Break down the barriers I erect,
Lord, so your love can get through and heal me.

"**M**ake certain you do not perform your religious duties in public so that people will see what you do. If you do these things publicly, you will not have any reward from your Father in heaven.

"So when you give something to a needy person, do not make a big show of it, as the hypocrites do in the houses of worship and on the streets. They do it so that people will praise them. I assure you, they have already been paid in full. But when you help a needy person, do it in such a way that even your closest friend will not know about it. Then it will be a private matter. And your Father, who sees what you do in private, will reward you."

Matthew 6: 1-6, 16-18

"…as the hypocrites do…"

Hypocrisy

When I was quite young, I remember finding out that a classmate was going to have a birthday party. This boy was not my friend, although we got along fine.

I don't know why, but I really wanted to go to that birthday party. So, for two weeks, I treated him as though he was my best friend. I ate lunch with him every day and played with him at recess. Sure enough, I got my party invitation.

I had a terrible time at that party. The games weren't fun, the food didn't taste good, and I felt like an outsider. I could hardly wait for it to end.

Hypocrisy and deceit – they rot the soul.

Lord, you know my deepest self.
Help me keep a clean heart.

"Today I am giving you a choice between good and evil, between life and death. If you obey the commands of the Lord your God, which I give you today, if you love him, obey him, and keep all his laws, then you will prosper and become a nation of many people.... But if you disobey and refuse to listen, and are led away to worship other gods, you will be destroyed – I warn you here and now.... I am now giving you the choice between life and death, between God's blessing and God's curse, and I call heaven and earth to witness the choice you make. Choose life. Love the Lord your God, obey him and be faithful to him, and then you and your descendants will live long in the land that he promised to give your ancestors, Abraham, Isaac, and Jacob."

Deuteronomy 30: 15-20

"Choose life."

Good and evil

Who wouldn't choose life over death, good over evil? When I consider the choices in such stark terms, my decision seems easy. But today I can choose to visit my aunt who is housebound, or I can telephone her, or I can do nothing. Neither choice is evil, but they are not equally loving or good.

Life is full of choices. I once read that life is a continuum and we constantly move either in the direction of good or in the direction of evil. Not every decision is definitive, but we need to be moving in the right direction.

This image is helpful when I want to choose good over evil with one grand, magnificent flourish, rather than inching along, one small step at a time.

Dear Lord, forgive my impatience.
Help me remain faithful to you in the little things.

The people ask, "Why should we fast if the Lord never notices? Why should we go without food if he pays no attention?" The Lord says, "The truth is that at the same time you fast, you pursue your own interests and oppress your workers. Your fasting makes you violent, and you quarrel and fight. Do you think this kind of fasting will make me listen to your prayers?

"The kind of fasting I want is this: Remove the chains of oppression and the yoke of injustice, and let the oppressed go free. Share your food with the hungry and open your homes to the homeless poor. Give clothes to those who have nothing to wear, and do not refuse to help your own relatives.

"Then my favour will shine on you like the morning sun, and your wounds will be quickly healed." *Isaiah 58: 1-9*

"The kind of fasting I want is this..."

Will power

My father used to say, "I've got a lot of will power; it's *won't* power that I'm a little short of."

I don't think of fasting when I think of my father. He liked eating and was a bit of a clown – so my picture is of someone acting foolish for us kids, or sleeping in the easy chair with butter tart crumbs on his shirt. Oh, he was also a bit of a butter tart thief.

Other pictures I have of my father are of him on the side of the road, fixing someone's car in sub-zero weather. And giving his brand new winter coat to a man hitchhiking to a job in Winnipeg in 1955.

Maybe Isaiah tells us "will" power is a little more important than "won't" power.

Lord, open my heart to those in need.

Jesus went out and saw a tax collector named Levi, sitting in his office. Jesus said to him, "Follow me." Levi got up, left everything, and followed him.

Then Levi had a big feast in his house for Jesus, and among the guests was a large number of tax collectors and other people. Some Pharisees and some teachers of the Law who belonged to their group complained to Jesus' disciples. "Why do you eat and drink with tax collectors and other outcasts?" they asked.

Jesus answered them, "People who are well do not need a doctor, but only those who are sick. I have not come to call respectable people to repent, but outcasts."

Luke 5: 27-32

"...Levi had a big feast in his house for Jesus."

Time to celebrate

Sometimes being a Christian seems overwhelming to me: "Sell all you have and give to the poor." "Forgive those who wrong you seventy times seven times!" "Love your enemies. Do good to those who hate you." How can I live up to all that? Christianity is for superheroes, not normal flesh-and-blood people – like me.

But wait a minute. Look at Levi. Jesus calls him to be a follower and what's the first thing he does? He throws a big party for Jesus and invites all his tax-collector friends. And, of course, Jesus shows up and everyone has a great time.

Maybe this Christianity is not quite what I thought. Maybe true conversion includes dancing and singing – as well as moral seriousness.

**Lord, help me remember the joy
of being one of your followers.**

"The Spirit led Jesus into the desert to be tempted by the Devil. After spending forty days and nights without food, Jesus was hungry. Then the Devil came to him and said, "If you are God's Son, order these stones to turn into bread." But Jesus answered, "The scripture says, 'Human beings cannot live on bread alone, but need every word that God speaks.'"

Then the Devil took Jesus to Jerusalem…. "If you are God's Son, throw yourself down, for the scripture says, 'God will give orders to his angels… they will hold you up, so that not even your feet will be hurt on the stones.'" Jesus answered, "But the scripture also says, 'Do not put the Lord your God to the test….'" The Devil left Jesus; and angels came and helped him.

Matthew 4: 1-11

> "The Spirit led Jesus into the desert…"

An inner desert

Jesus fasts and resists temptation. Food certainly tempts me. But I haven't found dieting (today's fasting!) too onerous. Once my clothes fit again, I can resume eating the forbidden foods. I know it's not forever.

But there are far greater temptations within me that I can't resist on my own. I'm impatient with my children; I'm quick to criticize; I can't admit my mistakes. Forty days' solitude wouldn't begin to conquer my failings!

Jesus went into the desert to face his tempter. I can journey into my inner desert and face my inadequacies each day in prayer. With God's help I can find the strength to work at overcoming my weaknesses. The first and hardest step is to hold out my hand for help.

**Lord, bring me with you into the desert,
so I may gain the strength and insight to conquer my demons.**

The law of the Lord
is perfect;
it gives new strength.
The commands of the Lord
are trustworthy,
giving wisdom to those who
lack it.
The laws of the Lord are right,
and those who obey them
are happy.
The commands of the Lord
are just
and give understanding
to the mind.
Reverence for the Lord is good;
it will continue forever.

The judgments of the Lord
are just;
they are always fair.
They are more desirable
than the finest gold;
they are sweeter
than the purest honey.
They give knowledge to me,
your servant;
I am rewarded
for obeying them.
None of us can see
our own errors;
deliver me, Lord,
from hidden faults!

Psalm 19: 7-12

"The judgments of the Lord are just…"

Life's lessons

"That's not fair!" Oh, the outrage of every child I have ever met who is not getting an equal share – of the pie, the swing or Mom's attention.

Well-known author Barbara Coloroso writes that there are three things I must teach my children: Life hurts. Life is unfair. Life is good. They will learn the first two; it is the third that challenges my parenting.

Despite the injustices they encounter, I want my children to experience the goodness of life. I want them to let go of those inequalities that don't really matter and find peace within. I want to teach them to help right wrongs, to make life fair for others. A daunting task.

**Loving God, guide me as I teach my children about life.
Help me work to make life good for all children.**

"When you pray, do not use a lot of meaningless words.... Your Father already knows what you need before you ask him. This, then, is how you should pray: 'Our Father in heaven: May your holy name be honoured; may your kingdom come; may your will be done on earth as it is in heaven. Give us today the food we need. Forgive us the wrongs we have done, as we forgive the wrongs that others have done to us. Do not bring us to hard testing, but keep us safe from the Evil One.'

"If you forgive others the wrongs they have done to you, your Father in heaven will also forgive you. But if you do not forgive others, then your Father will not forgive the wrongs you have done."

Matthew 6: 7-15

"...do not use a lot of meaningless words..."

Finding the right words

The drive seemed like an eternity, but I finally reached my anticipated destination. Finding the closest parking spot, I jumped from the car and hurried through the main doors of the hospital. Sorrow overwhelmed me when I reached my father's room: his doctors were not expecting him to live through the night.

If my father awoke from his coma, there might be an opportunity to say a few words. I would not have time for small talk or words with little meaning.

When his eyes suddenly opened, I was ready. "Dad, if I could be half the father you were to me," I whispered, pausing mid-sentence as his eyes closed. Sleep had overtaken him again, yet his lingering smile assured me I had used the right words.

Dear God, help me to speak with sincere and meaningful words in all my conversations.

51

Once again the Lord spoke to Jonah. He said, "Go to Nineveh, that great city, and proclaim to the people the message I have given you." So Jonah obeyed the Lord and went to Nineveh, a city so large that it took three days to walk through it. Jonah started through the city, and after walking a whole day, he proclaimed, "In forty days Nineveh will be destroyed!"

The people of Nineveh believed God's message. So they decided that everyone should fast, and all the people, from the greatest to the least, put on sackcloth to show that they had repented....

God saw what they did; he saw that they had given up their wicked behaviour. So he changed his mind and did not punish them as he had said he would.   *Jonah 3: 1-10*

> "So he changed his mind…"

Mercy and love

There is a tow truck that scours the streets of our neighbourhood. It gleams black and silver. Emblazoned above the cab in bright letters are the words "Expect No Mercy." Every time I see it, I imagine Jonah sitting behind the wheel. I think of him prowling the streets of Nineveh – warning of the severe judgment waiting for those whose meters have almost run out.

God's response in today's reading boggles my mind. Mercy is not something I'm very good at. I prefer to think about the just punishments waiting for those who have hurt me, rather than look for ways that I could be merciful.

Today I will look at my habit of judging harshly, and I will take one small step toward changing it.

Forgiving God, teach me to reach out to others
with a merciful touch.

" **A**sk, and you will receive; seek, and you will find; knock, and the door will be opened to you. For everyone who asks will receive, and anyone who seeks will find, and the door will be opened to those who knock. Would any of you who are fathers give your son a stone when he asks for bread? Or would you give him a snake when he asks for a fish? As bad as you are, you know how to give good things to your children. How much more, then, will your Father in heaven give good things to those who ask him!

"Do for others what you want them to do for you: this is the meaning of the Law of Moses and of the teachings of the prophets."

Matthew 7: 7-12

"...knock, and the door will be opened to you."

Food that satisfies

When I encounter a dilemma in my work, I often leave my computer and wander downstairs for a snack. When my daughter is upset or angry, I sometimes pull out her favourite food to either comfort or persuade her. I'm teaching my daughter to use food to avoid conflict just the way I do: "Knock, and the fridge door will be opened to you!"

Once I've eaten my snack, however, I still have to deal with my original dilemma. Leftovers don't satisfy; they don't give me what I really need.

Jesus' advice seems so easy to follow: just knock, seek or ask. While I am doing that already, perhaps I'm knocking at the wrong doors. I need to open myself to Jesus, the Bread of life – food that satsifies.

Help me to know what I really need, Lord,
and to trust that you will satisfy my every need.

From the depths of my despair I call to you, Lord.
Hear my cry, O Lord;
listen to my call for help!
If you kept a record of our sins,
who could escape being condemned?
But you forgive us,
so that we should stand in awe of you.
I wait eagerly for the Lord's help,
and in his word I trust.

Psalm 130: 1-6

"From the depths of my despair…"

Forgiveness

What was the psalmist's despair? And when was he feeling that despair? The dark, rainy days in early spring are the worst for me – when winter stretches its fingers, holding on. That's when I struggle with the memories of all I've done and can't undo, should have done and didn't. All the hurtful words I've spoken that can never be unsaid.

And what of those whose sins are more serious? Who got drunk, then killed someone while driving home? Seduced someone's spouse, and destroyed a family? Lost wife and kids through the bottle? What are the depths of their despair on dark, rainy nights? Those whom we would judge.

The psalmist says, "But you forgive us…." This is the great mystery: God forgives. We can be forgiven. And so must we forgive ourselves. And others.

Loving God, forgive my sins.
Give me the courage to forgive myself, and others.

" **Y**ou have heard that it was said, 'Love your friends, hate your enemies.' But now I tell you: love your enemies and pray for those who persecute you, so that you may become the children of your Father in heaven. For he makes his sun to shine on bad and good people alike, and gives rain to those who do good and to those who do evil. Why should God reward you if you love only the people who love you? Even the tax collectors do that! And if you speak only to your friends, have you done anything out of the ordinary? Even the pagans do that! You must be perfect – just as your Father in heaven is perfect."

Matthew 5: 43-48

> "...pray for those who persecute you..."

Love your enemies

Recently a good friend introduced me to a meditation practice called "Loving Kindness." Based on the Buddhist tradition, the meditations are meant to help me reach the point where I can truly send a positive prayer towards someone who has hurt me.

I must admit that I don't find it very easy. I start out well but I soon drift into revisiting wounds that have not healed. Before I know it I've spiralled into blame and accusation, and forgiveness is nowhere on the horizon.

And so I begin the meditation again. Some days I'm able to move a little further towards forgiveness before getting off track. Some days I don't get very far. Perhaps the desire to begin again is what is important.

God, help me to accept that even small steps towards forgiveness are steps headed in the right direction.

Jesus took with him Peter, James and John and led them up a high mountain where they were alone. As they looked on, a change came over Jesus: his face was shining like the sun, and his clothes were dazzling white. Then the three disciples saw Moses and Elijah talking with Jesus. So Peter spoke up and said to Jesus, "Lord, how good it is that we are here! If you wish, I will make three tents here...."

While he was talking, a shining cloud came over them, and a voice from the cloud said, "This is my own dear Son, with whom I am pleased – listen to him!"... As they came down the mountain, Jesus ordered them, "Don't tell anyone about this vision you have seen until the Son of Man has been raised from death." *Matthew 17: 1-9*

> "This is my own dear Son... listen to him!"

A sneak preview

Movie previews never tell their viewer the whole story. They entice with the glimpses they give, and they tease with what they leave out.

Peter, James and John get an important preview here on the mountain. They're enticed: pay attention, listen up. And they're teased: don't say anything yet. Having glimpsed Jesus' glory, they're cautioned against thinking they understand it well enough to talk about it – until after they've seen the whole story.

I, too, am reminded that this "preview" of Jesus' glory actually calls my attention to the rest of his life: his way of including the outcast, healing the sick, announcing forgiveness to sinners – and his acceptance of suffering along the way. More than this, I am invited to tell his whole story with my life.

Jesus, even as I recall your glory, keep my attention on serving you through the tasks before me this day.

"**B**e merciful just as your Father is merciful. Do not judge others, and God will not judge you; do not condemn others, and God will not condemn you; forgive others, and God will forgive you. Give to others, and God will give to you. Indeed, you will receive a full measure, a generous helping, poured into your hands – all that you can hold. The measure you use for others is the one that God will use for you."

Luke 6: 36-38

"The measure you use for others…"

Mercy upon mercy

Mairin works with the homeless with great courage and conviction. At twenty-five, she sometimes gets frustrated with systems and supervisors that put the process ahead of the people they claim to serve.

Recently she wrote, "I'm not asking 'Where is God?' like I have before. I know where God is, where God always is: with the unconscious, drunk man on the sidewalk whom people are just passing by, with the homeless, the hurting, those who are unwanted by our society. But why can't other people see that this is where God is? That these are our sisters and brothers, and God has charged all of us with their care?"

That's the question to be posed, measure for measure. Not "Where is God?" Rather, "Where are we?"

God, so many people live with quiet indifference.
Let me make a quiet difference today.

Jerusalem, your rulers and your people are like those of Sodom and Gomorrah. Listen to what the Lord is saying to you.... "Stop all this evil that I see you doing. Yes, stop doing evil and learn to do right. See that justice is done...."

The Lord says, "Now, let's settle the matter. You are stained red with sin, but I will wash you as clean as snow. Although your stains are deep red, you will be as white as wool. If you will only obey me, you will eat the good things the land produces. But if you defy me, you are doomed to die...."

Just as straw is set on fire by a spark, so powerful people will be destroyed by their own evil deeds, and no one will be able to stop the destruction. *Isaiah 1: 10, 16-20, 27-28, 31*

> "Stop all this evil that I see you doing."

Justice for all

It may seem impolite to talk about Middle East politics in a religious context, but apparently Isaiah doesn't know this. He doesn't mince his words here, and it's easy to hear the implications for today's world. There is no justification for Palestinian suicide bombers who target civilians. There is no justification for Israeli soldiers who bulldoze homes. There is no future that offers hope if it does not also promise both security for Israel and sovereignty for Palestine.

Yet neither side seems willing to entertain both possibilities. And, in the absence of this, Isaiah only foresees multitudes who will continue to be "destroyed by their own evil deeds." God help us all if we cannot imagine a justice that redeems not only ourselves, but also our adversaries.

Dear God, stretch my imagination today. Help me imagine a justice that is big enough for all your children.

Keep me safe from the trap that has been set for me;
shelter me from danger.
I place myself in your care.
You will save me, Lord;
you are a faithful God....
I hear many enemies whispering;
terror is all around me.
They are making plans against me,
plotting to kill me.
But my trust is in you, O Lord;
you are my God.
I am always in your care;
save me from my enemies,
from those who persecute me.

Psalm 31: 4-5, 13-15

"They are making plans against me..."

Blinded by suspicion

I'm not proud of this incident. When I was still in high school, an acquaintance telephoned: "Carl and I wanted to invite you over to join us." I didn't go. I thought they were up to something. I accused them of plotting ways to humiliate me. In truth, I had no grounds for my suspicions – except suspicion itself.

If the psalmist was writing about the nation of Israel, then I can understand the writer's suspicions. Israel was a small nation, a pawn of the larger powers that dominated the region.

But if it's about an individual, I can't help wondering if he, too, had bad days when he thought everyone was conspiring against him.

I trust you, God. I really do.
Free me from my secret doubts and fears.

"There was once a rich man and a poor man named Lazarus.... The poor man died and was carried by the angels to sit beside Abraham at the feast in heaven. The rich man died and was buried, and in Hades.... He called out, 'Father Abraham! Take pity on me, and send Lazarus to dip his finger in some water and cool off my tongue, because I am in great pain in this fire!' But Abraham said, 'Remember, my son, that in your lifetime you were given all the good things, while Lazarus got all the bad things. But now he is enjoying himself here, while you are in pain. Besides all that, there is a deep pit lying between us, so that those who want to cross over from here to you cannot do so.'"

Luke 16: 19-31

"There was once a rich man…"

A lesson from the street

Years ago I was involved with a radio program about ethics and religion. Should we give money to panhandlers, someone asked, or just to the organizations that help poor people?

Looking for an answer, we sent a researcher out on the street to "beg" for an hour. The worst thing, he said, was that everyone turned away from him. Even the people who gave him coins averted their gaze. Like the rich man, they preferred to ignore a beggar.

"I still haven't decided on the best way to help the poor," he said. "But I can tell you this: whether you say 'yes' or 'no,' look each beggar in the eye, and recognize another human being. Having your humanity denied is the worst thing of all."

Lord, you hold me responsible for the poor who cross my path.
Show me what to do.

J esus asked his disciples, "Who do people say the Son of Man is?" "Some say John the Baptist... others say Elijah, while others say Jeremiah or some other prophet." "What about you? Who do you say I am?" Simon Peter answered, "You are the Messiah, the Son of the living God." "Good for you, Simon son of John! For this truth did not come to you from any human being, but it was given to you directly by my Father in heaven. And so I tell you, Peter: you are a rock, and on this rock foundation I will build my church.... I will give you the keys of the Kingdom of heaven; what you prohibit on earth will be prohibited in heaven, and what you permit on earth will be permitted in heaven."

Matthew 16: 13-19

> "Who do you say I am?"

My true self

Who do people say I am? It's comforting to know that even the Son of God occasionally sought feedback, perhaps even reassurance, from those who shared his life!

The opinions of others have mattered to me more than I care to admit. In my years as a teacher and therapist, I have felt free to speak and act based on where my heart has led me. Unfortunately that's not been the case in my personal life! When I step out of my role as a confident professional, I am left with a broken, vulnerable core.

My challenge is to let people know what I'm really like. That's a frightening thought. But if I hide my real self, how can they truly love me – as I am?

**Loving God, grant me the courage and faith
to show others who I truly am.**

Praise the Lord, my soul!
All my being,
  praise his holy name!
Praise the Lord, my soul,
and do not forget
how kind he is.
He forgives all my sins
and heals all my diseases.
He keeps me from the grave
and blesses me with love and
mercy....
He does not keep on rebuking;
he is not angry forever.

He does not punish us
as we deserve
or repay us according to our
sins and wrongs.
As high as the sky
is above the earth,
so great is his love
for those who honour him.
As far as the east is from
the west,
so far does he remove our sins
from us.

Psalm 103: 1-4, 9-12

"...so great is his love..."

Faithfulness

My beloved Irish Setter, Brick, died last year, worn out by a lifetime of epilepsy. In one sense, his death freed me from a prison of pills and exercise regimes, of arranging for dog-sitters and, occasionally, repairing the damage caused by his playful spirit.

But I miss him terribly. He was always glad to see me. He always trusted me. He loved me unconditionally.

My daughter gave me a politically incorrect T-shirt. Its caption refers to a "dyslexic agnostic" pondering "if there is a Dog." Is it pure coincidence, I wonder, that "dog" and "God" use the same letters in English? Because the relationship between God and me, as portrayed in today's reading, sometimes seems uncommonly like the relationship I knew with my dog.

**I wish I could be as faithful to you, God, as my dog was to me.
Thank you for your unending love.**

The people complained to Moses: "Why did you bring us out of Egypt? To kill us and our children and our livestock with thirst?" Moses prayed earnestly to the Lord and said, "What can I do with these people? They are almost ready to stone me." The Lord said to Moses, "Take some of the leaders of Israel with you, and go on ahead of the people. Take along the stick with which you struck the Nile. I will stand before you on a rock at Mount Sinai. Strike the rock, and water will come out of it for the people to drink." Moses did so in the presence of the leaders of Israel.

The place was named Massah and Meribah, because the Israelites complained and put the Lord to the test.

Exodus 17: 3-7

"…and put the Lord to the test."

Gratitude for life

I've known Steph for years, and the one constant in her life has been *dissatisfaction*. From my point of view, her life has only gotten better. She found a good job; she met her husband there; and now they're expecting their first child.

But every time I talk to her, I hear about the latest thing that's gone wrong or needs fixing. Sometimes I think Steph is only happy when she has something to complain about.

I've heard it said that God let the Israelites wander in the desert for such a long time for a reason. After forty years, those who only knew a "slave mentality" would be replaced by a generation ready to accept the freedom and happiness that God was offering them.

**Lord, thank you for all you have done for me,
and for the many blessings in my life!**

" I tell you this," Jesus added, "prophets are never welcomed in their hometown. Listen to me: it is true that there were many widows in Israel during the time of Elijah, when there was no rain for three and a half years and a severe famine spread throughout the whole land. Yet Elijah was not sent to anyone in Israel, but only to a widow living in Zarephath in the territory of Sidon. And there were many people suffering from a dreaded skin disease who lived in Israel during the time of the prophet Elisha; yet not one of them was healed, but only Naaman the Syrian."

When the people in the synagogue heard this, they were filled with anger. They dragged Jesus out of town, and... meant to throw him over the cliff. *Luke 4: 24-30*

> "When the people... heard this, they were filled with anger."

Beyond divisions

Imagine a hockey game. The sides are clearly defined: us and them, good guys and bad. It's all a nice, comfortable illusion. Now imagine a hometown boy taking "their" side, saying, "Wake up, guys! They're just like us."

In life I tend to look for certainty. I want to be able to define my reality, to "know" the way things are. But there's a danger in certainty. For instance, it can make religion into a club: "I'm a member, so I'm OK." The people in today's reading seem to be saying, "We 'know,' therefore we're saved."

But Jesus says, "Open your eyes to the illusion. Don't think you're saved because you're on the right team. It's what you *do*, not what team you're on that counts."

**Lord, help me see each person as one of your children –
especially when I start to divide the world into "us and them."**

Peter came to Jesus and asked, "Lord, if my brother keeps on sinning against me, how many times do I have to forgive him? Seven times?"

"No, not seven times," answered Jesus, "but seventy times seven, because the kingdom of heaven is like this. Once there was a king who decided to check on his servants' accounts…. The king said to the servant, 'I forgave you the whole amount you owed me, just because you asked me to. You should have had mercy on your fellow servant, just as I had mercy on you.' The king was very angry, and he sent the servant to jail to be punished…."

Jesus concluded, "That is how my Father in heaven will treat every one of you unless you forgive your brother from your heart." *Matthew 18:21-35*

"You should have had mercy on your fellow servant…"

Pass it on

In so many areas of life I rarely get to keep what I have received. I am blessed in receiving and I am blessed in passing it on. To keep something for myself is to interrupt the flow.

Much like a pipe that carries water from one spot to another: in receiving the water and passing it along, the pipe is washed. If one end of the pipe is blocked and the water cannot pass on, then the water stagnates and the pipe rusts.

No doubt, it costs to give to and to forgive others… as the Lord gives to and forgives me. But, for me to hold onto what I have received not only deprives others, it also blocks God's saving action in my life.

**Open my hands, Lord,
to receive *and* to share what I have been given.**

Praise your God, O Zion!
He keeps your borders safe
and satisfies you with the finest wheat.
He gives a command to the earth,
and what he says is quickly done.
He spreads snow like a blanket
and scatters frost like dust.
He sends hail like gravel;
no one can endure the cold he sends!
Then he gives a command, and the ice melts;
he sends the wind, and the water flows.
He gives his message to his people,
his instructions and laws to Israel.   *Psalm 147: 12-20*

> "...and the ice melts..."

New growth

These days of teetering between winter and spring are challenging ones – especially for a gardener. It's been a long winter, and I'm just itching to get my fingers into some warm earth. It's hard to believe that the possibility of green, new life exists underneath these last vestiges of snow.

And then it happens. The first shoots of a crocus nudge me out of my winter ill-humour. My faith is restored. I believe again. My energy is renewed, and anything is possible!

Each year it is the same. I know spring will return, but my faith is fragile. The bright crocuses are like miracles. They remind me to be patient, to be attentive, and to be open to the surprise of God's presence and power.

**Creator God, open my heart to possibilities of new growth.
Indeed, with you all things are possible!**

" I did command them to obey me, so that I would be their God and they would be my people. And I told them to live the way I had commanded them, so that things would go well for them. But they did not obey or pay any attention. Instead, they did whatever their stubborn and evil hearts told them to do, and they became worse instead of better. From the day that your ancestors came out of Egypt until this very day I have kept on sending to you my servants, the prophets. Yet no one listened or paid any attention. Instead, you became more stubborn and rebellious than your ancestors.

"So, Jeremiah, you will speak all these words to my people, but they will not listen to you; you will call them, but they will not answer."

Jeremiah 7: 23-28

> "…speak all these words to my people…"

Keep trying

Sometimes I feel that no one is listening to me. Not my kids (muddy boots left in the hall), my husband (gym clothes rotting away beside the washer), my students (homework left at home). Even the cat seems bent on breaking my spirit (fur balls heaved onto the living room carpet)! How can I build a bridge of faith over the anger and disappointment I feel?

At first glance today's reading offers little solace. God's anger is deep; it is painful. And yet, despite angry words, God does not abandon the people of Israel. God sends Jeremiah in… again. At least the lines of communication are open.

The next time I feel like turning away, I might try to use Jeremiah as a model of my own.

God, I know you understand my disappointments.
Help my actions reflect a love that is deeper than my anger.

A teacher of the Law came to Jesus with a question: "Which commandment is the most important of all?"

Jesus replied, "The most important one is this: 'Listen, Israel! The Lord our God is the only Lord. Love the Lord your God with all your heart, with all your soul, with all your mind, and with all your strength.' The second most important commandment is this: 'Love your neighbour as you love yourself.' There is no other commandment more important than these two."

The teacher of the Law said to Jesus, "Well done, Teacher! It is true, as you say, that only the Lord is God and that there is no other god…. And it is more important to obey these two commandments than to offer on the altar animals and other sacrifices to God."

Mark 12: 28-34

> "Love your neighbour as you love yourself."

As you love yourself

The car became airborne on the last hill. It took hours to get Mary out of the wreck. After six months of reconstructive surgery and physio-therapy, she landed in my class unable to remember anything of that drug- and alcohol-filled night.

I had known Mary as a child – the perfect straight-A student who never disappointed anyone. After the accident, she went back to her life of drinking and drugs. One day I finally asked her, "Why?" She said she'd spent her whole life loving and pleasing others. She had never learned to love herself.

Jesus seems to assume that his comparison will be understood: "Love your neighbour as you love yourself." For some, love of neighbour is easier than love of self.

God, may I love myself enough to truly love others.

" I will abandon my people until they have suffered enough for their sins and come looking for me. Perhaps in their suffering they will try to find me."

The people say, "Let's return to the Lord! He has hurt us, but he will be sure to heal us; he has wounded us, but he will bandage our wounds, won't he…?"

But the Lord says, "Israel and Judah, what am I going to do with you? Your love for me disappears as quickly as morning mist; it is like dew, that vanishes early in the day. That is why I have sent my prophets to you…. What I want from you is plain and clear: I want your constant love, not your animal sacrifices. I would rather have my people know me than burn offerings to me." *Hosea 5: 15 – 6: 6*

"What I want from you is plain and clear…"

Simplicity itself

I am, without a doubt, part of the best-educated generation that has ever lived. I know about history, science, math, great works of art and literature. I even know how computers work! I have read my fill of theological and spiritual works to help me try to understand who God is and what God wants of me.

But I'm not sure that this knowledge has helped me very much. There are even times when I feel paralyzed by the vast stores of information to which I have access. I sometimes think that knowing so much has taken me further from the truth, not closer.

But here it is, simple as can be: God wants to be known and loved. And that's it. The rest is details.

Lord, the road to you is cluttered with thoughts and words.
Help me clear a simple path to walk along.

Jesus saw a man who had been born blind…. Jesus spat on the ground and made some mud with the spittle; he rubbed the mud on the man's eyes and told him, "Go and wash in the Pool of Siloam." So the man went, washed and came back seeing. [His neighbours] took to the Pharisees the man who had been blind….

Some of the Pharisees said, "The man who did this cannot be from God, for he does not obey the Sabbath law." Others, however, said, "How could a man who is a sinner perform such miracles as these?" And there was a division among them. So the Pharisees asked the man once more, "You say he cured you of your blindness – well, what do you say about him?" "He is a prophet," the man answered. *John 9: 1-41*

"…what do you say about him?"

The big picture

I love to garden. However, in the busyness of spring time work, I often forget to stand back and look at the overall picture. I am too involved with details, the day-to-day work. Yet someone arriving in my garden is aware, right away, of what I have been too preoccupied to see.

Jesus' critics are like this. They are unable to see the whole picture; their commitment to the Law blinds them to the purpose of the Law. The Law points the way; it is not the Way.

I act like the Pharisees, too. I get so involved with observances that I fail to see the real things that will help my neighbour: praise instead of criticism; a wave and a smile in greeting; saying "I'm sorry. Let's try again."

**Lord, open my eyes! Give me the ability
to see my neighbour as part of your creation.**

A government official went to Jesus and asked him to go to Capernaum and heal his son, who was about to die. Jesus said to him, "None of you will ever believe unless you see miracles and wonders."

"Sir," replied the official, "come with me before my child dies." Jesus said to him, "Go; your son will live!" The man believed Jesus' words and went. On his way home his servants met him with the news, "Your boy is going to live!"

He asked them what time it was when his son got better, and they answered, "It was one o'clock yesterday afternoon when the fever left him." Then the father remembered that it was at that very hour when Jesus had told him, "Your son will live." So he and all his family believed.   *John 4: 43-54*

"None of you will ever believe unless…"

From the heart

Jesus a little frustrated, maybe? Another request for a miracle! When will they ever get it? Maybe a little tired, too, after a long, hot day of walking and listening to the disciples arguing. And then, the cry of desperation, "Miracle or no miracle. Please save my son. Please!"

I think of my children and how often I say "No" when they ask for something. Then the way they ask catches my attention and I hear how much it means to them. And I just can't say "No."

Here Jesus performs a miracle – not to prove himself, but because he can't resist that cry, "Please! I need your help!" A comforting thought: Jesus, though tired and frustrated, when someone asks from the heart, just can't say "No."

Lord, let me hear, as you did, the real cries for help and respond when I hear them.

Near the Sheep Gate in Jerusalem there is a pool with five porches; in Hebrew it is called Bethzatha. A large crowd of sick people were lying on the porches – the blind, the lame, and the paralyzed. A man was there who had been sick for thirty-eight years. Jesus saw him lying there, and he knew that the man had been sick for such a long time; so he asked him, "Do you want to get well?"

The sick man answered, "Sir, I don't have anyone here to put me in the pool when the water is stirred up; while I am trying to get in, somebody else gets there first." Jesus said to him, "Get up, pick up your mat, and walk." Immediately the man got well; he picked up his mat and started walking.
John 5: 1-16

> "Do you want to get well?"

Asking for healing

"Do you want to get well?" Maybe the answer is not so obvious. This man had been sick for 38 years, and was often at the pool. What would be left of his life if he were cured? He'd lose his friends at the pool, his daily routine, his identity. As much as he sought an end to his pain, he also must have feared the unknown which loomed before him.

We all have some excuse for our failings: ill health, family concerns, fear, betrayal or bad luck.

If my crutches are taken away, then I must stand alone before Jesus. Do I have the courage to answer Jesus' question with a firm "yes"? Do I really want this new, unknown life of wholeness that Jesus promises? Yes!

Lord, let me not cling to my crutches.
Let me put my broken life in your healing hands.

The Lord says to his people,
"I will guard and protect you
and through you make a covenant with all peoples...."
But the people of Jerusalem said,
"The Lord has abandoned us!
He has forgotten us."
So the Lord answers,
"Can a woman forget her own baby
and not love the child she bore?
Even if a mother should forget her child,
I will never forget you."

Isaiah 49: 8-15

"Can a woman forget her own baby?"

Dependent on God

Recently the newspaper carried a terrible story of a young mother who abandoned her two small children for more than a week. The children died as a result of her neglect. "How can this be?" I cried. "How could she forget her own babies?" As a mother, I found this impossible to fathom. It's unnatural; it's hard to accept. And yet, it happens.

When Isaiah tells me that God will not forget me, I am comforted. Like a child dependent on its mother for food, for warmth, for water, for love, I rely on God. While human parents may let their children down, I know that in God all my needs will be met, all my desires will be known, all my tears will be wiped away.

Lord, I depend on your love and care every day.
Thank you for always remembering me.

The Lord said to Moses, "Hurry and go back down, because your people, whom you led out of Egypt, have sinned and rejected me…. They have made a bull-calf out of melted gold and have worshipped it and offered sacrifices to it. They are saying that this is their god, who led them out of Egypt. I know how stubborn these people are. Now, don't try to stop me. I am angry with them, and I am going to destroy them. Then I will make you and your descendants into a great nation."

But Moses pleaded with the Lord his God and said, "Lord, why should you be so angry with your people whom you rescued from Egypt with great might and power? Stop being angry; change your mind and do not bring this disaster on your people…." So the Lord changed his mind and did not bring on his people the disaster he had threatened. *Exodus 32:7-14*

"So the Lord changed his mind…"

Challenging authority

I don't know if I'm more amazed with the courage of Moses (after all, who likes to challenge the boss?), or with the fact that, with a good argument, it's possible to change God's mind. Way to go, Moses!

In today's reading, God listens to Moses' challenge. God is open to suggestion and is *willing* to change. How different from the image of God that I grew up with! The God of my childhood was all knowing, all powerful, righteous and always right.

I wonder if I try to be that way with my students at school or with my children at home. Do they see me as someone who is not to be challenged, or am I someone who is willing to listen?

**God, give me the wisdom to listen with a heart
that is willing to change.**

Some of the people said, "Isn't this the man the authorities are trying to kill? Look! He is talking in public, and they say nothing against him! Can it be that they really know that he is the Messiah? But when the Messiah comes, no one will know where he is from. And we all know where this man comes from."

As Jesus taught in the Temple, he said in a loud voice, "Do you really know me and know where I am from? I have not come on my own authority. He who sent me, however, is truthful. You do not know him, but I know him, because I come from him and he sent me." Then they tried to seize him, but no one laid a hand on him, because his hour had not yet come.

John 7: 1-2, 10, 25-30

"Do you really know me and know where I am from?"

Do you really know me?

All my life, it seems, I have struggled one way or another with the question Jesus asked the people of Jerusalem: "Do you really know me and know where I am from?" For a long time – years, in fact – my answer was, "No, I don't. And who cares anyway?" As far as I was concerned, that was the end of it. I simply got on with living my life.

But Jesus asked the question in a loud voice – I guess for people like me – and so the question never really went away. Eventually it bubbled up from deep within me until I had to face it again.

Now my answer is both the same and completely different: "No, I don't. Please help me find out."

Jesus, you are the question I cannot answer, the mystery I cannot fathom. Help me stand on that uncertain ground.

Some of the people in the crowd heard him and said, "This man is really the Prophet!" Others said, "He is the Messiah!" But others said, "The Messiah will not come from Galilee! The scripture says that the Messiah will be a descendant of King David and will be born in Bethlehem, the town where David lived." So there was a division in the crowd because of Jesus....

When the guards went back, the chief priests and Pharisees asked them, "Why did you not bring him?"

The guards answered, "Nobody has ever talked the way this man does!"

"Did he fool you, too?" the Pharisees asked them.... "Study the Scriptures and you will learn that no prophet ever comes from Galilee." *John 7: 40-53*

> "Nobody has ever talked the way this man does!"

An unlikely prophet?

"Dear William, I want to thank you for the kind words that you spoke at Eric's funeral. I know that his parents were comforted by your thoughts, as were the other children and adults there.

"Words have great power, and I want to thank you for reminding me of this. When you said that Eric deserved to be remembered, it reminded me that every day I need to remember the people who are special to me.... You have a natural gift for touching other people's souls. Thank you, William, for touching mine. Susan."

Prophets come in all shapes and sizes. How wonderful that Susan recognized and affirmed this eleven-year-old boy's gift to her and to the community.

Lord, give me the ears to hear and the eyes to recognize the prophets I will meet today – especially those close to home.

From the depths of my despair I call to you, Lord. Hear my cry, O Lord; listen to my call for help! If you kept a record of our sins, who could escape being condemned? But you forgive us, so that we should stand in awe of you. I wait eagerly for the Lord's help, and in his word I trust.

I wait for the Lord more eagerly than sentries wait for the dawn – than sentries wait for the dawn. Israel, trust in the Lord, because his love is constant and he is always willing to save. He will save his people Israel from all their sins.

Psalm 130: 1-8

> But you forgive us…"

The courage to forgive

When I worked for him, I'd say he was in despair. Despair of there being any goodness in people. He trusted no one, and saw something self-serving behind every action. We knew he thought we were always slacking off. "I know what you young guys are like." He was so hard.

His wife had left him for another man. He couldn't forgive her for leaving, or forgive himself for being fooled. And so he imprisoned himself in cynicism and despair. I wish there were a happy ending. I saw him recently: same old stuff.

Our grudges hold us captive. I want to learn to cry out from the depths of my despair, "Forgive me! Help me forgive those who hurt me. Help me forgive myself."

God, free me. Forgive me my sins. Help me to forgive others.

The teachers of the Law and the Pharisees brought in a woman who had been caught committing adultery. "Teacher," they said to Jesus, "this woman was caught in the very act of committing adultery. In our Law Moses commanded that such a woman must be stoned to death. Now, what do you say?" They said this to trap Jesus, so that they could accuse him. But he bent over and wrote on the ground with his finger. As they stood there asking him questions, he straightened up and said to them, "Whichever one of you has committed no sin may throw the first stone at her." Then he bent over again and wrote on the ground. When they heard this, they all left, one by one, the older ones first…. Jesus straightened up and said, "I do not condemn you either. Go, but do not sin again." *John 8: 1-11*

> "Go, but do not sin again."

"Codependent No More!"

Jesus acts as a "change agent" for the woman living in an adulterous relationship – a situation that was hurting herself and others. His words challenge her to take the first step toward healing those relationships: "Go, but do not sin again."

In her book *Codependent No More*, Melody Beattie describes how people, living in unhealthy relationships, feel they can't change things by themselves. Often it takes someone outside the situation to identify the behaviour that holds them trapped. To name it with honesty, and with love.

Recently, a friend challenged me to look at some choices I'd made in my life. Like the woman in today's reading, I knew I had a decision to make: to stay in the unhealthy situation, or to start the journey towards wholeness.

Lord, help me to heed the voice that challenges.
It calls me to become stronger and more loving.

The Israelites left Mount Hor… but on the way the people lost their patience and spoke against God and Moses. They complained, "Why did you bring us out of Egypt to die in this desert, where there is no food or water?" Then the Lord sent poisonous snakes, and many Israelites were bitten and died. The people said to Moses, "We sinned when we spoke against the Lord and against you. Now pray to the Lord to take these snakes away." So Moses prayed…. Then the Lord told Moses to make a metal snake and put it on a pole, so that anyone who was bitten could look at it and be healed. So Moses made a bronze snake and put it on a pole. Anyone who had been bitten would look at the bronze snake and be healed.   *Numbers 21:4-9*

"…could look at it and be healed."

A painful lesson

Last fall my daughter was excited as she started her first day of kindergarten. But as the time went on, she became discouraged.

It turned out that at recess she'd stand alone – watching the others play, too shy to join in. I ended up literally having to drag her out the door in the mornings. She would cry bitterly, and I felt like crying, too. Why had I brought her into this wilderness? Surely she's too young to have to experience such loneliness and alienation.

Moses' bronze serpent was a symbol both of the dangers that surrounded the Israelites, and of God's faithfulness. I need that bronze serpent – to acknowledge my daughter's pain and to remind me that God is with her, and will lead her through it.

God, help me believe that you are with us on our journey, and that the evil in the world will not have the final word.

" If you obey my teaching, you are really my disciples; you will know the truth, and the truth will set you free." "We are the descendants of Abraham," they answered, "and we have never been anybody's slaves. What do you mean, then, by saying, 'You will be free'?"

Jesus said to them, "I am telling you the truth: everyone who sins is a slave of sin. A slave does not belong to a family permanently, but a [child] belongs there forever. If the Son sets you free, then you will be really free. I know you are Abraham's descendants. Yet you are trying to kill me, because you will not accept my teaching. I talk about what my Father has shown me, but you do what your father has told you."

John 8: 31-42

"If you obey my teaching, you are really my disciples..."

Obedience and choice

I find it hard to obey; I always have. I can be stubborn and so sure that my way is the only way. I have chosen to follow Jesus, to be his disciple, but when he says I need to obey… well, that feels different. As if I have no choice.

I go to the dictionary. Instead of "obey," I look up another word from today's reading – "disciple": one who accepts and assists in spreading the doctrines of another. Nearby is a word from the same root – "discipline": control gained by enforcing obedience. Obedience again, but with a different spin.

I'll look beyond the loaded word and focus on the term that offers me choices. I'll accept the teaching of Jesus and assist in spreading it: I'll really be his disciple.

Jesus, I want to be your disciple.
Help me to accept and spread your good news every day.

God said, "I make this covenant with you: I promise that you will be the ancestor of many nations. Your name will no longer be Abram, but Abraham, because I am making you the ancestor of many nations. I will give you many descendants, and some of them will be kings. You will have so many descendants that they will become nations.

"I will keep my promise to you and to your descendants.... I will be your God and the God of your descendants. I will give to you and to your descendants this land in which you are now a foreigner. The whole land of Canaan will belong to your descendants forever...."

God said to Abraham, "You also must agree to keep the covenant with me, both you and your descendants in future generations."

Genesis 17: 3-9

"...and the God of your descendants."

God lives here

One of my earliest childhood memories is of a visit to my great-grandmother's house. I was fascinated by the icons hanging on the walls in her tiny kitchen. There were images of Mary, Jesus and a few saints – but none of God!

When I asked my grandmother about this, she showed me a flickering flame dancing in a ruby red glass. God lived on a small shelf in my great-grandmother's kitchen.

Now, with my own daughters, I often light candles on our table. One of their favourite lights is a small red glass. A rosy glow warms their faces as they gaze on it. I recall the flickering ruby shadows that once lit my grandmother's profile. And I know God lives here, too.

God, you grace my home in light and shadow. Thank you.

The Lord is my protector;
he is my strong fortress.
My God is my protection,
and with him I am safe.
He protects me like a shield;
he defends me
and keeps me safe.
I call to the Lord,
and he saves me
from my enemies.
Praise the Lord!
The danger of death
was all around me;
the waves of destruction
rolled over me.
The danger of death
was around me,
and the grave set its trap for me.
In my trouble,
I called to the Lord;
I called to my God for help.
In his temple
he heard my voice;
he listened to my cry for help.

Psalm 18: 1-6

"My God is my protection…"

A good life

My grandmother was eighty-nine, lying in a hospital bed, suffering from cancer of the bone. "It's time for the Lord to come and get me," she said. "I've had a good life, but now it's time for me to go."

A good life! She and her young family survived on an isolated farm in primitive conditions. She lost two babies at birth, and another child as a toddler. Later, she spent years caring for my grandfather during his long decline with Alzheimer's disease. A good life?

And yet, like the psalmist, my grandmother learned from experience that God would give her the strength – not only to carry on but to build a good life. Now she was ready to meet God who had been her fortress.

Lord, teach me to trust in you – as the great women and men who have gone before me did.

E very year the parents of Jesus went to Jerusalem for the Passover Festival. When Jesus was twelve years old, they went to the festival as usual. When the festival was over, they started back home, but the boy Jesus stayed in Jerusalem. His parents did not know this; they thought that he was with the group, so they travelled a whole day and then started looking for him among their relatives and friends....

On the third day they found him in the Temple, sitting with the Jewish teachers, listening to them and asking questions.... His mother said to him, "Son, why have you done this to us? Your father and I have been terribly worried...." He answered them, "Why did you have to look for me? Didn't you know that I had to be in my Father's house?"   *Luke 2: 41-51*

"...they found him in the Temple..."

Anxious and worried

When I was four years old, I went to stay with my aunt on her farm. In spite of her watchful eye, I wandered off. You can imagine her horror when she saw my footprints in the snow lead towards a hole in the river ice! I can still see her ashen face when she found me safe at a neighbour's house.

The young people in my family may fail to phone when I have reason to worry about them; they may adopt attitudes and ideas I find repugnant. When that happens, I need to remember the story of the adolescent Jesus and his terrified parents, and even my own childhood experience. I'm not the first person to spend anxious hours or days worrying about the children I love.

**Lord, help me to find peace
when I'm anxious about the ones I love.**

Then Jesus said to them, "This very night all of you will run away and leave me, for the scripture says, 'God will kill the shepherd, and the sheep of the flock will be scattered.' But after I am raised to life, I will go to Galilee ahead of you."

Peter spoke up and said to Jesus, "I will never leave you, even though all the rest do!"

Jesus said to Peter, "I tell you that before the rooster crows tonight, you will say three times that you do not know me."

Peter answered, "I will never say that, even if I have to die with you!"

And all the other disciples said the same thing.

Matthew 26: 14 – 27: 66

"I will never leave you…"

Betrayals

I hear this familiar story and Peter's words echo within me: "I will never leave you." I am a faithful follower of Jesus. I am his hands to the needy, his voice to the lonely. Surely I will never betray him.

And yet…. Just the other day I noticed a woman who walks her child to school every day. There was something profoundly sad about the way she paused, lingering a moment or two, as the other parents dropped off their children.

I smiled and said, "Good morning," but I had three children to care for, errands to run, and a date for morning coffee with my comfortable crowd. As I turned away, leaving her standing there alone in the school yard, I found myself remembering Peter's words….

**Lord, I am quick to recognize Peter's betrayal,
but slow to understand that my acts of omission betray you, too.**

The Lord says,
"Here is my servant,
whom I strengthen –
the one I have chosen,
with whom I am pleased.
I have filled him with my Spirit,
and he will bring justice
to every nation....
He will not lose hope or courage;
he will establish justice
on the earth."...
God created the heavens
and stretched them out;
he fashioned the earth
and all that lives there;
he gave life and breath
to all its people.
And now the Lord God
says to his servant,
"I, the Lord, have called you
and given you power
to see that justice is done
on earth.
Through you I will make
a covenant with all peoples;
through you I will bring light
to the nations.
You will open the eyes
of the blind
and set free those who sit
in dark prisons."

Isaiah 42: 1-7

"You will open the eyes of the blind..."

The gift of sight

"Dr Jane," as I called her during the brief time we worked together, had difficulties with today's reading. Blind due to juvenile diabetes, for her blindness was not symbolic but linked to her unique genetic circumstances. Her blindness was not a metaphor, but a tedious fact of daily life, a litany of "smashing crack-ups" that could send objects flying and cause bruises on her arms and legs.

She reminded me that "sight" is indeed an interior concept, a gift. She worked tirelessly, finding her way as a blind physician in a seeing world.

I, too, must find a way, through my inner darkness and doubt.

**Dear God, I'm not looking for miracles – just a sense that
no matter where I drift, you will keep me safe.**

Jesus said, "Now the Son of Man's glory is revealed; now God's glory is revealed through him.... My children, I shall not be with you very much longer. You will look for me; but I tell you now what I told the Jewish authorities, 'You cannot go where I am going.' And now I give you a new commandment: love one another. As I have loved you, so you must love one another. If you have love for one another, then everyone will know that you are my disciples."

"Where are you going, Lord?" Simon Peter asked him.

"You cannot follow me now where I am going," answered Jesus; "but later you will follow me."

"Lord, why can't I follow you now?" asked Peter. "I am ready to die for you!"   *John 13: 21-33, 36-38*

> "…but later you will follow me."

Love one another

The day-to-day demands of parenting three young children alone had taken their toll. One night, after a particularly challenging day, I whispered my husband's name: "How I wish I could see you again. Can't I join you now?" And, in the stillness of the night, I heard him say, "No, not yet. The children still need you."

Just as Peter wanted to follow Jesus, I wanted to follow my husband – to the grave and beyond. And, like Peter, I received a gentle reminder, "As I have loved you, so you must love one another."

I know that I have been loved – and loved deeply – in my life. And I know I must find the strength to continue to give my children the love and support they need.

Dear Jesus, how hard it is to follow you in the everyday demands of life. Give me strength. Give me hope. Give me love.

The Sovereign Lord has taught me what to say, so that I can strengthen the weary. Every morning he makes me eager to hear what he is going to teach me. The Lord has given me understanding, and I have not rebelled or turned away from him. I bared my back to those who beat me. I did not stop them when they insulted me, when they pulled out the hairs of my beard and spit in my face. But their insults cannot hurt me because the Sovereign Lord gives me help.... Does anyone dare bring charges against me? Let us go to court together! Let him bring his accusation! The Sovereign Lord himself defends me – who, then, can prove me guilty?

Isaiah 50: 4-9

> "…so that I can strengthen the weary."

Being there

Fair enough for Isaiah, a prophet. Or Jesus, who healed with a touch or a word. But then, there's me, wondering, "What can I say? Where's the magic word that will make it all better?"

Teaching English to refugees, I am often surrounded by sad, sometimes horrific stories: homes lost; children killed; lives over in a moment, never to return. And I seek a word "to strengthen the weary" – to offset the disillusionment of those who have seen the evil that can live in human beings, and felt it turned on them.

I have no way to go back and change things. No magic word. All I can do is be there. It's often not enough, but it's all I can do.

**God, give me the strength to stay and listen,
when I want to run away.**

Jesus and his disciples were at supper…. Jesus knew that the Father had given him complete power; he knew that he had come from God and was going to God. So he rose from the table, took off his outer garment, and tied a towel around his waist. Then he poured some water into a washbasin and began to wash the disciples' feet…. He came to Simon Peter, who said, "Are you going to wash my feet, Lord?"

Jesus answered him, "You do not understand now what I am doing, but you will understand later." Peter declared, "Never at any time will you wash my feet!" "If I do not wash your feet," Jesus answered, "you will no longer be my disciple." Simon Peter answered, "Lord, do not wash only my feet, then! Wash my hands and head, too!"   *John 13: 1-15*

> "Never at any time will you wash my feet!"

Accepting help

I have always been very self-sufficient. As a child, I could amuse myself for hours; as an adult, I have always been employed, able to take care of myself, and motivated. I have good friends, but I never used to bother them with my personal crises.

Then my life hit a rough patch. People began offering to help. I reacted like Simon Peter did. "What? Wash my feet? I don't need that kind of service, especially from someone I love and respect. Really, I'm fine on my own."

After some time, though, I had to admit that I desperately needed my friends' help. It was a revelation to me – that we are all to serve each other, and that in being served I can be healed.

Lord, I've always taken care of myself.
Help me to accept help when I need it.

Simon Peter and another disciple followed Jesus. That other disciple went with Jesus into the courtyard of the High Priest's house, while Peter stayed outside by the gate. Then the other disciple went back out, spoke to the girl at the gate, and brought Peter inside. The girl at the gate said to Peter, "Aren't you also one of the disciples of that man?"

"No, I am not," answered Peter....

The High Priest questioned Jesus about his disciples and about his teaching. Jesus answered, "I have always spoken publicly to everyone.... I have never said anything in secret. Why, then, do you question me? Question the people who heard me...." Then Annas sent him, still tied up, to Caiaphas the High Priest.

John 18: 1 – 19: 42

"Aren't you also one of the disciples of that man?"

Facing the pain

My Congolese friends tell me about the war that's tearing their country apart. They say the lucky ones are those who make it to refugee camps. Those who don't, mostly women and children, are living in a kind of hell on earth. I don't want to hear these stories – I try not to believe them, or try to find relief in blaming someone.

In today's reading, Pilate is intrigued by Jesus, but he doesn't even give Jesus the dignity of a full hearing, his "day in court." Guilty of avoidance, he hands him over to Caiaphas. Peter pretends he never knew the man who changed his life.

Today, of all days, I'll try not to flinch from looking deep into my Lord's eyes as he dies.

Lord, give me the courage to head straight into suffering until I find you.

After the Sabbath, as Sunday morning was dawning, Mary Magdalene and the other Mary went to look at the tomb. Suddenly there was a violent earthquake; an angel of the Lord came down from heaven, rolled the stone away, and sat on it....

The angel spoke to the women. "You must not be afraid," he said. "I know you are looking for Jesus, who was crucified. He is not here; he has been raised.... Go quickly now, and tell his disciples...." So they left the tomb in a hurry, afraid and yet filled with joy, and ran to tell his disciples. Suddenly Jesus met them and said, "Peace be with you." They came up to him, took hold of his feet, and worshipped him. "Do not be afraid," Jesus said to them.   *Matthew 28: 1-10*

"...afraid and yet filled with joy..."

Deep joy

A sunny spring morning in Ireland: I stood in the library of Trinity College, Dublin. In the display case before me was the Book of Kells, an ancient gospel of great beauty. As I gazed upon it, I was filled with joy, awe and wonder.

Experiences like this help me to imagine the feelings of the women at the tomb on Easter morning. Moments of generous love, awesome beauty and quiet peace help me to translate the overwhelming message of Easter into ordinary human language. I am given a tiny insight into a mystery beyond human comprehension.

Thanks to these flashes of light and grace, I can, however dimly, imagine the feelings of those who once knelt before their Lord, dead and now alive.

**Risen Lord, thank you for the special moments
when I see your glory reflected around me in this world.**

Early on Sunday morning, while it was still dark, Mary Magdalene went to the tomb and saw that the stone had been taken away from the entrance. She went running to Simon Peter and the other disciple, whom Jesus loved, and told them, "They have taken the Lord from the tomb, and we don't know where they have put him!"

Then Peter and the other disciple went to the tomb. The two of them were running, but the other disciple ran faster than Peter and reached the tomb first. He bent over and saw the linen cloths, but he did not go in. Behind him came Simon Peter, and he went straight into the tomb. He saw the linen cloths lying there and the cloth which had been around Jesus' head…. Then the other disciple, who had reached the tomb first, also went in; he saw and believed.

John 20: 1-18

"…and he went straight into the tomb."

The empty tomb

Over time, Christianity has come to be symbolized by the *cross*. However, it's the *empty tomb* that has most challenged and shaped my thinking about my faith.

Because "emptiness" cannot be given a shape, we don't reflect on it as easily as we do on the symbol of the cross. We don't talk about the emptiness that we experience. We often fill our lives with noise, activity and people – to avoid confronting that emptiness.

I've experienced God's love most deeply when I am most empty. First, I had to be willing to enter the emptiness, to confront the possibility of God not being there. Yet, in that searching, I've discovered the truth – that God gives me new life where all I've known is death. And that I am deeply loved.

Lord, help me to enter the emptiness I experience deep within me, and to trust that you are there already.

Protect me, O God;
I trust in you for safety.
I say to the Lord,
"You are my Lord;
all the good things I have
come from you...."
I praise the Lord,
because he guides me,
and in the night my conscience
warns me.
I am always aware of the Lord's
presence;
he is near,
and nothing can shake me.
And so I am thankful and glad,
and I feel completely secure,
because you protect me
from the power of death.
I have served you faithfully,
and you will not abandon me
to the world of the dead.
You will show me the path
that leads to life;
your presence fills me with joy
and brings me pleasure forever.

Psalm 16: 1-2, 5-11

"...and in the night my conscience warns me."

Sleepless nights

Strange that in this joyous song, the psalmist mentions his conscience hunting him down in his sleep. I, too, am one for whom the night is often difficult. Be it something I'm anxious about doing, or something I regret, in the night it comes, waking me. No escape.

How many nights did Jesus spend alone, his conscience saying, "No, you must not stop. You must drink from this cup." Yet his anxious nights ended, along with his agony. In the morning, the tomb was empty. Resurrection! Resurrection that's not possible without the agony.

For me, too, the night often brings not only the sleepless rumination, but the answer I seek. Resurrection. The dawn does come.

Lord, when you send me sleepless nights,
let me strain to hear the sound of your voice.

Mary stood crying outside the tomb…. "Woman, why are you crying?" Jesus asked her. "Who is it that you are looking for?"

She thought he was the gardener, so she said to him, "If you took him away, sir, tell me where you have put him, and I will go and get him." Jesus said to her, "Mary!" She turned toward him and said in Hebrew, "Rabboni!" (This means "Teacher.") "Do not hold on to me," Jesus told her, "because I have not yet gone back up to the Father. But go to my brothers and tell them that I am returning to him who is my Father and their Father, my God and their God."

So Mary Magdalene went and told the disciples that she had seen the Lord and related to them what he had told her.   *John 20: 11-18*

"Jesus said to her, 'Mary!'"

No more doubts

When our son died, we couldn't get our hearts and our heads in sync. Our heads knew he was dead – we had stayed with his body long enough to feel his hands, his feet, starting to turn as cold and stiff as plastic. But our hearts had trouble accepting that reality.

So we kept watching for a lanky blond kid striding up the sidewalk, listening for a familiar voice at the back door. We would have given anything to see him once more, to hear his voice, to know he was all right.

Mary came to the tomb with similar feelings. And through her tears, she heard her name. If I had her experience, I know that I would have no doubts either. Ever again.

Jesus, I long to hear your voice speaking to me, too.
Open my ears, and eyes, to your unexpected presence.

There was a man who had been lame all his life. Every day he was carried to the gate to beg for money from the people who were going into the Temple. When he saw Peter and John going in, he begged them to give him something. Peter said, "Look at us!" So he looked at them, expecting to get something from them. But Peter said to him, "I have no money at all, but I give you what I have: in the name of Jesus Christ of Nazareth I order you to get up and walk!" Then he took him by his right hand and helped him up. At once the man's feet and ankles became strong; he jumped up, stood on his feet, and started walking around…. When the people recognized him as the beggar who had sat at the Beautiful Gate, they were all surprised and amazed at what had happened to him.

Acts 3: 1-10

> "…expecting to get something from them."

Comfort or challenge

Frank McNair established the first mental health clinic in British Columbia's interior. When he died, the church was jammed with people who came to pay their respects. But not because he had a soft touch. The doctor giving the eulogy commented, "If people needed to be challenged, we referred them to Frank. If they needed comforting, we referred them to his colleague."

The beggar at the gate expected comforting. Peter challenged him. He took the beggar's hand and hoisted him to his feet. And the man danced around rejoicing.

How did Peter do it? All we know is that it could not have been a psychosomatic illness because the people *knew* this man. He really had been crippled, and now was healed.

I find it so hard to know whether to comfort someone or challenge them. Guide me, Lord.

O Lord, our Lord,
your greatness is seen
in all the world!
Your praise reaches up
to the heavens;
it is sung by children
and babies....
When I look at the sky,
which you have made,
at the moon and the stars,
which you set in their places
– what are human beings,
that you think of them;
mere mortals,
that you care for them?

Yet you made them inferior
only to yourself;
you crowned them with glory
and honour.
You appointed them rulers
over everything you made;
you placed them
over all creation:
sheep and cattle,
and the wild animals too;
the birds and the fish
and the creatures in the seas.
O Lord, our Lord,
your greatness is seen
in all the world!   *Psalm 8: 1-9*

> "You appointed them rulers..."

Ruler over all?

When I was a child, I couldn't wait to be a grown-up. I thought, "Then I'll be able to do whatever I want." As an adult, I soon came to realize the truth about my illusion!

I seem to have "rule" over some things – like the daffodils I planted last fall, which I now see outside my window. I planted them, but what control do I really have over the forces that make them grow? I can help, but my "rule," in this case, is illusory.

And what of the "rule" we, as a human race, have shown over our planet's air and water? The species we have rendered extinct? How have we exercised this sacred trust?

**God, help me live responsibly on this planet
you have entrusted to us.**

J esus appeared once more to his disciples. Simon Peter, Thomas, Nathanael, the sons of Zebedee, and two other disciples of Jesus were all together. Simon Peter said, "I am going fishing."

"We will come with you," they told him. So they went out in a boat, but all that night they did not catch a thing. As the sun was rising, Jesus stood at the water's edge, but the disciples did not know that it was Jesus. Then he asked them, "Young men, haven't you caught anything?"

"Not a thing," they answered. He said, "Throw your net out on the right side of the boat, and you will catch some." So they threw the net out and could not pull it back in, because they had caught so many fish. The disciple whom Jesus loved said to Peter, "It is the Lord!"   *John 21: 1-14*

> "I am going fishing."

Within the familiar

The day after my father's funeral, my sister and I took my mother for a walk in the park. We retraced the route that we used to follow so many years ago, when both parents would take us into the park: around the fountain, through the rockery, over to the lookout post for the dramatic view down toward the Welsh border. And then out through the rose garden, with its glorious fragrances.

But this day is different: my mother now uses a wheelchair, and this is her first day out without her husband there to push her. Happily, the scent of roses still welcomes us.

Like the disciples, in the face of catastrophe, we choose a familiar activity for consolation and security. And Jesus continues to break through in wonder.

Jesus, may I always be ready to welcome your surprising, yet gentle, tap on the shoulder.

After Jesus rose from death early on Sunday, he appeared first to Mary Magdalene, from whom he had driven out seven demons. She went and told his companions. They were mourning and crying; and when they heard her say that Jesus was alive and that she had seen him, they did not believe her.

After this, Jesus appeared in a different manner to two of them while they were on their way to the country. They returned and told the others, but these would not believe it.

Last of all, Jesus appeared to the eleven disciples as they were eating. He scolded them, because they did not have faith and because they were too stubborn to believe those who had seen him alive. He said to them, "Go throughout the whole world and preach the gospel to all people."   *Mark 16: 9-15*

"...he appeared first to Mary Magdalene..."

Outsiders

Today we might say Mary Magdalene had a mental illness. Perhaps she used to wander the streets shouting unintelligibly. Perhaps her family had locked her up. Whatever her affliction, she almost certainly lived as an outsider.

On Easter morning, she went looking for Jesus. And Jesus gave her a message for the leaders of his soon-to-be-born church. And where were those leaders? We know from the gospels that they were cowering behind barricaded doors back in the city.

When we feel that our religious leaders have barricaded themselves behind closed doors, we have only to look to Easter morning to see that it is nothing new. Sometimes it's the outsiders – the people who have no reputation or power – who recognize Jesus first.

Lord, open my heart to hear the good news – even when the messenger is someone dispossessed or reviled.

O ne of the twelve disciples, Thomas, was not with them when Jesus came. So the other disciples told him, "We have seen the Lord!" Thomas said, "Unless I see the scars of the nails in his hands and put my finger on those scars and my hand in his side, I will not believe."

A week later the disciples were together again indoors, and Thomas was with them. The doors were locked, but Jesus came and stood among them and said, "Peace be with you." Then he said to Thomas, "Put your finger here, and look at my hands; then reach out your hand and put it in my side. Stop your doubting, and believe!" Thomas answered him, "My Lord and my God!"

Jesus said, "Do you believe because you see me? How happy are those who believe without seeing me!" *John 20: 19-31*

> "Peace be with you."

Abiding peace

In Burundi, where she lives, my sister has a friend called Déo. He is in prison for a crime he did not commit. He is suffering from AIDS, and now also from cancer. He is married with young children. Yet, she says, he is deeply at peace. What kind of peace can that be?

I can only think that it is the very same peace that Jesus gave to his disciples, consumed with fear in their locked room – a peace that isn't just an absence of danger or pain or suffering. As Jesus said the word "peace," he was showing them the marks of pain and death on his body.

Perhaps if I trust that injustice and pain and death will not win, if I can trust Jesus' love, I will know Déo's peace, too.

Lord, peel away all pretence of false security, and teach me true peace.

You do not want sacrifices and offerings;
    you do not ask for animals burned whole on the altar
    or for sacrifices to take away sins.
Instead, you have given me ears to hear you,
and so I answered, "Here I am;
your instructions for me are in the book of the Law.
How I love to do your will, my God!
I keep your teaching in my heart."
In the assembly of all your people, Lord,
I told the good news that you save us.
You know that I will never stop telling it.
I have not kept the news of salvation to myself;
I have always spoken of your faithfulness and help.
In the assembly of all your people I have not been silent
about your loyalty and constant love.   *Psalm 40: 6-10*

"You do not want sacrifices and offerings..."

Self-sacrifice

Our dog sauntered down to the water to get a drink and disturbed a family of ducks. The mother duck thrashed just beyond the dog's nose, quacking furiously. "Chase me," she seemed to say, "not my little ones!" Self-sacrifice seems to be a theme of motherhood.

I wonder how different Christianity might be, had its interpreters through the ages been mothers rather than fathers. The mother duck's self-sacrifice had nothing to do with ritual, with ransom to pay off an authority, or with punishment. It was a totally voluntary act to distract attention from those she loved, those she felt responsible for.

I don't hear many echoes of that motivation in traditional Christianity.

**Lord, when I make sacrifices,
why do I calculate the cost when those I love are priceless?**

" I tell you that you must all be born again. The wind blows wherever it wishes; you hear the sound it makes, but you do not know where it comes from or where it is going. It is like that with everyone who is born of the Spirit."

How can this be?" asked Nicodemus.... Jesus answered, "I am telling you the truth: we speak of what we know and report what we have seen, yet none of you is willing to accept our message. You do not believe me when I tell you about the things of this world; how will you ever believe me, then, when I tell you about the things of heaven? And no one has ever gone up to heaven except the son of Man, who came down from heaven."

John 3: 7-15

"The wind blows wherever it wishes..."

The Spirit's presence

"Who Has Seen the Wind?" The title of this well-known novel by W. O. Mitchell captures the elusive yet compelling search for life's meaning that often absorbs our attention.

I can't "see" the wind, but I can observe its effects. I can't "know" the wind – hold it within my grasp to examine it – but I can feel its presence.

God's Spirit is just as elusive *and* just as real as the wind. I've seen God's Spirit when my children were born, when death visited our family, and in the concern friends have shown us in our time of need. I've known the Spirit's presence as I struggle to live a life of integrity and justice. An unseen God? Yes, but a God that is as close to me as the wind.

**Loving Spirit, guide my words and actions
when I cannot see clearly the way to go.**

The High Priest and all his companions, members of the local party of the Sadducees, became extremely jealous of the apostles; so they decided to take action. They arrested the apostles and put them in the public jail. But that night an angel of the Lord opened the prison gates, led the apostles out, and said to them, "Go and stand in the Temple, and tell the people all about this new life." The apostles obeyed, and at dawn they entered the Temple and started teaching.

Acts 5: 17-26

"…an angel of the Lord opened the prison gates…"

Angels

It's hard to think of angels when it's cold and dark outside, and when you're preparing to bury a young girl just sixteen. That's where I find myself now.

Several years ago I survived a very serious illness. Someone told me that I was "lucky to have dodged the bullet." This young girl was not so "lucky."

I know people will say, "But the angels have come for her. They have opened the gates…." But I can't see that right now. What I see is a grandma looking into the distance, young girls with tear-stained faces, and a mother still in shock. And it is dark, and cold.

Maybe, in the face of human tragedy, we have to be angels for one another.

**God, give me the strength to bring a little light
into someone's darkness.**

They brought the apostles in, made them stand before the Council, and the High Priest questioned them. "We gave you strict orders not to teach in the name of this man," he said; "but see what you have done! You have spread your teaching all over Jerusalem, and you want to make us responsible for his death!"

Peter and the other apostles answered, "We must obey God, not men. The God of our ancestors raised Jesus from death, after you had killed him by nailing him to a cross. God raised him to his right side as Leader and Saviour, to give the people of Israel the opportunity to repent and have their sins forgiven. We are witnesses to these things – we and the Holy Spirit, who is God's gift to those who obey him."

Acts 5: 27-33

> "We are witnesses to these things…"

Good news

Michael, who has severe cerebral palsy, does not speak in words. He also needs a wheelchair to get around. But this has not prevented him from being part of a liturgical dance group at L'Arche Daybreak called "The Spirit Movers." That is where Michael shines! When his dance partner, Steve, whirls him around, Michael has a smile that lights up the whole room. His joy is irrepressible.

When Michael and Steve go places, people sometimes look at Michael critically, as if he doesn't have a right to be there – especially if he makes noises. But Steve insists that Michael participate. He knows Michael has something to say – a "good news" to share that cannot be stifled.

**O Holy Spirit, give me the courage to speak up
for what I know to be true.**

J esus asked Philip, "Where can we buy enough food to feed all these people? Philip answered, "For everyone to have even a little, it would take more than two hundred silver coins to buy enough bread." Then Andrew said, "There is a boy here who has five loaves of barley bread and two fish. But they will certainly not be enough for all these people."

"Make the people sit down," Jesus told them…. He took the bread, gave thanks to God, and distributed it to the people who were sitting there. He did the same with the fish, and they all had as much as they wanted. When they were all full, he said, "Gather the pieces left over." So they gathered them all and filled twelve baskets with the pieces left over from the five barley loaves which the people had eaten.   John 6: 1-15

> "There is a boy here who has five loaves…"

Not much to offer

My brother and sister-in-law got married twenty years ago. Each doubted that they were lovable enough, or that they had enough to offer the other. Yet with that wonderfully foolish bravery that lovers have, the question was asked and the answer was Yes!

Since then they have brought forth three children; as well, they have made their home into a place of welcome for many beyond their own family.

Perhaps they each felt a bit like Andrew, who mentions that there are a few loaves and fishes available, but then immediately feels foolish for having suggested it. This simple and innocent offering, made with many doubts, is transformed by Jesus into abundance, enough for everyone with plenty to spare. This is the miracle of love.

Lord, I don't feel I have much to offer.
But take it: you can work miracles with it.

When evening came, Jesus' disciples went down to the lake, got into a boat, and went back across the lake toward Capernaum. Night came on, and Jesus still had not come to them. By then a strong wind was blowing and stirring up the water. The disciples had rowed about three or four miles when they saw Jesus walking on the water, coming near the boat, and they were terrified. "Don't be afraid," Jesus told them, "it is I!" Then they willingly took him into the boat, and immediately the boat reached land at the place they were heading for.

John 6: 16-21

> "Don't be afraid."

Unexpected hope

Sometimes I have difficulty with the miracle accounts. They're so different from my own experience. But I like the hope they give – that the natural way can be turned miraculously on its ear. And sometimes I feel I could use a miracle in my own life!

I met a Cambodian woman who forgave the man who murdered her parents. "We have to forgive," she said. "It was the times, the war." Her words were sincere; she was at peace. To this man, her attitude must have seemed, as it did to me, a miracle.

It gives me hope to think that even in hopeless cases, when I can't see how things can change, Jesus says, "Don't be afraid." Miracles can happen when we're least expecting them.

**God, help me. Let me know that there is always hope.
Miracles can happen.**

Two of Jesus' followers were going to a village named Emmaus.... As they talked and discussed, Jesus himself drew near and walked along with them; they saw him, but somehow did not recognize him. Jesus said, "What are you talking about to each other, as you walk along?"

One of them asked him, "Are you the only visitor in Jerusalem who doesn't know the things that have been happening there these last few days?"

"What things?" he asked. "The things that happened to Jesus of Nazareth," they answered. "This man was a prophet and was considered by God and by all the people to be powerful in everything he said and did. Our chief priests and rulers handed him over to be sentenced to death, and he was crucified. And we had hoped that he would be the one who was going to set Israel free." *Luke 24: 13-35*

> "...they saw him, but somehow did not recognize him."

Seeing Jesus

First, the disciples don't recognize Jesus; then he has to explain everything to them again. "Somehow they didn't recognize him...." I mean, really.

We've heard it all before: we need to see Jesus in other people. Do we need to hear it again? Maybe.

There was this kid. By the way, I'm a teacher. Man, that kid ran me ragged. Never took responsibility. Always somebody else's fault. Very nice until things didn't go his way. No matter what I did, I couldn't get through. That's when it's hard to stay open. That's when it's hard to see Jesus. It's great to say, but sometimes it's confusing, and hard to do.

"Somehow they didn't recognize him...." Maybe we *do* need to hear it all again.

Lord, let me see you in the faces of your children.

Next day the crowd that had stayed on the other side of the lake realized that there had been only one boat there. They knew that Jesus had not gone in it with his disciples, but that they had left without him. Other boats, which were from Tiberias, came to shore…. When the crowd saw that Jesus was not there, they got into those boats and went to Capernaum, looking for him.

When the people found Jesus on the other side of the lake, they said, "Teacher, when did you get here?" Jesus answered, "I am telling you the truth: you are looking for me because you ate the bread and had all you wanted, not because you understood my miracles. Do not work for food that spoils; instead, work for the food that lasts for eternal life."

John 6: 22-29

"…work for the food that lasts…"

Food that lasts

"You are looking for me because you ate the bread and had all you wanted, not because you understood my miracles." I have to admit that there are times when I eat for the wrong reasons. Even though I'm not hungry, I fill myself with "food that spoils." Trying to fill an emptiness that exists within me. Trying to convince myself that these "small indulgences" will make me happy. Trying to silence an inner voice that cries out to be heard.

Fearful, I turn away from Jesus' challenge to "work for the food that lasts for eternal life."

When I *have* chosen to listen to that inner voice, it has shown me hurts that need healing. And it has shown me how love can heal those hurts, making my emptiness less frightening.

Dearest Lord, out of fear I turn from your truth.
Give me the courage to be still, to listen,
and to allow your love to heal the hurt in my heart.

They replied, "What miracle will you perform so that we may see it and believe you? What will you do? Our ancestors ate manna in the desert, just as the scripture says, 'He gave them bread from heaven to eat.'"

"I am telling you the truth," Jesus said. "What Moses gave you was not the bread from heaven; it is my Father who gives you the real bread from heaven. For the bread that God gives is he who comes down from heaven and gives life to the world."

"Sir," they asked him, "give us this bread always." "I am the bread of life," Jesus told them. "Those who come to me will never be hungry; those who believe in me will never be thirsty."   *John 6: 30-35*

> "What miracle will you perform...?"

More proof

What a bold crowd, demanding another miracle of Jesus. He's just fed the five thousand, after all!

Would I have asked for more proof? Probably. I often bargain with God: "If you'll get me over this hurdle," I say, "I promise to be more patient, less judgmental." The crisis passes, and my promises vanish. The next time there's trouble, I vow to believe *if* God will do one more miracle for me. Just like the crowd.

The one miracle that can change my life forever has already happened. So, no more deals, no more proof required! The Spirit of Jesus dwells in my heart. If I follow the Spirit's promptings, I will find the nourishment I need to face each crisis – without demanding new miracles.

> **Lord, may I be aware of the rich blessings**
> **you have given me today and every day.**

" I am the bread of life…. Those who come to me will never be hungry; those who believe in me will never be thirsty…. Everyone whom my Father gives me will come to me. I will never turn away anyone who comes to me, because I have come down from heaven to do not my own will but the will of him who sent me. And it is the will of him who sent me that I should not lose any of all those he has given me, but that I should raise them all to life on the last day. For what my Father wants is that all who see the Son and believe in him should have eternal life. And I will raise them to life on the last day."

John 6: 35-40

"And I will raise them to life on the last day."

Raised to life

I can barely wrap words around this mystery. Five months into their pregnancy, Steve and Laurie received the tragic news that the baby in Laurie's womb was dead.

When no natural miscarriage occurred, doctors induced labour. Laurie pushed and breathed and groaned like any mother-to-be in labour – and all the while she knew that she was giving birth… to death.

Laurie and Steve cradled this stillborn baby, and in the very face of death, they named him. They were moved in part by grief, for how could they grieve a nameless child? But more than this, they were moved by the conviction that, on the last day, this child, too, would be called by name and raised to life.

**Jesus, in matters both great and small,
help me act with confidence in your promise of life.**

An Ethiopian eunuch, who was an important official in charge of the treasury of the queen of Ethiopia, was on his way home. As he rode along, he was reading from the book of the prophet Isaiah. The Holy Spirit said to Philip, "Go over to that carriage and stay close to it." Philip ran over and heard him reading from the book of the prophet Isaiah. He asked him, "Do you understand what you are reading…?"

The official asked Philip, "Tell me, of whom is the prophet saying this? Of himself or of someone else?" Then Philip began to speak; starting from this passage of scripture, he told him the Good News about Jesus. As they travelled down the road, they came to a place where there was some water, and the official said, "Here is some water. What is to keep me from being baptized?"… Both Philip and the official went down into the water, and Philip baptized him.   *Acts 8: 26-40*

> "What is to keep me from being baptized?"

Time to act

In April 1963 Martin Luther King was arrested in Birmingham, Alabama for participating in a non-violent protest against racial segregation. After his arrest, several local clergymen published a letter in the city's newspaper criticizing King's "impatience" and suggesting that segregation would take care of itself "in time." King penned a response – scribbling notes on the margins of the newspaper – that would become a classic in the literature of non-violence.

In his letter, King wrote, "Time itself is neutral. We must use time creatively, in the knowledge that the time is always ripe to do good." In his own way, King is like the eunuch who, upon seeing water, knew it was the moment to act.

God, each day brings with it moments when the time is right to act. Help me see – and seize – that moment today.

Friday | **APRIL 11**

As Saul was coming near the city of Damascus, suddenly a light from the sky flashed around him. He fell to the ground and heard a voice saying to him, "Saul, Saul! Why do you persecute me?"

"Who are you, Lord?" he asked. "I am Jesus, whom you persecute," the voice said. "But get up and go into the city, where you will be told what you must do."

Saul got up from the ground and opened his eyes, but could not see a thing. So [the men who were travelling with Saul] took him by the hand and led him into Damascus. For three days he was not able to see....

Ananias entered the house where Saul was, and placed his hands on him. "Brother Saul," he said, "the Lord has sent me... so that you might see again and be filled with the Holy Spirit."   *Acts 9: 1-20*

> "...a light from the sky flashed around him."

In a new light

By the time I reached the lake the sky had completely clouded over. Having been up all night with work, I hoped that a few moments of sun near the water would restore my soul. Agitated, overtired and anxious to finish my work, I turned away from the lake. I really didn't have time for this.

I'm not sure what made me turn around to take one last glance. There, above the water, the sky opened. A shaft of sunlight slowly appeared and grew in intensity. Within moments I was completely surrounded by light. There was no voice, no directive from above. I knew, however, that I was in the presence of something great, something holy. Suddenly my work fell into perspective, and I was grateful.

God, open my eyes and soul to your presence all around me.

J esus said, "I am telling you the truth: if you do not eat the flesh of the Son of Man and drink his blood, you will not have life in yourselves…." Many of his followers heard this and said, "This teaching is too hard. Who can listen to it?"

Without being told, Jesus knew that they were grumbling about this, so he said to them, "Does this make you want to give up? What gives life is God's Spirit; human power is of no use at all…."

Because of this, many of Jesus' followers turned back and would not go with him any more. So he asked the twelve disciples, "And you – would you also like to leave?" Simon Peter answered him, "Lord, to whom would we go? You have the words that give eternal life. And now we believe and know that you are the Holy One who has come from God."   *John 6: 53, 60-69*

"And you – would you also like to leave?"

Tough love

If I asked my friends to eat my flesh and drink my blood, I bet they'd go away, too. The idea is unreasonable; it's uncivilized.

Jim Loney is a Canadian who went to Iraq as a peacemaker and was kidnapped. Rather than interpreting "peace" as that safe feeling we get from sitting at home and staying out of trouble, Jim risked his life – his body and blood – for the life that Jesus is talking about. His life is a witness to a power that goes beyond the flesh, beyond what is reasonable and "civilized."

Today's reading challenges me: Does the thought of eating the flesh of Jesus offend me? Do I also wish to go away? Today, with a witness like Jim Loney, I have to answer with Peter, Where else would I go?

**Lord, give me the courage to be ready
to give up my life for love.**

J esus said, "I am telling you the truth: the man who does not enter the sheep pen by the gate, but climbs in some other way, is a thief and a robber. The man who goes in through the gate is the shepherd of the sheep. The gatekeeper opens the gate for him; the sheep hear his voice as he calls his own sheep by name, and he leads them out. When he has brought them out, he goes ahead of them, and the sheep follow him, because they know his voice. They will not follow someone else; instead, they will run away from such a person, because they do not know his voice."   *John 10: 1-5*

"...a thief and a robber."

A culture of thieves

Some evenings I like to sit in front of the television and flip from station to station. It's a bad habit. I don't watch much of anything. I just sit in limbo catching glimpses and fragments of different images and voices. In no time at all, I notice that an hour has stolen away.

I am like the sheep that don't have enough sense to recognize the voice that calls them to a restful place. I am so easily misled by the thieves of this culture.

How can I hear Jesus' voice when I give attention to so many other voices? I would like to change this habit. With more quiet time I might hear and recognize Jesus' voice at the end of the day.

Jesus, help me make time to hear your voice each day.

Jesus said, "The man who goes in through the gate is the shepherd of the sheep. The gatekeeper opens the gate for him; the sheep hear his voice as he calls his own sheep by name, and he leads them out. When he has brought them out, he goes ahead of them, and the sheep follow him, because they know his voice. They will not follow someone else; instead, they will run away from such a person, because they do not know his voice....

"All others who came before me are thieves and robbers, but the sheep did not listen to them. Those who come in by me will be saved; they will come in and go out and find pasture. I have come in order that you might have life – life in all its fullness."   *John 10: 1-10*

> "...he calls his own sheep by name."

Called by name

Once, as a child, I was separated from my mother in a department store. I was so small that I could only see under the racks of clothing. I searched desperately among strange footwear for a sign of her familiar boots. Tears flowed as sadness, fear and panic overwhelmed me. I was lost!

Then came the wondrous moment when I heard Mom's familiar voice calling my name. Her voice led me to her. Relief and joy launched me into her waiting arms. There was no doubt that I was safely home, that place where I knew I was forever precious, beloved, called and known by name.

Jesus, the shepherd, calls me in the same way. Do I listen for his voice? Will I recognize him speaking my name?

Lord, many voices compete for my time, attention and talents. Today, help me to listen for your voice.

J esus was walking in Solomon's Porch in the Temple, when the people gathered around him and asked, "How long are you going to keep us in suspense? Tell us the plain truth: are you the Messiah?"

Jesus answered, "I have already told you, but you would not believe me. The deeds I do by my Father's authority speak on my behalf; but you will not believe, for you are not my sheep. My sheep listen to my voice; I know them, and they follow me. I give them eternal life, and they shall never die. No one can snatch them away from me. What my Father has given me is greater than everything, and no one can snatch them away from the Father's care. The Father and I are one."

John 10: 22-30

"...are you the Messiah?"

Beyond the title

Ever since the beginning, Jesus' identity has provoked controversy. Wandering prophet? Ordinary human person? Messiah? Son of God? Sides have been drawn; wars fought. Women and men have been killed: some condemned as heretics, others hailed as martyrs.

Whatever title I might decide to give Jesus, when I read the Good News stories, I discover the truth about his life. He was an individual who reached out to others – healing, forgiving, challenging and accepting. He knew the source of his love, and was always ready to tell others about God.

Like Jesus, I hope that I will be known – not by any title or position I have – but by my words and actions, and by my belief in the God of love.

**God, give me the courage to let my words
and actions speak of your love.**

Jesus said, "Whoever believes in me believes not only in me but also in him who sent me. Whoever sees me sees also him who sent me. I have come into the world as light, so that everyone who believes in me should not remain in the darkness. If people hear my message and do not obey it, I will not judge them. I came, not to judge the world, but to save it. Those who reject me and do not accept my message have one who will judge them. The words I have spoken will be their judge on the last day! This is true, because I have not spoken on my own authority, but the Father who sent me has commanded me what I must say and speak. And I know that his command brings eternal life." *John 12: 44-50*

> "I have come into the world as light…"

Light and life

Every night, when my children were very young, I'd go to their rooms and look in on them before going to bed. And every night, my visit to my youngest son's room was the same. He'd be fast asleep, but every single light would be on, giving off enough illumination for a plane to land!

He never said he was afraid of the dark, and he didn't seem afraid of the dark, but clearly he needed lots of light in order to feel secure enough to fall asleep.

I never said anything to him about the lights, but as I turned them all off, I used to smile to myself, happy that he could so directly and easily address his anxieties and worries.

My own darkness has always been far more resistant.

**Lord, as I wander about in darkness,
show me your light and guide me home.**

" I have set an example for you, so that you will do just what I have done for you. I am telling you the truth: no slaves are greater than their master, and no messengers are greater than the one who sent them. Now that you know this truth, how happy you will be if you put it into practice!

"I am not talking about all of you; I know those I have chosen. But the scripture must come true that says, 'The man who shared my food turned against me.' I tell you this now before it happens, so that when it does happen, you will believe that 'I Am Who I Am.' I am telling you the truth: whoever receives anyone I send receives me also; and whoever receives me receives him who sent me." *John 13: 16-20*

> "...whoever receives anyone I send..."

Anyone I send

As my dad once discovered, this "receiving anyone I send" thing can be risky.

One frigid winter morning in 1955, a lightly dressed man entered our small, rural post office in northwestern Ontario. He was broke, and he was hitchhiking to Winnipeg for work. Mom gave him lunch, even some money. But what he needed was a warmer coat.

Mom, having scrimped for a year, had recently bought Dad a new coat. So there were two winter coats hanging in the woodshed. Fortunately there is no photographic record of Mom's face – as she looked out to see the stranger standing by the road, wearing Dad's new coat! It was, Dad thought, warmer.

To this day, I wonder if my dad's actions changed the way that hitchhiker lived his life.

Dear God, let me give the best of what I have.

"**D**o not be worried and upset," Jesus told them. "Believe in God and believe also in me. There are many rooms in my Father's house, and I am going to prepare a place for you. I would not tell you this if it were not so. And after I go and prepare a place for you, I will come back and take you to myself, so that you will be where I am. You know the way that leads to the place where I am going."

Thomas said to him, "Lord, we do not know where you are going; so how can we know the way to get there?"

Jesus answered him, "I am the way, the truth, and the life; no one goes to the Father except by me."

John 14: 1-6

> "I am the way..."

The way

Julius helped me see how easily words intended to comfort can become tools of exclusion. Julius grew up as a black child under apartheid in Namibia. He remembers missionaries explaining that Jesus' reference to "many mansions" proved that there would be apartheid even in heaven – with mansions for whites, blacks, coloured and other racial groups.

When Jesus reassures his disciples that "I am the way," he seeks to comfort followers who fear they will be lost without him. Yet I often hear these words used to *exclude* non-Christians from salvation.

Then I remember Julius' story and how easily we turn consolation into isolation. I am thankful for "the way" that I have come to know in Jesus. But I refuse to use that which comforts me to exclude others.

> **Dear God, help me see the fine line between words that offer comfort and words that create exclusion.**

S ing a new song to the Lord;
he has done wonderful things!
By his own power and holy strength
he has won the victory.
The Lord announced his victory;
he made his saving power known to the nations.
He kept his promise to the people of Israel
with loyalty and constant love for them.
All people everywhere have seen the victory of our God.
Sing for joy to the Lord, all the earth;
praise him with songs and shouts of joy!

Psalm 98: 1-4

"The Lord announced his victory…"

God's saving power

Over the centuries, the fate of many people has been influenced by powerful empires. Decisions made by one country often meant life or death for people living in other, far off countries.

Today, that superpower is the United States and its president often mentions his own belief in "the Lord's saving power." God is on America's side in the War against Terror, he claims.

But when I look at the fruits of that war: the prison camps, the torture and the untold civilian deaths, I realize that this president is looking at God from the wrong direction. Maybe the nation's prayer should be more like the words attributed to another American president, Abraham Lincoln: "My concern is not whether God is on our side; my greatest concern is to be on God's side."

Lord, help me to know and to do your will.

"Do not be worried and upset," Jesus told them. "Believe in God and believe also in me. There are many rooms in my Father's house, and I am going to prepare a place for you. I would not tell you this if it were not so. And after I go and prepare a place for you, I will come back and take you to myself, so that you will be where I am. You know the way that leads to the place where I am going."

Thomas said to him, "Lord, we do not know where you are going; so how can we know the way to get there?"

Jesus answered him, "I am the way, the truth, and the life; no one goes to the Father except by me."

John 14: 1-12

"...I am going to prepare a place for you."

A place for you

I know a man who has a small house and a large family. As his children got older, their shared rooms grew more and more cramped. Finally, the man and his wife decided that they had to create a new room for their oldest son out of the attic. The work was very expensive, even though they did what they could themselves.

When their son first went up the ladder to his new room – the first time he had ever had a room of his own – the smile on his face and the excitement in his voice made his parents realize how important it was that they had "prepared a place" for their son, that preparing a place said, "I love you. You are important. I want you with me."

Lord, help me to know how and when
to prepare a place for those who need one.

"Those who accept my commandments and obey them are the ones who love me. My Father will love those who love me; I, too, will love them and reveal myself to them."

Judas (not Judas Iscariot) said, "Lord, how can it be that you will reveal yourself to us and not to the world?"

Jesus answered him, "Those who love me will obey my teaching. My Father will love them, and my Father and I will come to them and live with them. Those who do not love me do not obey my teaching. And the teaching you have heard is not mine, but comes from the Father, who sent me.

"I have told you this while I am still with you. The Helper, the Holy Spirit, whom the Father will send in my name, will teach you everything and make you remember all that I have told you."

John 14: 21-26

> "…I, too, will love them and reveal myself to them."

Revealing

Jesus doesn't say, "I'll show myself so you'll love me, then you'll obey my commandments." In fact, he does the opposite.

I met my wife a long time ago. One day, I said, "I love you." Love, it seems, is like that: you say it. But you don't know what you're saying. And you really don't know the person you're saying it to.

Then come the years. The learning to obey the commandment of love. Nursing sick children. Walking the floor, exhausted: "No, you need your rest." Enduring the dark nights. Accepting each other's blind insistence on holding onto odd habits, repeating the same mistakes, on being who they are. Just being there. And staying. And gradually revealing, and learning to know. And then… to love.

Lord, help me live your commandments.
Reveal yourself to me.

"Peace is what I leave with you; it is my own peace that I give you. I do not give it as the world does. Do not be worried and upset; do not be afraid. You heard me say to you, 'I am leaving, but I will come back to you.' If you loved me, you would be glad that I am going to the Father; for he is greater than I. I have told you this now before it all happens, so that when it does happen, you will believe. I cannot talk with you much longer, because the ruler of this world is coming. He has no power over me, but the world must know that I love the Father; that is why I do everything as he commands me.

"Come, let us go from this place." *John 14: 27-31*

"…it is my own peace that I give you."

True peace

My sister works in Burundi, Africa, with children in need. Every year she comes back to Canada for a few precious weeks of holiday.

The disciples feared letting Jesus go to Jerusalem. Similarly, when my sister's holiday comes to an end, I have a hard time seeing her go. She returns to a country that is very unstable, where the rebels are now launching attacks in the township next to hers.

Jesus had courage to go to Jerusalem where he knew he faced imprisonment and death. My sister has courage in going back to Burundi. Both are considered foolish in the eyes of the world. But I have to trust my sister's courage, and entrust her to Jesus' care, in order to receive the peace that he offers.

Help me to know your peace, Jesus,
when the world seems menacing and harsh.

" I am the real vine, and my Father is the gardener. He breaks off every branch in me that does not bear fruit, and he prunes every branch that does bear fruit, so that it will be clean and bear more fruit. You have been made clean already by the teaching I have given you. Remain united to me, and I will remain united to you. A branch cannot bear fruit by itself; it can do so only if it remains in the vine. In the same way, you cannot bear fruit unless you remain in me.

"I am the vine, and you are the branches. Those who remain in me, and I in them, will bear much fruit; for you can do nothing without me.... My Father's glory is shown by your bearing much fruit; and in this way you become my disciples." *John 15: 1-8*

> "...and in this way you become my disciples."

Becoming a disciple

Sonny, as we all called him, was the janitor at the school I attended as a child. I suppose he knew that we called him that, but he never heard us. Sonny couldn't hear or speak.

And while Sonny was a fine janitor, I'm not sure any of us kids even noticed that fact. What we did notice was his smiling face, his twinkling eyes, his cheerful greeting, and his unremitting kindness toward us.

Around the school and playground, Sonny was as close as we would ever come to seeing the embodiment of God's love. I don't know if he was baptized or even attended church. But judging from the fruit he bore, Sonny spent a lifetime becoming a disciple.

**Jesus, help me to see that my simple deeds
can bear fruit in the lives of others.**

T he apostles and the elders met together to consider the conversion of the Gentiles. After a long debate Peter stood up and said, "God, who knows the thoughts of everyone, showed his approval of the Gentiles by giving the Holy Spirit to them, just as he had to us. He made no difference between us and them; he forgave their sins because they believed. So then, why do you now want to put God to the test by laying a load on the backs of the believers which neither our ancestors nor we ourselves were able to carry? No! We believe and are saved by the grace of the Lord Jesus, just as they are." The whole group was silent as they heard Barnabas and Paul report all the miracles and wonders that God had performed through them among the Gentiles. *Acts 15: 7-21*

"He made no difference between us and them…"

Finding fault

One of my children tends to get "under my skin" more than the others. I'm quick to tell him how he is too judgmental, too impulsive, or too critical. I label and categorize his behaviour; I tell him how he needs to change.

I cringe when I think about some of the things I've said. If I'm honest with myself, I must admit that many of the criticisms I level at my son are, in fact, a reflection of what I see in myself.

It's easy to find faults in my children. Then I don't have to look at my own limitations. It's much harder to pause in silence, to look and to discover "all the miracles and wonders" that God is performing in our family.

**Lord, before I point the finger,
may I remember to pause and look in the mirror first.**

J esus said to the disciples, "Go throughout the whole world and preach the gospel to all people. Whoever believes and is baptized will be saved; whoever does not believe will be condemned. Believers will be given the power to perform miracles: they will drive out demons in my name; they will speak in strange tongues; if they pick up snakes or drink any poison, they will not be harmed; they will place their hands on sick people, and these will get well."

After the Lord Jesus had talked with them, he was taken up to heaven and sat at the right side of God. The disciples went and preached everywhere, and the Lord worked with them and proved that their preaching was true by the miracles that were performed.

Mark 16: 15-20

"Go throughout the whole world…"

Preaching the gospel

Every Friday, the light in Doug's kitchen comes on early – at five in the morning! Doug rises early – as he has done every Friday for many years – to bake bread for friends and colleagues who are his regular customers. His baking project began as a way of raising money for L'Arche communities in poorer parts of the world.

In just over eight years, he has sent more than $30,000 to communities in India, Poland, Nigeria, Haiti and Honduras. I am amazed by how much one person can do – quietly and faithfully – to make a difference.

Doug is an example of someone who is preaching the gospel with his life. He shows me how the Good News is going out to the ends of the earth.

**Lord, help me to preach the Good News of your love –
by the way I live my life.**

" If the world hates you, just remember that it has hated me first. If you belonged to the world, then the world would love you as its own. But I chose you from this world, and you do not belong to it; that is why the world hates you. Remember what I told you: 'Slaves are not greater than their master.' If people persecuted me, they will persecute you too; if they obeyed my teaching, they will obey yours too. But they will do all this to you because you are mine; for they do not know the one who sent me."

John 15: 18-21

"If you belonged to the world…"

Owned by the world

I had a book published last month. The launch was held on the top floor of the tallest building in our city. I was praised for my book, my speech went well, wine was poured, the media took pictures. It was great!

A week later, I went to the launch of a little, alternative Christian magazine. It was held in a tiny, dark, messy basement apartment. I was given a mug of water to drink, and we sat around the kitchen table listening to a young man, tattooed and much-pierced, who had left school when he was twelve years old. He was reading out his *Manifesto for a Just Society*.

I knew at which of the launches Jesus would have felt more at home, and it wasn't mine.

Lord, let me not be seduced by the world's opinion, but only by your burning tenderness.

" **I**f you love me, you will obey my commandments. I will ask the Father, and he will give you another Helper, who will stay with you forever. He is the Spirit, who reveals the truth about God. The world cannot receive him, because it cannot see him or know him. But you know him, because he remains with you and is in you.

"When I go, you will not be left all alone; I will come back to you. In a little while the world will see me no more, but you will see me; and because I live, you also will live. When that day comes, you will know that I am in my Father and that you are in me, just as I am in you."

John 14: 15-21

> "...he remains with you and is in you."

The living Spirit

When I was fourteen, my father died of cancer. I now have lived more than two-thirds of my life without him. Yet, the spirit of my father lives on in me. The choices I have made in life, and the person I've become, have all been affected not only by my father's physical death, but also by his enduring presence in my heart. He is still a big part of who I am.

My father's death helps me understand what Jesus was trying to tell his disciples about the Holy Spirit. While I can try to make sense of what this means by reading books on theology, it's more important to just take time to be still and to feel the Spirit within me.

Lord, open my ears and my heart to hear the Spirit who will reveal the truth about you.

"The Helper will come – the Spirit, who reveals the truth about God and who comes from the Father. I will send him to you from the Father, and he will speak about me. And you, too, will speak about me, because you have been with me from the very beginning.

"I have told you this, so that you will not give up your faith. You will be expelled from the synagogues, and the time will come when those who kill you will think that by doing this they are serving God. People will do these things to you because they have not known either the Father or me. But I have told you this, so that when the time comes for them to do these things, you will remember what I told you.

"I did not tell you these things at the beginning, for I was with you."   *John 15: 26 – 16: 4*

"You will be expelled from the synagogues…"

Speaking the truth

Lucy speaks the truth as she sees it. Sometimes her voice trembles because it takes everything she's got to go up against others' opinions. She's willing to speak even when she is not absolutely sure of herself – because she stands up for the poor and the marginalized.

Jesus warned us that it would be hard to witness to the truth. Sometimes our family, our friends, our community will reject us if we do.

I can learn from Lucy how to practise the little, day-to-day acts of courage needed to keep from backing away from the truth. When I am called to bigger acts of truth-telling, I hope that the Spirit of God will lead me to the truth, and give me strength to speak it.

Lord, give me courage when I am tempted to duck out of my responsibility to speak your word.

thank you, Lord,
with all my heart;
I sing praise to you
before the gods.
I face your holy Temple,
bow down,
and praise your name
because of your constant love
and faithfulness,
because you have shown
that your name
and your commands
are supreme.
You answered me
when I called to you;
with your strength
you strengthened me....
When I am surrounded
by troubles,
you keep me safe.
You oppose my angry enemies
and save me by your power.
You will do everything
you have promised;
Lord, your love is eternal.
Complete the work
that you have begun.

Psalm 138: 1-3, 7-8

> "...you strengthened me."

Strength in weakness

My children and I have been watching a spider that has stretched her web between the garage and our honeysuckle tree. We've become quite attached to her. Each day we go to check on her progress. The last few nights have been windy and I've been afraid that we'll find her gossamer strands in tatters.

And yet the web remains. Some strands have been broken but the spider persists: she repairs and rebuilds. What seems so vulnerable, so fragile is actually strong, surprisingly resilient.

There are times when my resources are stretched. Rather than panicking, I might think of this little spider that lets the web of her life stretch and bend through the windy days, believing that the calm days for repairing will come.

Thank you, God, for the small signs of strength that inspire me.

" I have much more to tell you, but now it would be too much for you to bear. When, however, the Spirit comes, who reveals the truth about God, he will lead you into all the truth. He will not speak on his own authority, but he will speak of what he hears and will tell you of things to come. He will give me glory, because he will take what I say and tell it to you. All that my Father has is mine; that is why I said that the Spirit will take what I give him and tell it to you."

John 16: 12-15

"...he will lead you into all the truth."

Live the question

When my husband was diagnosed with terminal cancer, a close friend asked, "Where is your God of love?" Now, several years later, I can say with deep conviction, that God has never been far from me.

Within the pain and the loss, the confusion, the searching for inner peace (and outer stability!), I have discovered new truths about myself, others and God. It hasn't been easy. I've wanted to "know," to have the answers to my many questions... now! But each new question has kept me straining to discover God's Spirit, to be open to the "things to come."

I know there won't be black and white answers to my questions. But when I live the questions, I discover the many, vibrant colours that life has to offer!

Lord, help me to "be patient toward all that is unsolved in my heart and help me to try to love the questions themselves."
(Rainer Maria Rilke)

Thursday | MAY 1

" In a little while you will not see me any more, and then a little while later you will see me." Some of his disciples asked among themselves, "He tells us that in a little while we will not see him, and then a little while later we will see him; and he also says, 'It is because I am going to the Father.' What does this 'a little while' mean?"

Jesus knew that they wanted to question him, so he said, "I said, 'In a little while you will not see me, and then a little while later you will see me.' Is this what you are asking about among yourselves? I am telling you the truth: you will cry and weep, but the world will be glad; you will be sad, but your sadness will turn into gladness."

John 16: 16-20

"In a little while you will not see me any more…"

A puzzling truth

A friend has been practising his magic tricks. Since retirement, he's had time on his hands. Gradually, he has perfected some sleight of hand. "Now you see it," he says, flashing a playing card at me. "Now you don't!" And the card vanishes.

I'm fascinated. "How did you do that?" I demand. But he won't show me. He just does another trick.

Jesus seemed to be promising his disciples a vanishing act: "Soon you won't see me, then you will." Like me, they were fascinated. "How will you do that?" they demanded.

But like my friend the magician, Jesus didn't tell them. Instead, he gave them another riddle to puzzle over. Only later, after his resurrection, did his verbal sleight of hand make sense.

Like your disciples, Jesus, I keep on fumbling in the dark for your truth. Show me the way.

" I am telling you the truth: you will cry and weep, but the world will be glad; you will be sad, but your sadness will turn into gladness. When a woman is about to give birth, she is sad because her hour of suffering has come; but when the baby is born, she forgets her suffering, because she is happy that a baby has been born into the world. That is how it is with you: now you are sad, but I will see you again, and your hearts will be filled with gladness, the kind of gladness that no one can take away from you.

"When that day comes, you will not ask me for anything. I am telling you the truth: the Father will give you whatever you ask of him in my name."

John 16: 20-23

"...her hour of suffering has come..."

No gain without pain

I'm almost jealous. As a male, I have never given birth to a child. I have held our newborn children in my arms; I have comforted them in the dark hours of the night; I have marvelled at their fragile perfection.

But I've also missed a significant learning about life, because women recognize that the birth of anything new always comes as a painful experience. There's no way of easing into a new life. Rather, at some point, the new life takes over. It tears you apart. It demands to be born. And you cannot stay as you were.

That's as true for spiritual birth as for physical birth. It's a hard lesson for a man to learn.

Lord, I usually try to avoid pain.
Help me to see it instead as a gateway to new life.

Hﾠow clearly the sky reveals God's glory!
How plainly it shows what he has done!
Each day announces it to the following day;
each night repeats it to the next.
No speech or words are used,
no sound is heard;
yet their message goes out to all the world
and is heard to the ends of the earth.
God made a home in the sky for the sun.

Psalm 19: 1-4

"How clearly the sky reveals God's glory!"

Gratitude and praise

It just doesn't get much better than the first Saturday in the month of May! In most parts of the country, winter is just a memory – and the first leaves and new grass are proof of that.

It's no wonder that the poet who wrote today's psalm chose to invoke nature to show the goodness of the Creator. No church, no worship can compete with these soft, illuminated spring evenings when the birds are back and life seems as if it will go on forever.

Birds and crickets – even frogs – all cry, "Thanks!" The new grass, the leaves in bud, the first flowers of spring are all signs of "Praise!" The words of this beautiful psalm roll around in my senses, awakening my need for gratitude and praise.

**When I cannot find the words, O God,
your creation speaks them for me. Thank you.**

The eleven disciples went to the hill in Galilee where Jesus had told them to go. When they saw him, they worshipped him, even though some of them doubted. Jesus drew near and said to them, "I have been given all authority in heaven and on earth. Go, then, to all peoples everywhere and make them my disciples: baptize them in the name of the Father, the Son, and the Holy Spirit, and teach them to obey everything I have commanded you. And I will be with you always, to the end of the age."

Matthew 28: 16-20

> "...even though some of them doubted."

Praising God

As I watch my daughter skip along, I recall skipping in my Nanna's home. Her home was always warm and open; she welcomed visitors, prayed often, and was certain about *everything* – in my eyes.

I now see how her life of 106 years must have been full of worries and doubts. She raised seven children through the Depression, and went on to live through many changes within the circle of her family and friends.

Nanna praised God in love and service amid the doubts and questions of her life. Both Nanna and the apostles inspire me not to let doubts take over my life, but to find room in it for praising God. Perhaps, one small act of praise I make today could help to dispel the doubts of another.

God, amid life's troubles, refresh me with your spirit of joy and energy. Help me show my love in simple ways.

While Apollos was in Corinth, Paul travelled through the interior of the province and arrived in Ephesus. There he found some disciples and asked them, "Did you receive the Holy Spirit when you became believers?"

"We have not even heard that there is a Holy Spirit," they answered.

"Well, then, what kind of baptism did you receive?" Paul asked. "The baptism of John," they answered.

Paul said, "The baptism of John was for those who turned from their sins; and he told the people of Israel to believe in the one who was coming after him – that is, in Jesus."

When they heard this, they were baptized in the name of the Lord Jesus. Paul placed his hands on them, and the Holy Spirit came upon them; they spoke in strange tongues and also proclaimed God's message. *Acts 19: 1-8*

> "We have not even heard that there is a Holy Spirit."

The gift of tongues

Paul meets a group of believers, and after he baptizes them, they begin to speak "in strange tongues" and to proclaim "God's message" – even though they had already been believers.

"Speaking in tongues" sounds like such a bizarre response to God's personal intervention in life – if we take it literally. But what if it means being able to understand the needs of people we had previously considered "foreigners."

To *speak* in tongues would mean to *understand* in tongues. That is, to recognize foreigners as our own kin – which of course they are in the sight of God. What barriers would fall!

**Lord, give me the gift of the Holy Spirit
that I may see all people as sisters and brothers.**

Y ou caused abundant rain to fall
and restored your worn-out land;
your people made their home there;
in your goodness you provided for the poor....
Praise the Lord,
who carries our burdens day after day;
he is the God who saves us.
Our God is a God who saves;
he is the Lord, our Lord,
who rescues us from death.

Psalm 68: 9-10, 19-20

"...who carries our burdens day after day..."

A heavy load

One afternoon, on our way home from
school, my daughter felt overwhelmed. It
had not been a good day in Grade One. Small woes had plagued her
all day: a spilled juicebox in her knapsack, a scraped knee at recess,
a lost library book.... She poured out her troubles as we walked home
together. As she struggled with her knapsack, she reached her breaking point. Dropping it on the ground, she burst into tears.

Usually when my daughter balks at carrying her bag, I launch
into the lecture about "responsibility." That day I picked up her bag
without saying a word. Her hand slipped into mine and we continued
on our way.

How easy it was for me to lighten her load! How often I forget
that God offers to do the same for me.

**God, I know you will help me carry my burdens today,
and every day.**

Paul said, "Keep watch over yourselves and over all the flock which the Holy Spirit has placed in your care.... I know that after I leave, fierce wolves will come among you, and they will not spare the flock....

"I commend you to the care of God and to the message of his grace, which is able to build you up and give you the blessings God has for all his people. I have not wanted anyone's silver or gold or clothing. You yourselves know that I have worked with these hands of mine to provide everything that my companions and I have needed. I have shown you in all things that by working hard in this way we must help the weak, remembering the words that the Lord Jesus himself said, 'There is more happiness in giving than in receiving.'"

Acts 20: 28-38

"...we must help the weak..."

Helping the weak

In today's reading, Paul exhorts us to selflessness and a commitment to the weak. I think of my childhood friend John who was mature beyond his years. There was no social safety net then so he worked evenings throughout high school to help support his family. He also did things the rest of us did only in our fantasies – such as standing up to bullies. He really did help the weak.

The thing you would notice most about John was his contentment, despite his life – which was mostly work to earn money, not for himself, but for his family. In a way, his childhood was taken from him. Yet, to this day, he remains calm and happy.

It's easy to write about these things; it's much harder to do them myself.

**God, give me the courage to actually do something,
not just talk about it.**

" I pray that they may all be one. Father! May they be in us, just as you are in me and I am in you. May they be one, so that the world will believe that you sent me. I gave them the same glory you gave me, so that they may be one, just as you and I are one: I am in them and you in me, so that they may be completely one, in order that the world may know that you sent me and that you love them as you love me.

"Father! You have given them to me, and I want them to be with me where I am, so that they may see my glory, the glory you gave me; for you loved me before the world was made." *John 17: 20-26*

> "I pray that they may all be one."

United in love

Today's reading is a complicated expression of Jesus' deepest desire for us to know the intimacy with God which Jesus himself knew: an intimacy to be shared with one another, as well.

But yesterday, after reading the newspaper, I simply couldn't imagine the caring relationship Jesus describes. I laid my head on the table – in despair over the state of our world.

That night, when I went out, a friend put my three-year-old to bed. At four in the morning, my daughter awoke and called for me. I picked her up and she threw her arms around me, saying, "You came back!" We stood by the window in the dark, holding each other – a moment of paradise. I think I got a glimpse of what Jesus meant.

**God, help me to keep my senses alert
for the signs of your love around me.**

Afer they had eaten, Jesus said to Simon Peter, "Simon son of John, do you love me more than these others do?"

"Yes, Lord," he answered, "you know that I love you." Jesus said to him, "Take care of my lambs." A second time Jesus said to him, "Simon son of John, do you love me?"

"Yes, Lord," he answered, "you know that I love you." Jesus said to him, "Take care of my sheep." A third time Jesus said, "Simon son of John, do you love me?" Peter became sad because Jesus asked him the third time, "Do you love me?" and so he said to him, "Lord, you know everything; you know that I love you!" Jesus said to him, "Take care of my sheep...." Then Jesus said to him, "Follow me!"

John 21: 15-19

> "A third time Jesus said, 'Do you love me?'"

Three times

Threes have an amazing power. I teach English to would-be writers and editors. Three examples are enough to convince anyone, I tell them – additional examples become overkill. Three characteristics will give readers a thumbnail sketch of any character. The most basic English sentence has three elements: subject, verb, object.

In religion, we have the Holy Trinity: Father, Son and Holy Spirit. At Christmas, the "three wise men" came from the east to see Jesus. In the wilderness, Jesus faced three temptations.

And here, in this passage, Jesus asked Simon Peter three times: "Do you love me?" Perhaps he wanted three questions to balance the three times Peter denied knowing Jesus in the high priest's courtyard.

The rule of three must have worked. Peter got a second chance. He didn't need a third one.

Dear God, I wish I had only denied you three times.
Thank you for giving me so many second chances.

P aul called the local Jewish leaders to a meeting, and he said to them, "My fellow Israelites, even though I did nothing against our people or the customs that we received from our ancestors, I was made a prisoner in Jerusalem and handed over to the Romans. After questioning me, the Romans wanted to release me, because they found that I had done nothing for which I deserved to die…. That is why I asked to see you and talk with you. As a matter of fact, I am bound in chains like this for the sake of him for whom the people of Israel hope…."

For two years Paul… welcomed all who came to see him. He preached about the kingdom of God and taught about the Lord Jesus Christ, speaking with all boldness and freedom.

Acts 28: 16-20, 30-31

"…I am bound in chains like this…"

Freedom to love

Freedom is one of our most precious gifts. So, how could giving up my freedom and being bound in chains achieve anything?

I think of Nelson Mandela, imprisoned for so many years in a South African jail, seemingly for no purpose at all. And yet, upon his release, the world watched in wonder as he became a major political player once again. All that waiting spoke volumes to those who feared that justice would never prevail.

I can be bound by chains, too – chains of responsibility, of doing what I believe is right. At times, I would love to throw them off. But I know that, even though I keep the chains, I can be free to live and love the way Jesus did.

Lord, I long to be free of my chains.
Give me the strength to wear them with faith and love.

When the day of Pentecost came, all the believers were gathered together in one place. Suddenly there was a noise from the sky which sounded like a strong wind blowing, and it filled the whole house where they were sitting. Then they saw what looked like tongues of fire which spread out and touched each person there. They were all filled with the Holy Spirit and began to talk in other languages, as the Spirit enabled them to speak.

There were Jews living in Jerusalem, religious people who had come from every country in the world. When they heard this noise, a large crowd gathered. In amazement and wonder they exclaimed, "These people who are talking like this are Galileans! How is it, then, that all of us hear them speaking in our own native languages… about the great things that God has done?"   *Acts 2: 1-11*

> "…all of us hear them speaking in our own native languages…"

Rooted in love

At times I feel that I'm from a different country – or even a different planet – from my teenagers! On those occasions, we seem to talk different languages, making it impossible to "hear" what the other is saying.

But there are times when we truly connect and we have the most amazing exchanges about what is happening in the world, our community, or in our family. Why are we able to "hear" one another in these instances, and not at other times?

It occurs to me that when we are rooted in love – in what binds us together – we are able to truly communicate. Perhaps that is what was happening when the Holy Spirit enabled the disciples to speak and the crowd to listen.

God, when you spoke, you brought order from chaos.
May my words bring love and healing rather than division.

Some Pharisees came to Jesus and started to argue with him. They wanted to trap him, so they asked him to perform a miracle to show that God approved of him. But Jesus gave a deep groan and said, "Why do the people of this day ask for a miracle? No, I tell you! No such proof will be given to these people!"

He left them, got back into the boat, and started across to the other side of the lake.

Mark 8: 11-13

"Why do the people of this day ask for a miracle?"

Show me!

The Pharisees are usually synonymous with trickery and ill-will. So I'm a bit surprised to find myself siding with them today.

Maybe they were trying to trap Jesus. But then again, maybe they were simply trying to find out the truth. After all, *if* Jesus had performed a miracle for them, wouldn't that have answered their question, once and for all?

If I stood on a hill tomorrow and said to Jesus, "Cure cancer," or "End world poverty," and it happened instantly, wouldn't that resolve my own doubts and prove that Jesus was God's chosen one?

But then I hear Jesus' heartfelt groan and watch his back as he sails to the other side of the lake. And I realize that I still don't get it.

**Lord, give me understanding,
and help me see who you are.**

Happy are those who remain faithful under trials, because when they succeed in passing such a test, they will receive as their reward the life which God has promised to those who love him. If we are tempted by such trials, we must not say, "This temptation comes from God." For God cannot be tempted by evil, and he himself tempts no one. But we are tempted when we are drawn away and trapped by our own evil desires….

Do not be deceived, my dear friends! Every good gift and every perfect present comes from heaven; it comes down from God, the Creator of the heavenly lights, who does not change or cause darkness by turning. By his own will he brought us into being through the word of truth, so that we should have first place among all his creatures. *James 1: 12-18*

> "…who remain faithful under trials…"

Choosing to believe

Reeling from the news that my husband only had six to twelve months to live, I realized that I was faced with a choice. I could either deny and try to escape from that harsh reality, becoming bitter about what was "being done to me," or I could live fully whatever difficulties lay ahead, believing that life is good. While I couldn't change the final outcome, I could decide *how* I would face its challenges.

Nine years later, I realize that I face that same choice… every day. I want to live believing that life is a gift from a loving God. But it's not always easy. There are times when I feel I can barely get through the day.

Deciding to believe in God's loving kindness is a conscious choice I must make – each and every day.

Lord, help me to meet my trials head on,
believing that you are with me in the midst of it all.

" I love you just as the Father loves me; remain in my love. If you obey my commands, you will remain in my love, just as I have obeyed my Father's commands and remain in his love.

"I have told you this so that my joy may be in you and that your joy may be complete. My commandment is this: love one another, just as I love you. The greatest love you can have for your friends is to give your life for them. And you are my friends if you do what I command you. I do not call you servants any longer, because servants do not know what their master is doing. Instead, I call you friends, because I have told you everything I heard from my Father."

John 15: 9-17

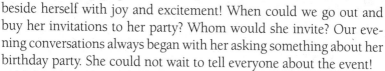

> "...and that your joy may be complete."

Full of joy

Last fall, my daughter turned seven. During the months leading up to this event, she was beside herself with joy and excitement! When could we go out and buy her invitations to her party? Whom would she invite? Our evening conversations always began with her asking something about her birthday party. She could not wait to tell everyone about the event!

I have experienced moments of joy: at my wedding and at the births my children. But a young child's joy is so pure; it lacks the sophistication, the self-restraint of an older person's joy.

Christ wants to provide me with a joy that is all-encompassing, totally freeing and life-giving. Like the joy of an "almost seven-year-old girl"!

Lord, free me to embrace the joy that only you can provide.

esus and his disciples went away to the villages near Caesarea Philippi. On the way he asked them, "Tell me, who do people say I am?"

"Some say that you are John the Baptist," they answered; "others say that you are Elijah, while others say that you are one of the prophets."

"What about you?" he asked them. "Who do you say I am?"

Peter answered, "You are the Messiah."

Then Jesus ordered them, "Do not tell anyone about me."

Then Jesus began to teach his disciples: "The Son of Man must suffer much and be rejected by the elders, the chief priests, and the teachers of the Law. He will be put to death, but three days later he will rise to life."   *Mark 8: 27-33*

> "Who do you say I am?"

Asking the question

A few years ago I moved far away from family and friends to an isolated community in Northern Ontario. It was a challenging year for me: making new friends, starting a new job, adapting to a new language and culture.

In the silence and stillness of those long winter nights, I had lots of time for reflection and prayer. Looking back over those months, I see that God's love was working in me – prodding me, guiding me, asking me the question that Jesus asked the disciples.

That time spent in reflection helped me to grow in my spiritual life. And when asked to give Jesus my answer to his question, I was able to respond with deep conviction: "Jesus, you are my Saviour, my Beloved."

**Jesus, continue to instill in me the desire
for silence and reflection.**

J esus told the crowd: "If any of you want to come with me, you must forget yourself, carry your cross, and follow me. For if you want to save your own life, you will lose it; but if you lose your life for me and for the gospel, you will save it. Do you gain anything if you win the whole world but lose your life? Of course not! There is nothing you can give to regain your life. If you are ashamed of me and of my teaching in this godless and wicked day, then the Son of Man will be ashamed of you when he comes in the glory of his Father with the holy angels.

"I tell you, there are some here who will not die until they have seen the kingdom of God come with power."   *Mark 8: 34 – 9: 1*

"If any of you want to come with me, you must carry your cross..."

Cross or resurrection?

My crosses tend to be people. People with one-track minds. People who prejudge issues. People who whine constantly. They sit beside me on planes. They single me out in a crowd. They put me on committees.

To balance that, my resurrections also tend to be people. Resurrections happen when an acquaintance unexpectedly turns into a friend. When a face lights up with a smile. When, on the telephone, I hear delight in someone's voice.

Crosses drain life; resurrections restore it. Sometimes there's not much difference between my crosses and my resurrections. Some of these people can't return much for what I try to give them. But spending time with them makes me feel good.

And I hope I'm not one of the crosses that they have to bear.

**God, let me take up my crosses gladly,
confident that they can turn into resurrections.**

J ust think how large a forest can be set on fire by a tiny flame! And the tongue is like a fire. It is a world of wrong, occupying its place in our bodies and spreading evil through our whole being. It sets on fire the entire course of our existence with the fire that comes to it from hell itself. We humans are able to tame and have tamed all other creatures – wild animals and birds, reptiles and fish. But no one has ever been able to tame the tongue. It is evil and uncontrollable, full of deadly poison. We use it to give thanks to our Lord and Father and also to curse other people, who are created in the likeness of God. Words of thanksgiving and cursing pour out from the same mouth. My friends, this should not happen! *James 3: 1-10*

"And the tongue is like a fire."

The power of words

Once, when my daughter was three, she was angry at me and said something hurtful. Like the good parent I was trying to be, I gently reminded her that words are powerful and that hers had hurt my feelings. She looked me straight in the eye and said, "Good. I wanted them to."

Somehow I managed to keep from laughing, and made a mental note not to be so smarmy next time. But I also noted that my young daughter clearly understood the effect words can have on others.

I, too, know the power of words. Yet sometimes I forget or, even worse, like my daughter, I deliberately speak words meant to hurt. Harsh words come so easily and can be so hard to undo.

Lord, words can be used like a sharp knife.
Give me wise judgment in my use of them.

F or God loved the world so much that he gave his only Son, so that everyone who believes in him may not die but have eternal life. For God did not send his Son into the world to be its judge, but to be its saviour. Those who believe in the Son are not judged; but those who do not believe have already been judged, because they have not believed in God's only Son.

John 3: 16-18

"...he gave his only Son..."

Love unto death

I try to imagine God as a parent: choosing to stand back and to let go of his son. Watching as Jesus approaches the blackness, the emptiness of death. Watching in hope, believing in the strength of his love.

I think of a time when my son had some problems at school. It was tempting to step in and try to solve things for him. Instead I chose to stand back, watching as he flailed his way through the darkness and confusion he experienced. I stood back, hoping that my love would sustain him in his searching.

I've learned that we have to grapple with the darkness in our lives. It doesn't make the struggle any easier, but I believe that new life waits for us there.

God, you know what it is to love – to the point of death. Help me to let love shape my life, even when it hurts.

A man in the crowd [said], "Teacher, I brought my son to you, because he has an evil spirit in him and cannot talk…. Have pity on us and help us, if you possibly can!" "Yes," said Jesus, "if you yourself can! Everything is possible for the person who has faith." The father at once cried out, "I do have faith, but not enough. Help me have more!"

Jesus… gave a command to the evil spirit. "Deaf and dumb spirit," he said, "I order you to come out of the boy and never go into him again!" The spirit screamed, threw the boy into a bad fit, and came out….

The disciples asked Jesus privately, "Why couldn't we drive the spirit out?" "Only prayer can drive this kind out," answered Jesus; "nothing else can."   *Mark 9: 14-29*

"Everything is possible for the person who has faith."

Faith and healing

This story sounds so out of sync in our age of scientific explanations. How am I to understand this story?

I think of a friend who, on two occasions, attempted suicide. Real attempts, not "just calls" for help. Now, some years later, still in a twelve-step program, still recovering, he credits his success as a husband and father to a greater power and his faith in that power. When he talks he sounds different: there's a ring of reality to what he says. He is changed.

If you'd asked him some years ago how he could shake the abysmal darkness he experienced, how he could exorcise his demons, he would have said (and did): "I can't believe I ever will."

"Everything is possible for the person who has faith."

**God, I struggle with my own demons, and I can't seem
to change. Help me when I despair and lose faith.**

Jesus and his disciples left that place and went on through Galilee.... They came to Capernaum, and after going indoors Jesus asked his disciples, "What were you arguing about on the road?"

But they would not answer him, because on the road they had been arguing among themselves about who was the greatest. Jesus sat down, called the twelve disciples, and said to them, "Whoever wants to be first must place himself last of all and be the servant of all." Then he took a child and had him stand in front of them. He put his arms around him and said to them, "Whoever welcomes in my name one of these children, welcomes me; and whoever welcomes me, welcomes not only me but also the one who sent me."   *Mark 9: 30-37*

"...one of these children..."

A child's love

Not long ago, as I walked down a hospital corridor, I found myself approaching an elderly woman. Bound to her wheelchair, she looked quite unhappy. I wondered what words of comfort I could offer her.

A young boy, who could not have been more than four, was coming from the other end of the hallway. He happily bounced towards the wheelchair, holding his mother's hand. When he came alongside of it, he gave the wheelchair-bound woman a huge smile, a cheery wave, and a bright two note "Hi."

I marvelled at his spontaneous and loving ministry that came straight from the heart. I felt that I was standing in the presence of pure and genuine life. Yes, in welcoming the children, I welcome Jesus.

**May I welcome all children with open arms,
recognizing your life-giving spirit in their eyes.**

Now listen to me, you that say, "Today or tomorrow we will travel to a certain city, where we will stay a year and go into business and make a lot of money." You don't even know what your life tomorrow will be! You are like a puff of smoke, which appears for a moment and then disappears. What you should say is this: "If the Lord is willing, we will live and do this or that." But now you are proud, and you boast; all such boasting is wrong.

So then, if we do not do the good we know we should do, we are guilty of sin.

James 4: 13-17

"…we will live and do this or that."

Campfire smoke

A men's night out: around a campfire, for us "forty-somethings." Our fire crackled warmly as we chatted together about everything and nothing. "Can you believe life's turned out like this?" someone ventured to say. "Never in a million years did I ever dream I'd be…," replied someone else. And we filled in the blanks: without my partner, with a disabled daughter, with no money…. We covered all the bases.

Listening to us, you could feel the absolute disbelief about how life had shaped us to date. None of us could have planned it this way. And yet, we were dead sure that next year was going to be this way or that….

God must laugh. Arrogant puffs of campfire smoke!

Lord, grant me true wisdom for my living this day.

nd now, you rich people, listen to me! Weep and wail over the miseries that are coming upon you! Your riches have rotted away, and your clothes have been eaten by moths. Your gold and silver are covered with rust, and this rust will be a witness against you and will eat up your flesh like fire. You have piled up riches in these last days. You have not paid any wages to those who work in your fields. Listen to their complaints! The cries of those who gather in your crops have reached the ears of God, the Lord Almighty. Your life here on earth has been full of luxury and pleasure. You have made yourselves fat for the day of slaughter. You have condemned and murdered innocent people, and they do not resist you.   *James 5: 1-6*

> ## "Listen to their complaints!"

Recognizing the other

At a recent poetry gathering, one of the participants read a poem she had written about a couple going out to dinner for a special occasion. Their spirits were dampened when they walked by a homeless person on their way into the restaurant.

Although the situation was described poignantly, the instructor challenged her. He asked who she thought the reader would sympathize with: the homeless person, callously passed by, or the rich couple whose illusions were momentarily interrupted?

How many times have I been in a similar situation: not just bypassing a person in need, but feeling sorry for myself that I felt uncomfortable?

The instructor's reaction was mild compared to James' in today's reading. It leaves no doubt about the power of the purse to destroy the spirit.

Lord, I am selfish.
Please open my heart to people in need everywhere.

S ome Pharisees came to Jesus and tried to trap him. "Tell us," they asked, "does our Law allow a man to divorce his wife?" Jesus answered with a question, "What law did Moses give you?" Their answer was, "Moses gave permission for a man to write a divorce notice and send his wife away." Jesus said to them, "Moses wrote this law for you because you are so hard to teach. But in the beginning, at the time of creation, 'God made them male and female,' as the scripture says. 'And for this reason a man will leave his father and mother and unite with his wife, and the two will become one.'

So they are no longer two, but one. No human being must separate, then, what God has joined together."   *Mark 10: 1-12*

"…what God has joined together."

Brokenness and hope

Some texts in scripture lend themselves to reflection more easily than others. But some are downright forbidding because they hit so close to home. I am divorced. Recently.

Is there any good news for me in today's reading? I think so. Behind Jesus' very specific words about divorce is the message that brokenness – within persons, relationships and whole societies – is not God's plan. I kid myself if I think otherwise.

But the good news – lurking at the edges of this passage, and seeping in from all aspects of Jesus' ministry – gives me hope. In Jesus, God opens up new possibilities for healing and wholeness – even in the midst of the brokenness that can be so evident in my own life.

**Jesus, in the midst of my brokenness
help me to receive the hope and healing you offer.**

I call to you, Lord; help me now!
Listen to me when I call to you.
Receive my prayer as incense,
my uplifted hands as an evening sacrifice.
Lord, place a guard at my mouth,
a sentry at the door of my lips....
But I keep trusting in you, my Sovereign Lord.
I seek your protection;
don't let me die!

Psalm 141: 1-3, 8

"...place a guard at my mouth..."

A guard at my mouth

It's interesting that this psalm is subtitled "An Evening Prayer." Often it's after a particularly trying day that my words do the most damage. I hear myself saying things that I know I'll regret later: sarcastic barbs and snide remarks – well-aimed, where I know they'll do the most damage.

I know these words are hurtful. I've been hurt by them myself. But sometimes, out of frustration or just plain fatigue, I say them anyway, and later wish I hadn't.

How do I turn back before I go too far? How can I express my hurt without being hurtful? This psalm reminds me to ask for help. I hope I'll remember to ask for help before the end of the day arrives.

**God, guide my words so that they reflect
your loving presence to others.**

"Remember how the Lord your God led you on this long journey through the desert these past forty years, sending hardships to test you, so that he might know what you intended to do and whether you would obey his commands....

"Be sure that you do not become proud and forget the Lord your God who rescued you from Egypt, where you were slaves. He led you through that vast and terrifying desert where there were poisonous snakes and scorpions. In that dry and waterless land he made water flow out of solid rock for you. In the desert he gave you manna

to eat, food that your ancestors had never eaten. He sent hardships on you to test you, so that in the end he could bless you with good things." *Deuteronomy 8: 2-3, 14-16*

"...your God led you on this long journey..."

Signs of hope

Forty years seems like a long time. Where were the signs of hope for the desert people? How did they keep from giving up? God knows, the next *four* years ahead of me seem a burden!

I look over my world and see an increasing gap between rich and poor. I see a worrisome tendency for leaders to use their own agendas to exacerbate conflicts. I experience a technological culture that claims to connect people, yet most of us are much better off when we are "unplugged" for a bit.

Where are the signs of hope for us? There are days when they seem few and far between. I ask God to help me scan the horizon with hopeful eyes.

God, this journey is not an easy one.
Open my eyes to recognize signs of hope.

A man knelt before [Jesus] and asked, "What must I do to receive eternal life?" ... Jesus looked straight at him with love and said, "You need only one thing. Go and sell all you have and give the money to the poor, and you will have riches in heaven; then come and follow me." When the man heard this, gloom spread over his face, and he went away sad, because he was very rich.

Jesus said, "It is much harder for a rich person to enter the kingdom of God than for a camel to go through the eye of a needle."

At this the disciples were completely amazed: "Who, then, can be saved?" Jesus looked straight at them and answered, "This is impossible for human beings but not for God; everything is possible for God."

Mark 10: 17-27

"Jesus looked straight at him with love..."

The challenge

I often feel like that rich young man in today's reading. I say that I want to follow Jesus and, to show my good intentions, I make some dramatic gestures. But then the thought of Jesus looking "straight at me with love" reminds me of all that I still cling to, all that I don't *really* want to give up.

At different periods throughout my life, I've clung to money, an unhealthy relationship, the habit of self-pity. Could I really give up everything to which my heart secretly clings?

However often I turn away, with gloom spread over my face, I know that Jesus waits for me – to let go and to follow him. When I finally do, I'll realize how poor I really was.

Jesus, look straight at me with love: show me what I cling to, and help me to let it go and follow you.

Sing a new song
to the Lord;
he has done
wonderful things!
By his own power
and holy strength
he has won the victory....
All people everywhere have
seen the victory of our God.
Sing for joy to the Lord,
all the earth;
praise him with songs
and shouts of joy!

Play music on the harps!
Blow trumpets and horns,
and shout for joy to the Lord,
our king.
Roar, sea, and every creature
in you;
sing, earth, and all who live
on you!
Clap your hands, you rivers;
you hills, sing together with joy
before the Lord, because
he comes to rule the earth.

Psalm 98: 1-9

"Sing a new song to the Lord..."

Sing a new song

With much care and attention, my husband and I chose today's psalm for our wedding liturgy. Its words captured the joy, the laughter, the music and the happiness we hoped our life together would hold.

A few years later, my husband and I were to re-visit this psalm – as we planned his funeral liturgy. Though in a vastly different context, we felt it expressed the love we shared. The love that we believed would extend beyond his death.

Today, several years have passed and I find myself face-to-face with this psalm – again. In some way, I realize that I've never stopped living its words – even in my darkest times. A new song is emerging – with a different shape and form – at this new point in my journey.

**Loving God, when all seems dark, help me look for
the spark of joy that gives me reason to believe... and to sing.**

James and John came to Jesus. "Teacher, when you sit on your throne in your glorious kingdom, we want you to let us sit with you...." Jesus said, "You don't know what you are asking for. Can you drink the cup of suffering that I must drink?" "We can," they answered.

Jesus said, "You will indeed drink the cup I must drink.... But I do not have the right to choose who will sit at my right and my left. It is God who will give these places to those for whom he has prepared them.... If one of you wants to be great, you must be the servant of the rest.... For even the Son of Man did not come to be served; he came to serve and to give his life to redeem many people."

Mark 10: 32-45

> "...you must be the servant of the rest..."

Servant-leader

I have worked for many bosses in my life, and most have liked the sense of power they had over their employees. For them, this "power over others" seemed to be one of the perks of the job.

Once, however, I did work for a man who really took the gospel seriously. I will always remember him saying, "Power has only one real purpose: service. If power is not used to help others, then that power is wasted."

I was raised to believe status was partly determined by how many people you had "under you." What a radical idea to suggest that the boss is there to help and serve! I am challenged to look at how I use my power to serve others – at work and at home.

Dear God, teach me a spirit of service
– both at work and at home.

B e like newborn babies, always thirsty for the pure spiritual milk, so that by drinking it you may grow up and be saved. As the scripture says, "You have found out for yourselves how kind the Lord is."

Come to the Lord, the living stone rejected by people as worthless but chosen by God as valuable. Come as living stones, and let yourselves be used in building the spiritual temple, where you will serve as holy priests to offer spiritual and acceptable sacrifices to God through Jesus Christ....

But you are the chosen race, the King's priests, the holy nation, God's own people, chosen to proclaim the wonderful acts of God, who called you out of darkness into his own marvellous light.

1 Peter 2: 2-5, 9-12

"Be like newborn babies…"

Food for the soul

All three of my children were big eaters when they were babies. They didn't sleep much, but, boy, did they eat. They were always either nursing, about to nurse, or had just finished nursing. There were days when they seemed to grow right before my eyes.

But I could see that their mother's milk didn't just give them the nutrients necessary to help their bodies grow. That reliable and inexhaustible spring was the source of nourishment for the hunger of the whole being. Everything – body, soul, mind, spirit – was fed.

I like to think of myself as an adult looking for the hard truths. It's humbling to realize that I'm truly just a spiritual newborn looking for the mother's milk of God's word.

Lord, I am your child, hungry for nourishment. Feed me.

"Father, Lord of heaven and earth! I thank you because you have shown to the unlearned what you have hidden from the wise and learned. Yes, Father, this was how you were pleased to have it happen. My Father has given me all things. No one knows the Son except the Father, and no one knows the Father except the Son and those to whom the Son chooses to reveal him. Come to me, all of you who are tired from carrying heavy loads, and I will give you rest. Take my yoke and put it on you, and learn from me, because I am gentle and humble in spirit; and you will find rest. For the yoke I will give you is easy, and the load I will put on you is light."

Matthew 11: 25-30

> "Come to me... and I will give you rest."

A heavy load

Last week, my youngest son came home from school with his head hung low. I could see he was very upset, but he quickly went into the bathroom to hide his tear-filled eyes. When he came out, I held out my arms and invited him onto my lap for a hug. Being at that in-between stage and afraid of being thought a baby, he hesitated at first. But then he climbed up and put his head on my shoulder. He held on for a while, and then we talked about the problem.

Finding rest in another when the load gets too heavy won't make the problems disappear, but it will help ease the burden. I am awe-struck – and comforted – knowing that Jesus is there to help ease my burden.

**When the load gets too heavy, guide me,
O Lord, to find rest in you.**

When Elizabeth heard Mary's greeting, the baby moved within her. Elizabeth was filled with the Holy Spirit and said in a loud voice, "You are the most blessed of all women, and blessed is the child you will bear! For as soon as I heard your greeting, the baby within me jumped with gladness. How happy you are to believe that the Lord's message to you will come true!"

Mary said, "My heart praises the Lord; my soul is glad because of God my Saviour, for he has remembered me, his lowly servant.... He has stretched out his mighty arm and scattered the proud with all their plans. He has brought down mighty kings from their thrones, and lifted up the lowly. He has filled the hungry with good things, and sent the rich away with empty hands."   *Luke 1: 39-56*

> "You are the most blessed of all women…"

A powerful greeting

When Elizabeth greets Mary, she calls her "most blessed of all women." The words seem tame, but only two other women in Scripture are greeted this way: Jael (Judges 5: 24) and Judith (Judith 13: 18) each killed an enemy general, thereby liberating their people.

Recently a bumper sticker made me think of Solveig: "Well-behaved women rarely make history." Solveig never killed anyone, but for twenty years she was the most persistent, articulate and unwilling-to-be-well-behaved woman in North America, working to end apartheid. And during her lifetime, she saw the Magnificat happen: the kings brought down and the lowly lifted up.

Mary and Solveig deserve today's greeting – not for their readiness to use violence, but for their determination to sing the justice of God with their whole lives.

God, let me know when being well-behaved keeps me from being faithful to you.

"Not everyone who calls me 'Lord, Lord' will enter the kingdom of heaven, but only those who do what my Father in heaven wants them to do....

"So then, anyone who hears these words of mine and obeys them is like a wise man who built his house on rock. The rain poured down, the rivers flooded over, and the wind blew hard against that house. But it did not fall, because it was built on rock.

"But anyone who hears these words of mine and does not obey them is like a foolish man who built his house on sand. The rain poured down, the rivers flooded over, the wind blew hard against that house, and it fell. And what a terrible fall that was!"

Matthew 7: 21-27

> "But it did not fall, because it was built on rock…"

A true story

When he was small, maybe four years old, a boy's mother took him grocery shopping in the city, 25 miles from the village where they lived. While at the store, he took a peanut – one peanut – and put it in his pocket. At home when his mother discovered this, she took him back – 25 miles – to return the peanut. When the sales clerk raised her eyebrows, his mother simply stated, "It is not his."

Recently, when that young boy, now forty-five years old, bought $200 worth of theatre tickets, a harried clerk forgot to take his cheque. When he discovered it in his wallet one week later, he returned to the theatre, found the clerk and gave her the cheque. Why?

He remembered the peanut.

**Lord, help me take the time to hear your words
and give me the courage to act by them, whatever the cost.**

"Once there was a man who planted a vineyard… [and] rented the vineyard to tenants. When the time came to gather the grapes, he sent a slave to the tenants to receive from them his share of the harvest. The tenants grabbed the slave, beat him, and sent him back without a thing…. The owner sent another slave, and they killed him; and they treated many others the same way, beating some and killing others. Last of all, then, he sent his son to the tenants…. The tenants said, 'Come on, let's kill him, and his property will be ours!'

"What, then, will the owner of the vineyard do?" asked Jesus. "He will come and kill those tenants and turn the vineyard over to others…."

The Jewish leaders tried to arrest Jesus, because they knew that he had told this parable against them. But they were afraid of the crowd, so they left him and went away.   *Mark 12: 1-12*

"But they were afraid of the crowd…"

Speaking out

Jesus wasn't one to avoid speaking out against injustice when he saw it.

I find it hard to speak out, no matter how just and important my concerns. It's much safer to speak about the truth in private, behind closed doors. Safer, and easier.

Anger at an unjust situation easily bubbles up in me. But often fear overwhelms me, rendering me silent. I debate within myself, wondering, "Will my speaking out make any difference?"

Sixteen hundred years ago, Saint Augustine understood these conflicting feelings when he wrote: "Hope has two daughters, anger that things are not what they should be and courage to make them what they should be."

**O God, help me to speak out when I see an injustice,
even when I'm afraid.**

S ome Pharisees and some members of Herod's party were sent to Jesus to trap him with questions. They came to him and said, "Teacher, we know that you tell the truth, without worrying about what people think. You pay no attention to anyone's status, but teach the truth about God's will for people. Tell us, is it against our Law to pay taxes to the Roman Emperor? Should we pay them or not?"

But Jesus saw through their trick and answered, "Why are you trying to trap me? Bring a silver coin, and let me see it." They brought him one, and he asked, "Whose face and name are these?" "The Emperor's," they answered. So Jesus said, "Well, then, pay to the Emperor what belongs to the Emperor, and pay to God what belongs to God."   *Mark 12: 13-17*

> "...pay to God what belongs to God."

Paying the emperor

The question the Pharisees asked, while not sincere, was fairly straightforward. Jesus' answer to their question was both sincere and straightforward: Pay those you owe what they are due.

Sometimes life is not so straightforward. I'm a middle-aged guy with a family, and often there's just not enough money, time and energy to go around. There are simply too many emperors! What do I owe my employer? How many times must I volunteer at the school? And my kids' needs...? After all, they won't be with me forever. And, oh yeah, take some "quality" time for yourself. Right!

I have a good life. A great life! It's just hard sometimes to know what belongs to the emperor, and how much I should be paying.

God, may I have the wisdom
to know how much I can truly give.

163

Some Sadducees said, "Teacher, Moses wrote this law for us: 'If a man dies and leaves a wife but no children, that man's brother must marry the widow so that they can have children who will be considered the dead man's children.' Once there were seven brothers; the oldest got married and died without having children. Then the second one married the woman, and he also died without having children. The same thing happened to the rest: all seven brothers married the woman and died without having children.... Now, when all the dead rise to life on the day of resurrection, whose wife will she be?"

Jesus answered, "How wrong you are!... It is because you don't know the Scriptures or God's power.... He is the God of the living, not of the dead."

Mark 12: 18-27

"...you don't know the Scriptures or God's power."

Seeking truth

My, how "clever" these guys were. Clever at hiding behind a question designed to trick: a question designed to preserve the "truth" that they already "knew"; a question protecting them from having to look for a new way of "seeing," from being challenged to grow.

These guys would have been "clever" lawyers – working, perhaps, for an insurance company that wanted to keep money from an accident victim who everyone knew deserved and needed the money.

And what about me? I turn discussions into fencing matches; I spar over trivial points; I try to keep from seeing the other person's point of view. My mind is focused on winning rather than on understanding. I don't want to see the truth if it means I have to say, "Maybe I was wrong."

God, let me try to understand those who disagree with me – to see the world in a new way.

A teacher of the Law came to Jesus with a question: "Which commandment is the most important of all?" Jesus replied, "The most important one is this: 'The Lord our God is the only Lord. Love the Lord your God with all your heart, with all your soul, with all your mind, and with all your strength.' The second most important commandment is this: 'Love your neighbour as you love yourself.' There is no other commandment more important than these two."

The teacher of the Law said, "Well done, Teacher! It is more important to obey these two commandments than to offer on the altar animals and other sacrifices to God." Jesus noticed how wise his answer was, and so he told him, "You are not far from the kingdom of God."

Mark 12: 28-34

> "Which commandment is the most important of all?"

From the heart

I won't ask serious questions of just anyone. I want to know something about the other's knowledge, integrity and expertise in my area of concern. I want to be able to trust the answers, especially if I choose to act on them.

Similarly, the teacher of the Law notes Jesus' own growing reputation as a teacher before asking him the most important question of all. He is thrilled when Jesus' answer echoes his own. He is eager to apply it. What a meeting of two great minds!

But Jesus wants more than the meeting of minds. To enter God's kingdom requires a meeting of hearts. "Surrender your heart," he says, "first to God and then to each other." Further questions are pointless if love is always the answer!

Lord, help me to trust you with all my questions.
Teach me that love is the response to each one.

As Jesus was teaching in the Temple, he asked the question, "How can the teachers of the Law say that the Messiah will be the descendant of David? The Holy Spirit inspired David to say: 'The Lord said to my Lord: Sit here at my right side until I put your enemies under your feet.' David himself called him 'Lord'; so how can the Messiah be David's descendant?" *Mark 12: 35-37*

"...how can the Messiah be David's descendant?"

The human face of God

Here we see Jesus under fire: the lawyers and scribes are trying to entangle him in a confusion of questions and accusations.

Jesus cannot abide anyone who tries to use God. To be committed to Jesus' vision of God is to be in solidarity with and to show compassion for our neighbour.

And it is Jesus' vision of neighbour that challenges me. I need to expand my vision of neighbour to include others – the less-than-likable colleague, my bawling preschooler, the seemingly snobby woman who sits in front of me at church, the irritating squeegee kid cleaning my car's windshield at a downtown intersection – and to recognize them as my neighbour, as the human face of God. And to recognize that I am theirs.

God, grant me the courage to reach beyond my fear and arrogance, to touch and to be touched by my neighbour.

A ll day long I praise you
   and proclaim your glory.
   Do not reject me now that I am old;
do not abandon me now that I am feeble....
I will always put my hope in you; I will praise you more and more.
I will tell of your goodness;
all day long I will speak of your salvation,
though it is more than I can understand....
You have taught me ever since I was young,
and I still tell of your wonderful acts....
I will indeed praise you with the harp;
I will praise your faithfulness, my God.

Psalm 71: 8-9, 14-17, 22

"You have taught me ever since I was young…"

My whole life long

I'm not old, but I'm older than I used to be. As the years go by and life experiences accumulate, I'm beginning to see a pattern – to see mountains and valleys in my personal story of faith.

When I was a child, faith shaped our family and our social life. During adolescence and young adulthood, when I thought I was in charge of my life, faith played a lesser role. Now that I am a parent and have hit a few potholes along the way, I rely on God more and more to get me through the hard times. And I take time to praise and thank God for the good times.

Now, more than ever, I see God's faithfulness at work in my life each and every day – my whole life long.

**Lord, I praise you for your faithfulness to me –
in good times and in hard times.**

A s Jesus walked along, he saw a tax collector, named Matthew, sitting in his office. He said to him, "Follow me." Matthew got up and followed him.

While Jesus was having a meal in Matthew's house, many tax collectors and other outcasts came and joined Jesus and his disciples at the table. Some Pharisees saw this and asked his disciples, "Why does your teacher eat with such people?"

Jesus heard them and answered, "People who are well do not need a doctor, but only those who are sick. Go and find out what is meant by the scripture that says: 'It is kindness that I want, not animal sacrifices.' I have not come to call respectable people, but outcasts."

Matthew 9: 9-13

"Follow me."

Trust the process

While forming a sculpture from a lump of clay, instead of trusting my instincts, at times I choose instead to make something I know I'll be able to sell. But these pieces never seem to turn out right. My best works come from following my intuition.

So I throw the clay and begin shaping it, pushing and pulling, trying not to think too much about what will happen, staying present to the moment. When I'm on the right track, I get a special feeling that tells me to go on. I don't need to have all my questions answered; I simply allow myself to trust the process.

I think that's the feeling Matthew had when he got up and followed Jesus. When things are right, you just know it.

God, help me to recognize and to trust your call.

I look to the mountains;
where will my help
come from?
My help will come
from the Lord,
who made heaven and earth.
He will not let you fall;
your protector is always awake.
The protector of Israel
never dozes or sleeps.
The Lord will guard you;
he is by your side
to protect you.

The sun will not hurt you
during the day,
nor the moon during the night.
The Lord will protect you
from all danger;
he will keep you safe.
He will protect you
as you come and go
now and forever.

Psalm 121: 1-8

"The Lord will protect you from all danger."

God's loving care

A few years ago, my mother was close to death in another city. I spent most days in the hospital at her side. My husband and our three young children tried but were unable to join me. They had started out by car, but had been forced by freezing rain to turn back. I was grateful that they were safe.

Alone and far from home, I felt helpless as I watched my mother. Widowed as a young woman, she had been so independent. Now frail, she depended on me.

In the midst of this, I felt sustained by something beyond my own strength. Just as my family had been shielded from danger on the road, I knew that my mother and I were surrounded by God's loving care.

O God, may I always place my trust in you.

"You are like salt for the whole human race. But if salt loses its saltiness, there is no way to make it salty again. It has become worthless, so it is thrown out and people trample on it.

"You are like light for the whole world. A city built on a hill cannot be hid. No one lights a lamp and puts it under a bowl; instead it is put on the lampstand, where it gives light for everyone in the house. In the same way your light must shine before people, so that they will see the good things you do and praise your Father in heaven."

Matthew 5: 13-16

"But if salt loses its saltiness…"

Thinking metaphorically

My friend John takes things literally. He has never seen salt lose its saltiness – though he wishes sometimes it would, such as when the city works crews spread it on the streets in winter and it rots the bottom of his car. So he treats these words as meaningless.

I tell him, "Don't ask whether it can happen – ask what it would be like if it could happen. If salt could lose its saltiness. Or if paint lost its colour. If food lost its taste. If springs lost their bounce. If light bulbs lost their light. They'd become useless. You'd throw them out."

John has trouble thinking metaphorically. But sometimes, it's the only way to understand the Bible's message for us.

God, help me to nurture whatever it is that makes me what I am, so that I don't become useless to you.

"**G**o and preach, 'The kingdom of heaven is near!' Heal the sick, bring the dead back to life, heal those who suffer from dreaded skin diseases, and drive out demons. You have received without paying, so give without being paid. Do not carry any gold, silver, or copper money in your pockets; do not carry a beggar's bag for the trip or an extra shirt or shoes or a walking stick. Workers should be given what they need.

"When you come to a town or village, go in and look for someone who is willing to welcome you, and stay with him until you leave that place. When you go into a house, say, 'Peace be with you.' If the people in that house welcome you, let your greeting of peace remain; but if they do not welcome you, then take back your greeting."

Matthew 10: 7-13

"When you come to a town or village…"

Places to go

When I was growing up there was no greater thrill than coming home from school and finding that Joe Tom Burke had arrived at our farm. Sixty years ago we did not know about "hoboes" or "knights of the road." Joe Tom was just a man who walked all over the place and relied on people's hospitality.

When we sat down to supper he would have stories of the places he'd been or was planning to visit. Expressions like: "I think I'll take a little jaunt down to Nova Scotia…" filled his young listeners with dreams of a much wider world.

The next day he would be gone with freshly laundered clothes and, unlike the apostles, extra socks. He had other places to go – to spread the news.

O God, let me welcome strangers at my door.
Help me listen to their good news.

"You have heard that people were told in the past, 'Do not commit murder; anyone who does will be brought to trial.' But now I tell you: if you are angry with your brother you will be brought to trial, if you call your brother 'You good-for-nothing!' you will be brought before the Council, and if you call your brother a worthless fool you will be in danger of going to the fire of hell. So if you are about to offer your gift to God at the altar and there you remember that your brother has something against you, leave your gift there in front of the altar, go at once and make peace with your brother, and then come back and offer your gift to God."

Matthew 5: 20-26

"…and make peace with your brother…"

Saying "I'm sorry"

Some time ago, two mothers won the Nobel Prize for their efforts to bring peace to Northern Ireland. It's not surprising that they were mothers. Maybe it was all those years of telling their children, "Go and say you're sorry."

I think of childhood fights in the sandbox when my mother would say to me, "Go and tell Johnny you're sorry." I remember thinking, "But I'm not sorry." It was so hard to say, and so much harder to mean.

It's hard for husbands to say, "I'm sorry," to their wives. It's hard for parents to say it to children. It's hard to say it at work; it's hard to say it at home. And it's hard when, as in so many places, the ghosts of loved ones hover close by, listening.

Dear God, help me to forgive others.
Help me to work for peace in our world today.

There he went into a cave to spend the night. Suddenly the Lord spoke to him, "Elijah, what are you doing here?" He answered, " Lord God Almighty, I have always served you – you alone. But the people of Israel have broken their covenant with you, torn down your altars, and killed all your prophets. I am the only one left – and they are trying to kill me!"

"Go out and stand before me on top of the mountain," the Lord said to him. Then the Lord passed by and sent a furious wind that split the hills and shattered the rocks – but the Lord was not in the wind. The wind stopped blowing, and then there was an earthquake – but the Lord was not in the earthquake. After the earthquake there was a fire – but the Lord was not in the fire. And after the fire there was the soft whisper of a voice.

I Kings 19: 9-16

> "...the Lord was not in the fire."

Seeing God

When disasters strike we often hear the question: "Where was God?" Few who ask that question take time to look for God's presence. That's because it becomes most evident after the disaster.

I visited Thailand a month after the 2004 tsunami. God was there in the hands and hearts of the members of small Thai churches who reached out with practical assistance and a message of hope to those who had lost everything.

In Canada and the U.S., we saw the people of God become messengers of hope following Hurricane Katrina. It is in our quiet moments, in small acts of kindness, that the evidence of God's love is best seen and experienced.

Lord, show me opportunities to demonstrate your love.
Give me the strength to follow through.

"You have also heard that people were told in the past, 'Do not break your promise, but do what you have vowed to the Lord to do.' But now I tell you: do not use any vow when you make a promise. Do not swear by heaven, for it is God's throne; nor by earth, for it is the resting place for his feet; nor by Jerusalem, for it is the city of the great King. Do not even swear by your head, because you cannot make a single hair white or black. Just say 'Yes' or 'No' – anything else you say comes from the Evil One."

Matthew 5: 33-37

"Just say 'Yes' or 'No.'"

Words, words, words

Today I received a gift. An unexpected gift. A generous gift. A thoughtful gift. While I struggled to find the right words, all that came out was, "Thank you." Nothing more. But, I suppose nothing more was needed.

Today's reading seems to be telling me to keep it simple: say "Yes" or "No." I know how I tend to use too many words… when fewer would do. Words serve to distract, to obscure the truth.

Funny how life's deepest experiences can be expressed with so few words: "I'm sorry," and "I love you." And how often I say too much: "I'm sorry, but…"; "I'll love you, if…." What a challenge: to say what I mean. To mean what I say. Nothing more. Nothing less.

Dear God, give me the words to say how I feel, what I think.
May I speak with love and integrity.

C hrist died for the wicked at the time that God chose. It is a difficult thing for someone to die for a righteous person. It may even be that someone might dare to die for a good person. But God has shown us how much he loves us – it was while we were still sinners that Christ died for us! By his blood we are now put right with God; how much more, then, will we be saved by him from God's anger! We were God's enemies, but he made us his friends through the death of his Son. Now that we are God's friends, how much more will we be saved by Christ's life! But that is not all; we rejoice because of what God has done through our Lord Jesus Christ, who has now made us God's friends. *Romans 5: 6-11*

"Now that we are God's friends..."

Friend of God

Every summer, I am amazed to see the monarch butterflies return home after spending the winter in a warmer, southern climate. They return to fields that, a few months before, had lain frozen and lifeless. Now they flit among the milkweed in the sunlight as if they know they belong.

My own life is rarely as peaceful or predictable as theirs. I so often struggle, redefine myself and my goals, search for my true "identity."

Today's reading offers me an identity that will not change: friend of God through the saving grace of Christ's life. No matter how much my fortunes seem to ebb and flow, I can know my place with the same serenity as the monarch butterflies – if only I accept this truth.

Lord, centre me in the knowledge that I am yours.

"You have heard that it was said, 'An eye for an eye, and a tooth for a tooth.' But now I tell you: do not take revenge on someone who wrongs you. If anyone slaps you on the right cheek, let him slap your left cheek too. And if someone takes you to court to sue you for your shirt, let him have your coat as well. And if one of the occupation troops forces you to carry his pack one mile, carry it two miles. When someone asks you for something, give it to him; when someone wants to borrow something, lend it to him."

Matthew 5: 38-42

"Do not take revenge on someone who wrongs you."

A peaceful response

Over the centuries, Christians have wrestled with this passage. How difficult it is to live!

But we see how Gandhi, a devout Hindu, used it as the basis for his life-stance of non-violence. Martin Luther King also used it to develop his political platform of civil disobedience. What enormous reserves of love it must take: not to retaliate when faced with physical violence!

I don't have anyone physically compelling me to do things. But what about the grudging way that I take on chores? When criticized, why do I fire back with angry words? What patience and humility this passage asks of me – to move out of my self-centredness and to try to see the other person more clearly!

Dear Lord, give me the courage to live with peace and goodwill throughout this day.

"You have heard that it was said, 'Love your friends, hate your enemies.' But now I tell you: love your enemies and pray for those who persecute you, so that you may become the children of your Father in heaven. For he makes his sun to shine on bad and good people alike, and gives rain to those who do good and to those who do evil. Why should God reward you if you love only the people who love you? Even the tax collectors do that! And if you speak only to your friends, have you done anything out of the ordinary? Even the pagans do that! You must be perfect – just as your Father in heaven is perfect."

Matthew 5: 43-48

"...pray for those who persecute you..."

May he be well

He was at it again. My colleague's sarcasm and vicious barbs were reaching their mark and I was shaken to the core. My confidence and composure were crumbling. Why me? Of course, he didn't always treat me this way. Other times he was overflowing with praise. It was a roller coaster ride working with him. I was angry, hurt and confused. I would awaken at night with terrible dreams about him.

Praying for myself didn't seem to help. So I decided to pray for him. I wanted to pray that he would be sucked off the planet by aliens! But, instead, in a moment of grace, I prayed for his well-being.

Empathy moved me to a new position. Not quite love, but at least closer to his side.

**Loving God, open my heart to your love so I may find
the stability, humility and compassion needed to go on.**

"Make certain you do not perform your religious duties in public so that people will see what you do. If you do these things publicly, you will not have any reward from your Father in heaven.

"So when you give something to a needy person, do not make a big show of it, as the hypocrites do in the houses of worship and on the streets. They do it so that people will praise them. I assure you, they have already been paid in full. But when you help a needy person, do it in such a way that even your closest friend will not know about it. Then it will be a private matter. And your Father, who sees what you do in private, will reward you."   *Matthew 6: 1-6, 16-18*

> "...do not perform your religious duties in public..."

A quiet giving

I have a friend, George, who came from Lebanon a few years ago. I first met George when I taught his English class, and since then we've become friends. George is one of those quiet guys – the one who, when a few of us go out, gets teased; and he just shrugs and smiles.

Once, during night school, the coffee machine broke. At the time, I also worked days, and I looked forward to my coffee at the break. Mysteriously, a cup appeared on my desk from a place down the street. Later, I found out it was George. No fanfare – just a little shrug when I said, "Thanks."

When George does things in his quiet way, it makes me feel good – because he did it for me, not for himself.

Lord, let me be quiet in my giving.

"When you pray, do not use a lot of meaningless words.... Your Father already knows what you need before you ask him. This, then, is how you should pray: 'Our Father in heaven: may your holy name be honoured; may your kingdom come; may your will be done on earth as it is in heaven. Give us today the food we need. Forgive us the wrongs we have done, as we forgive the wrongs that others have done to us. Do not bring us to hard testing, but keep us safe from the Evil One.'

"If you forgive others the wrongs they have done to you, your Father in heaven will also forgive you. But if you do not forgive others, then your Father will not forgive the wrongs you have done."   *Matthew 6: 7-15*

> "...as we forgive the wrongs that others have done to us."

True prayer

I pray the Lord's Prayer each day, but often I don't pay attention to what I'm saying.

My mother claims she isn't a very religious person. Recently she broke her leg in a fall, and as she has osteoporosis, the bone broke into three pieces. The emergency ward was so crowded that after being x-rayed, she had to wait for twelve hours lying on a gurney before being seen by a doctor. My temptation would have been to lie there cursing myself, my bones and the medical system.

She told me later that as she waited, she stared up at the ceiling panels and assigned to each one something for which she was grateful. "There were so many things," she said, "that I ran out of panels."

**Lord, deepen my understanding of your prayer,
and keep drawing me to your goodness.**

"Do not store up riches for yourselves here on earth, where moths and rust destroy, and robbers break in and steal. Instead, store up riches for yourselves in heaven, where moths and rust cannot destroy, and robbers cannot break in and steal. For your heart will always be where your riches are.

"The eyes are like a lamp for the body. If your eyes are sound, your whole body will be full of light; but if your eyes are no good, your body will be in darkness. So if the light in you is darkness, how terribly dark it will be!"

Matthew 6: 19-23

"...your heart will always be where your riches are."

Hands to hold

We had gathered as an extended family to share a meal. As we prepared to give thanks for our food, my dad invited us to join hands (rather than fold them as is our usual custom). As soon as we said "Amen," and even before we could release our hands, three-year-old Susanna announced to me, with the thrill of genuine discovery, "Look, Dad, there's just enough hands for everyone to hold one!"

Much more than elementary math prompted her insight. With simple eloquence, Susanna named the treasure of the day: the gift of being present to one another.

And naming it so exuberantly, we heard in Susanna's wonder what Jesus might mean when he says, "the kingdom of God is at hand."

**Jesus, help me recognize the true treasures in my life,
and to take hold of them.**

"Y ou cannot be a slave of two masters; you will hate one and love the other. Do not be worried about food and drink, or about clothes for your body. After all, isn't life worth more than food? And isn't the body worth more than clothes? Look at the birds… your Father takes care of them! Aren't you worth much more than birds? And why worry about clothes? Look how the wild flowers grow…. It is God who clothes the wild grass.

"Instead, be concerned above everything else with the kingdom of God and with what he requires of you, and he will provide you with all these other things. So do not worry about tomorrow; it will have enough worries of its own. There is no need to add to the troubles each day brings."

Matthew 6: 24-34

"…do not worry about tomorrow…"

The gift of today

Oh yes! This sounds so good when I hear it Sunday morning. But then Sunday becomes Monday and the car breaks down, or I have a final exam, or I can't seem to get that computer to work and a deadline is staring at me!

Sometimes it's hard to really stop and take this wisdom seriously. I can almost hear, "Well, that sounds good, but really…" echoing in my brain. It's so easy to be trapped by the "here and now." It is hard to free myself from anxiety when the responsibilities, for myself and for others, are so real and so pressing. But then life is so quickly gone.

How hard to give the world what it deserves, but not be a prisoner of it.

God, help me live for today, realizing that this day is a gift to be revelled in, not a weight to be borne.

S in came into the world through one man, and his sin brought death with it. As a result, death has spread to the whole human race because everyone has sinned…. From the time of Adam to the time of Moses, death ruled over all human beings, even over those who did not sin in the same way that Adam did when he disobeyed God's command.

Adam was a figure of the one who was to come. But the two are not the same, because God's free gift is not like Adam's sin. It is true that many people died because of the sin of that one man. But God's grace is much greater, and so is his free gift to so many people through the grace of the one man, Jesus Christ.

Romans 5: 12-15

"Sin came into the world through one man…"

A personal choice

Sin: what an old-fashioned concept. Like guardian angels, limbo for unbaptized babies, and indulgences. A little embarrassing. Too pious. Just not done anymore. But here is Paul, making it the foundation for the coming of the Messiah. What am I, an educated, sophisticated, thoroughly modern person, supposed to do with that claim?

I believed that a non-nurturing environment, especially in early childhood, forced people to make bad choices. And that unjust social structures caused social harm. Surely political theorists, sociologists and psychologists have more to say than this ancient tent-maker!?

Perhaps not. Maybe the reason I don't like to talk of sin is that it's personal. If I sin, that means I choose to do wrong. And who wants to face up to that?

**Lord, give me the courage and humility to accept
the responsibility for my own life.**

Y ou have rejected us, God, and defeated us;
you have been angry with us – but now turn back to us.
You have made the land tremble, and you have cut it open;
now heal its wounds, because it is falling apart.
You have made your people suffer greatly;
we stagger around as though we were drunk.
You have warned those who have reverence for you,
so that they might escape destruction.
Save us by your might; answer our prayer,
so that the people you love may be rescued....
Have you really rejected us?
Aren't you going to march out with our armies?
Help us against the enemy;
human help is worthless.

Psalm 60: 1-5, 10-11

"...now heal its wounds..."

The courage to hope

This psalm is striking in the way it weaves
its way between despair and hope.

How painful to hear the voice behind this lament – a voice
I recognize. This is the voice of the wound that never seems to heal.
It is the voice that trembles as it tries to move past rejection to find
the courage to ask for healing. It is the child asking to draw closer
to a parent who doesn't understand. It is the parent trying to carve
out some common ground with a teenager who lives a culture and a
world away. It is the voice that speaks with a fierce but fragile hope.

I can only imagine that God hears this voice, and responds with
compassion.

Loving God, hear the prayers of all those who need healing.

Lord, you have
examined me
and you know me.
You know everything I do;
from far away you understand
all my thoughts.
You see me, whether I am
working or resting;
you know all my actions.
You created every part of me;
you put me together
in my mother's womb.
I praise you because
you are to be feared;

all you do is strange
and wonderful.
I know it with all my heart.
When my bones
were being formed,
carefully put together
in my mother's womb,
when I was growing there
in secret,
you knew that I was there
– you saw me before
I was born.

Psalm 139: 1-3, 13-15

"When my bones were being formed…"

God's love revealed

Today's psalm makes me think of a friend who was born with a life-threatening birth defect. She tells me how, for many years, the words of this psalm made her sad, and even angry towards God.

Why did God – who knew her while her bones were being formed in her mother's womb – let her body develop as it did? What sort of loving God would allow this to happen?

Strangely enough, the answers to my friend's questions came from her body itself. The limitations she experienced taught her to face the challenges and setbacks that life brings us, and to turn them into opportunities for growth. Within her "birth defect," my friend discovered God truly loves her – as she is. And this gives her comfort.

**God, give me the courage to face the limitations
with which I live. Let me learn from them.**

Teach me, Lord, the meaning of your laws,
and I will obey them at all times.
Explain your law to me, and I will obey it;
I will keep it with all my heart.
Keep me obedient to your commandments,
because in them I find happiness.
Give me the desire to obey your laws
rather than to get rich.
Keep me from paying attention to what is worthless;
be good to me, as you have promised....
I want to obey your commands;
give me new life, for you are righteous.

Psalm 119: 33-37, 40

"...give me new life, for you are righteous."

New life

Joan wept as she told me about her grandson, Andrew. Stricken with
a rare brain condition, the little boy could not learn to read and had
developed paralysis in his left hand and leg. Joan felt her own anguish
and her daughter's pain. In a family of university graduates, Andrew
would not be able to learn. Left untreated, his condition would inevitably lead to death.

However, there was hope: a medical procedure that might treat
the brain anomaly and reverse the paralysis. Joan explained that only
three doctors in North America can perform this operation. Andrew
will see one of them in Baltimore next week.

We are all praying that Andrew will be one of the fortunate ones
to receive new life. I hope and trust that his grandmother's heart will
be lightened.

O God, we place all our trust in you.

"Not everyone who calls me 'Lord, Lord' will enter the kingdom of heaven, but only those who do what my Father in heaven wants them to do....

"So then, anyone who hears these words of mine and obeys them is like a wise man who built his house on rock. The rain poured down, the rivers flooded over, and the wind blew hard against that house. But it did not fall, because it was built on rock.

"But anyone who hears these words of mine and does not obey them is like a foolish man who built his house on sand. The rain poured down, the rivers flooded over, the wind blew hard against that house, and it fell. And what a terrible fall that was!"

Matthew 7: 21-29

"...anyone who hears these words of mine and obeys them..."

Built on rock

Socorro lives in one of the poorest neighbourhoods imaginable. On any given day, she may be seen helping a woman who'd been beaten by her husband, taking a sick baby to the hospital, or lobbying city hall for better living conditions for her neighbourhood.

Socorro visited me one day. She was perplexed about a lengthy conversation she'd had with some Christians. They wanted her to attend their church. She wondered aloud, "How can I say to church-goers that I don't believe we go to church.... We *do* church. We *are* church."

The truth of her words is etched in my mind, highlighted by the witness of her life. Her faith is built on solid rock: hearing the words of the gospel and living by them.

Dear God, may the foundation of my faith be the solid rock of knowing and living your values.

When Jesus came down from the hill, large crowds followed him. Then a man suffering from a dreaded skin disease came to him, knelt down before him, and said, "Sir, if you want to, you can make me clean." Jesus reached out and touched him. "I do want to," he answered. "Be clean!" At once the man was healed of his disease. Then Jesus said to him, "Listen! Don't tell anyone, but go straight to the priest and let him examine you; then in order to prove to everyone that you are cured, offer the sacrifice that Moses ordered."

Matthew 8: 1-4

"Sir, if you want to, you can make me clean."

A dreaded disease

Have you ever met a leper? No? Neither have I. Leprosy is the "dreaded skin disease" which Jesus cures in this touching scene.

While most of us have never seen leprosy up close, there are nevertheless plenty of "dreaded diseases" to fill us with fear and even revulsion.

Last night I visited my cousin, a 45-year-old father of four: a kind and decent man now seriously ill with an inoperable brain tumour. There he lay in the cancer hospital, heavily sedated and hooked up to tubes and machines.

How I wish there were some miracle waiting for him, a holy healer to reach out and touch him, so that he, too, would be cured of his disease!

Lord, comfort those who suffer today
as you comforted those who suffered in your time.

My eyes are worn out with weeping; my soul is in anguish.
I am exhausted with grief at the destruction of my people.
Children and babies are fainting in the streets of the city.
Hungry and thirsty, they cry to their mothers;
They fall in the streets as though they were wounded,
And slowly die in their mothers' arms.
O Jerusalem, beloved Jerusalem, what can I say?
How can I comfort you? No one has ever suffered like this.
Your disaster is boundless as the ocean; there is no possible hope....
O Jerusalem, let your very walls cry out to the Lord!
Let your tears flow like rivers night and day;...
All through the night get up again and again to cry out to the Lord;
Pour out your heart and beg him for mercy on your children.

Lamentations 2: 2, 10-14, 18-19

"Let your tears flow like rivers…"

Light in the dark

I feel torn about writing on this passage. People want something up-lifting – right? But then I consider our world: so many countries experience war and poverty. Even within the "developed world," there's great wealth alongside destitution. And spiritual poverty – I look at the values that television is selling my children. Today, one of my students started on anti-depressants again. "It's too much," he says.

But then, I hear Clara Hughes, after winning her 5000-metre Olympic speedskating race, saying that sport and play can give so much to the world. She has, I learn, given all her savings to "Right to Play," a charity for Third World children.

Find the light in the darkness. Find the hope. For the New Jerusalem.

Dear God, when I despair, show me reason to hope.

Jesus asked his disciples, "Who do people say the Son of Man is?" "Some say John the Baptist," they answered. "Others say Elijah, while others say Jeremiah or some other prophet." "What about you?" he asked them. "Who do you say I am?" Simon Peter answered, "You are the Messiah, the Son of the living God."

"Good for you, Simon son of John!" answered Jesus. "For this truth did not come to you from any human being, but it was given to you directly by my Father in heaven. And so I tell you, Peter: you are a rock, and on this rock foundation I will build my church, and not even death will ever be able to overcome it. I will give you the keys of the kingdom of heaven."

Matthew 16: 13-19

"Peter: you are a rock…"

Commitment

Peter: the "rock." Sometimes with a head like a rock! Stubborn and thick. Taking so long to understand. Before Jesus' death, he's so afraid that he even denies knowing Jesus. But then this rough, simple man is chosen from all of them. Why Peter? Why him?

I am reminded of a friend, named Peter, too. We played hockey together. He was far from being the best, but very probably was the most valuable. Why? He never stopped trying. Knock him down, he got up. Knock him down again, he got up again.

Maybe that's what Jesus saw in Peter, and what he asks of me: not perfection, not brilliance, but commitment. Being there and getting up one more time after I fall.

**God, give me the courage to pick myself up
each time I stumble and fall, and to carry on.**

The Lord says, "The people of Israel have sinned again and again, and for this I will certainly punish them…. They trample down the weak and helpless and push the poor out of the way….

"And yet, my people, I brought you out of Egypt, led you through the desert for forty years, and gave you the land of the Amorites to be your own…. And now I will crush you to the ground, and you will groan like a cart loaded with grain. Not even fast runners will escape; strong men will lose their strength, and soldiers will not be able to save their own lives. Archers will not stand their ground, fast runners will not get away, and men on horses will not escape with their lives. On that day even the bravest soldiers will drop their weapons and run." The Lord has spoken.   *Amos 2: 6-10, 13-16*

> "…and push the poor out of the way."

Quiet, prophetic fury

In 1917 my great-grandfather buried the second oldest of his six young children. They were a devout family – my great-grandfather served on the parish council – but they were far from wealthy.

When six-year-old Hans died, the church elders reviewed the family's record of donations to the church. They decided that Hans could have a church funeral but that the family hadn't given enough for the bell to be rung afterwards. So little Hans was laid to rest without the tolling of a church bell.

My great-grandfather remained a faithful, active member of the parish his entire life. But, to the end, he was adamant that no church bell would toll at his funeral, either. This was not bitterness on his part. It was quiet prophetic fury. My great-grandfather understood Amos' words – from the inside.

Dear God, how often institutions fail to mirror your mercy! Help me choose mercy every time the choice is mine.

J esus got into a boat, and his disciples went with him. Suddenly a fierce storm hit the lake, and the boat was in danger of sinking. But Jesus was asleep. The disciples went to him and woke him up. "Save us, Lord!" they said. "We are about to die!" "Why are you so frightened?" Jesus answered. "What little faith you have!" Then he got up and ordered the winds and the waves to stop, and there was a great calm. Everyone was amazed. "What kind of man is this?" they said. "Even the winds and the waves obey him!"

Matthew 8: 23-27

"Why are you so frightened?"

Peace amid the storm

The storm breaks suddenly. My company announces it may lay me off. My child becomes very ill. The person I've trusted more than anyone else on earth betrays me. Whatever the storm, I behave the way the disciples did. I scream, "Save me, Lord, I'm going down!"

As the powerful waves batter me in the darkness, I feel that all is lost. It seems to me that God is asleep.

But Jesus urges me to have faith. The one who calmed the wind and waves of a vicious storm on the Sea of Galilee has the power to bring healing and peace into my life.

Clinging to that hope, I can keep my balance as the storm crashes against me.

Teach me, Lord, to trust in you!

Make it your aim to do what is right, not what is evil, so that you may live. Then the Lord God Almighty really will be with you, as you claim he is. Hate what is evil, love what is right, and see that justice prevails in the courts. Perhaps the Lord will be merciful to the people of this nation who are still left alive....

The Lord says, "I hate your religious festivals; I cannot stand them! When you bring me burnt offerings and grain offerings, I will not accept them; I will not accept the animals you have fattened to bring me as offerings. Stop your noisy songs; I do not want to listen to your harps. Instead, let justice flow like a stream, and righteousness like a river that never goes dry."   *Amos 5: 14-15, 21-24*

> "I hate your religious festivals..."

True worship

The little church I attend is in trouble. Attendance is dropping. Church school consists of three families. Half our annual income comes from people over the age of seventy, and they're starting to die off or move away.

Obviously, what we're doing is not attracting new people. Yet whenever we attempt something new, the pressure grows to go back to the old ways, whatever they were.

Contemporary worship? "It doesn't feel reverent." Contemporary music? "Why don't we sing any of the good old hymns any more?" Midweek services? "We'll split into two congregations. We must stay together." Project words on a screen? "I can't see them from the back."

I suspect that if Amos – or Jesus – wandered into a worship service today, he'd fall asleep at best, or at worst, walk out in disgust.

> **Help me set aside my preconceptions,**
> **God, and worship as you want to be worshipped.**

C hrist preached the Good News of peace to all – to you Gentiles, who were far away from God, and to the Jews, who were near to him. It is through Christ that all of us, Jews and Gentiles, are able to come in the one Spirit into the presence of the Father. So then, you Gentiles are not foreigners or strangers any longer; you are now citizens together with God's people and members of the family of God. You, too, are built upon the foundation laid by the apostles and prophets, the cornerstone being Christ Jesus himself. He is the one who holds the whole building together and makes it grow into a sacred temple dedicated to the Lord. In union with him, you too are being built together with all the others into a place where God lives through his Spirit.   *Ephesians 2: 17-22*

> "...not foreigners or strangers any longer..."

No longer strangers

Ancient hatreds are rekindled for political gain; people leave their countries as new boundaries are drawn, boundaries intended to include and to exclude.

I know two people, one a Muslim and the other a Christian. One is young, and Canada has become home. The other is old enough to know that she may never feel "at home" again. Her children will, and that is enough for her. Both have told me they love this country. "Here I can pray in my way, without fear." As they speak, I see tears in their eyes.

Today's reading strikes a chord in me as we, the children of the conquerors and the conquered – the old and the new – are still trying to live together. Trying to become "us," not "us and them."

Lord, help me share my world with my brothers and sisters.

As Jesus walked along, he saw a tax collector, named Matthew, sitting in his office. He said, "Follow me." Matthew got up and followed him.

While Jesus was having a meal in Matthew's house, many tax collectors and other outcasts came and joined Jesus and his disciples at the table. Some Pharisees saw this and asked his disciples, "Why does your teacher eat with such people?"

Jesus answered, "People who are well do not need a doctor, but only those who are sick. Go and find out what is meant by the scripture that says: 'It is kindness that I want, not animal sacrifices.' I have not come to call respectable people, but outcasts."

Matthew 9: 9-13

"Why does your teacher eat with such people?"

At home

When Juan, a young man from South America, first came to live in our L'Arche home, he was very quiet at the dinner table. Everything was so new to him.

But Mike, a man with disabilities who speaks very slowly and with great difficulty, kept talking to him, calling him "funny guy." At the end of the meal Nancy would throw a napkin at him, and Francis would perform his magic tricks. Gradually Juan started smiling and joining in the jokes. He found he could be himself; he began to feel at home.

When Jesus invited himself to Matthew's house for dinner, it changed Matthew's life. He discovered a new way of being, and he formed an important friendship with Jesus.

Lord, may I welcome at my table those who are in need.

The followers of John the Baptist asked Jesus, "Why is it that we and the Pharisees fast often, but your disciples don't fast at all?"

Jesus answered, "Do you expect the guests at a wedding party to be sad as long as the bridegroom is with them? Of course not! But the day will come when the bridegroom will be taken away from them, and then they will fast.

"No one patches up an old coat with a piece of new cloth, for the new patch will shrink and make an even bigger hole in the coat. Nor does anyone pour new wine into used wineskins, for the skins will burst, the wine will pour out, and the skins will be ruined. Instead, new wine is poured into fresh wineskins, and both will keep in good condition."   *Matthew 9: 14-17*

> "…new wine is poured into fresh wineskins…"

A new day dawns

Today, when I awoke, the sun was rising. The birds were singing. It seemed everything was new… except me. I feel myself becoming, in T. S. Eliot's words, "an old man in a dry month." The challenge Jesus gives me is not only to hear a new message, but to "be new" so his message can be heard.

But it's hard. The burdens of yesterday, the scars of old hurts, unfulfilled dreams and broken promises conspire against me. They make it so much easier to cling to my old penances and to cut myself off from the world of people and change. It is more difficult to see the world as it is: ever new and open to my own creative response to Jesus' call to love, to joy.

God, help me be "new" each day – to see the gifts you have given me. Help me to share them with others.

Rejoice, rejoice,
people of Zion!
Shout for joy,
you people of Jerusalem!
Look, your king is coming
to you!
He comes triumphant
and victorious, but humble
and riding on a donkey –
on a colt, the foal of a donkey.
The Lord says,
"I will remove the war chariots
from Israel
and take the horses
from Jerusalem;
the bows used in battle
will be destroyed.
Your king will make peace
among the nations;
he will rule from sea to sea,
from the Euphrates River
to the ends of the earth."

Zechariah 9: 9-10

"...but humble and riding on a donkey..."

Peace among the nations

As I write, Afghanistan is still being bombed, but some refugees are already trying to go home, on foot, or if they are lucky, by donkey. Will their home still be there? Will someone else be living in it? Will their neighbours welcome them? Will there be any work, any food? Will there be peace? For how long?

It suddenly struck me that Jesus was born in a situation very like that in which Afghan refugees find themselves. Mary and Joseph were refused lodging in his own home town, stayed in a shelter while Jesus was born, then were forced into Egypt as refugees. This is how "peace among the nations" was proclaimed.

Victory comes to the world humbly – on a donkey, not in warplanes.

**Lord, keep me from being cynical about our world.
Teach me to read the signs of hope around me.**

A Jewish official knelt before Jesus, and said, "My daughter has just died; but come and place your hands on her, and she will live."

Jesus got up and followed him. A woman who had suffered from severe bleeding for twelve years came up behind Jesus and touched the edge of his cloak. She said to herself, "If only I touch his cloak, I will get well." Jesus turned around and saw her, and said, "Courage, my daughter! Your faith has made you well." At that very moment the woman became well.

Then Jesus went into the official's house. He said, "The little girl is not dead – she is only sleeping!" As soon as the people had been put out, Jesus went into the girl's room and took hold of her hand, and she got up. *Matthew 9: 18-26*

"Courage, my daughter! Your faith has made you well."

Courage to change

Why the warning to have courage now? Surely this is a courageous woman! Though unclean, she dares to reach out and touch Jesus. She believes that simple contact will heal her. But perhaps even greater courage is needed to walk away – healed!

Many things in my life need healing: from major hurts to minor habits. But do I have any idea what letting go of them will really involve? Am I committed to living the new life Jesus wants to create in me?

Sometimes I choose to go on living with the familiar – unhealthy as it may be. It seems easier than risking the unknown! At other times, even when others around me scoff at the possibilities, I grasp the hand that offers new life.

Jesus, today I ask for the courage to take one small step in the direction of new life.

Why should the
nations ask us,
"Where is your God?"
Our God is in heaven;
he does whatever he wishes.
Their gods are made of silver
and gold,
formed by human hands.
They have mouths,
but cannot speak,
and eyes, but cannot see.
They have ears,
but cannot hear,
and noses, but cannot smell.
They have hands,
but cannot feel,
and feet, but cannot walk;
they cannot make a sound.
May all who made them
and who trust in them
become like the idols
they have made.
Trust in the Lord,
you people of Israel.
He helps you and protects you.

Psalm 115: 2-10

> "…become like the idols they have made."

Powerful gods

We are far more theologically advanced than the people for whom the psalmist wrote! Their gods were visible but powerless. Our gods are invisible but enormously powerful.

It's true that our gods are still made of silver and gold, but they no longer have actual body parts. Yet they see and touch us all the time and are never, ever silent.

A trip to their temple shows how clearly they see our secret hopes and fears and how they reach out to us with their soft and soothing words: "Buy me and you will be loveable." "Own me and you will never be alone." "Worship me and I will take care of you." And we who trust them have become like them – things to be bought and sold.

Lord, our gods are powerful gods.
Help me to keep my trust in you.

J esus called his twelve disciples together and gave them authority to drive out evil spirits and to heal every disease and every sickness. These are the names of the twelve apostles: first, Simon (called Peter) and his brother Andrew; James and his brother John, the sons of Zebedee; Philip and Bartholomew; Thomas and Matthew, the tax collector; James son of Alphaeus, and Thaddaeus; Simon the Patriot, and Judas Iscariot, who betrayed Jesus.

These twelve men were sent out by Jesus with the following instructions: "Do not go to any Gentile territory or any Samaritan towns. Instead, you are to go to the lost sheep of the people of Israel. Go and preach, 'The kingdom of heaven is near!'"

Matthew 10: 1-7

"These twelve men were sent out by Jesus..."

On our way

The disciples received their instructions and set out – some fearing failure (as we do); some doubting themselves (as we do); some brimming with confidence (as we are). Jesus watched them go. Each one different. Each with his own walk – some shuffle head down, others stride gracefully. Each special to him.

Recently I watched my son go – with his new driver's licence. I gave him my advice and watched him go. How strange to see him heading off alone, knowing how risky the first few trips will be. Yet, he must go. Only he can walk – or in this case, drive – his path.

And we, like the disciples, must walk ours. It is we who must carry the message, in our halting ways – as we shuffle, or stride, or limp toward our destiny.

Lord, let me bring goodness into the world this day, and always.

"Go and preach, 'The kingdom of heaven is near!' Heal the sick, bring the dead back to life, heal those who suffer from dreaded skin diseases, and drive out demons. You have received without paying, so give without being paid. Do not carry any gold, silver, or copper money in your pockets; do not carry a beggar's bag for the trip or an extra shirt or shoes or a walking stick. Workers should be given what they need.

"When you come to a town or village, go in and look for someone who is willing to welcome you, and stay with him until you leave that place. When you go into a house, say, 'Peace be with you.' If the people in that house welcome you, let your greeting of peace remain."

Matthew 10: 7-15

> "...so give without being paid."

Giving freely

Almost fifty years ago, my parents immigrated to this country. They arrived by boat with a few steamer trunks, leaving behind family and friends and all that was familiar.

Their new life in Canada was full – a growing family, new jobs, even night courses. Then, just a few years after their arrival, my mother contracted polio and had to be hospitalized. At the same time, my younger brother died, days after his birth. My parents grieved, but neither illness nor death overcame them.

Now I have children of my own, and I have experienced illness and death in my family. With this perspective I now recognize how much love and support my parents gave us as children. And I am challenged to give – as I have received – to my children.

Loving God, I have received so much and for that I am thankful. Help me to give to others – without expecting to be thanked.

Be merciful to me, O God,
because of your constant love.
Because of your great mercy
wipe away my sins!
Wash away all my evil
and make me clean from my sin!
Sincerity and truth are what you require;
fill my mind with your wisdom.
Remove my sin, and I will be clean;
wash me, and I will be whiter than snow.
Create a pure heart in me, O God,
and put a new and loyal spirit in me.
Do not banish me from your presence;
do not take your holy spirit away from me.

Psalm 51: 1-2, 6-7, 10-12, 15

"Create a pure heart in me, O God..."

Healing the heart

I spent years trying to "fix" my life. I felt hopelessly flawed, damaged beyond repair. I tried to heal painful childhood memories and bitter resentments through "self-help" and "self-improvement." But the more books I bought, the more workshops I attended, the more therapists I saw, the more confused I became.

Later I realized that only the grace of God could help me. And, to accept that grace, all I really needed was humility. This humility meant not thinking less of myself, but thinking of myself less.

As grace transformed my sense of humiliation to humility, I came to rely less upon my "self" and more upon God. That's when my healing really began.

God, grant me the humility to accept your healing grace.

"Do not be afraid of people. Whatever is now covered up will be uncovered, and every secret will be made known. What I am telling you in the dark you must repeat in broad daylight, and what you have heard in private you must announce from the housetops. Do not be afraid of those who kill the body but cannot kill the soul; rather be afraid of God, who can destroy both body and soul in hell. For only a penny you can buy two sparrows, yet not one sparrow falls to the ground without your Father's consent. As for you, even the hairs of your head have all been counted. So do not be afraid; you are worth much more than many sparrows!"

Matthew 10: 24-33

"...even the hairs of your head have all been counted."

Unconditional love

At one time or another in our lives, most of us have been badly criticized and our self-esteem hurt. A chance remark – "Look at you now. And you were such a pretty baby!" – can cut so deeply. Repeated negative messages – "Can't you ever get it right?" – create wounds that we may carry for years, making us believe that we're not worth much.

Yet Jesus says that I am so valuable to God that even the hairs of my head have been counted. I am known and loved by God.

People know me by my words and actions; God knows my heart and motives and loves me completely. That's enough to brighten the most miserable day!

**Lord, it is such a comfort to know you love me.
Help me comfort those I meet today with my love.**

I consider that what we suffer at this present time cannot be compared at all with the glory that is going to be revealed to us. All of creation waits with eager longing for God to reveal his children. For creation was condemned to lose its purpose.... Yet there was the hope that creation itself would one day be set free from its slavery to decay and would share the glorious freedom of the children of God. For we know that up to the present time all of creation groans with pain, like the pain of childbirth. But it is not just creation alone which groans; we who have the Spirit as the first of God's gifts also groan within ourselves as we wait for God to make us his children and set our whole being free.   *Romans 8: 18-23*

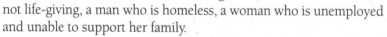

"...all of creation groans with pain..."

Pain and glory

Sometimes all I can see is the suffering around me: a friend with a debilitating chronic illness, another whose marriage is not life-giving, a man who is homeless, a woman who is unemployed and unable to support her family.

In my own life I, too, experience suffering: I lose heart and cry out to God. At those times, I am like a woman giving birth: I can experience nothing beyond my own pain.

But just as the miracle of a newborn baby follows a painful labour and birth, I believe that my suffering will give way to God's glory. The Spirit is leading me to a deeper understanding of suffering as a part of my experience, but not as its end.

Lord, sometimes I feel surrounded by suffering.
Help me see beyond it to the glory that awaits each one of us.

The Lord says, "Do you think I want all these sacrifices you keep offering to me? I have had more than enough of the sheep you burn as sacrifices and of the fat of your fine animals…. Who asked you to bring me all this when you come to worship me? Who asked you to do all this tramping around in my Temple? It's useless to bring your offerings….

"When you lift your hands in prayer, I will not look at you. No matter how much you pray, I will not listen, for your hands are covered with blood. Wash yourselves clean. Stop all this evil that I see you doing. Yes, stop doing evil and learn to do right. See that justice is done – help those who are oppressed, give orphans their rights, and defend widows."

Isaiah 1: 10-17

> "No matter how much you pray, I will not listen…"

Love and limits

How can I reconcile my image of God – as always patient and kind – with the one presented in today's reading? What would push a loving God to speak and act so strongly?

I think I've often confused loving with not imposing any limits. It's taken me a while to learn when to be patient and when to say, "Enough is enough! I won't take this any more!" Also, there have been times when I have pushed the patience and limits of those I love. Their willingness to challenge me has been the wake-up call I needed.

Perhaps today's reading is saying that, while there are no limits to God's love, when my words and actions are unloving and unacceptable, God will say, "Enough is enough." ·

**Loving God, help me to recognize your limits
so that I may act justly.**

Thehe people in the towns where Jesus had performed most of his miracles did not turn from their sins, so he reproached those towns. "How terrible it will be for you, Chorazin! How terrible for you too, Bethsaida! If the miracles which were performed in you had been performed in Tyre and Sidon, the people there would have long ago put on sackcloth and sprinkled ashes on themselves, to show that they had turned from their sins! I assure you that on the Judgment Day God will show more mercy to the people of Tyre and Sidon than to you! And as for you, Capernaum! Did you want to lift yourself up to heaven? You will be thrown down to hell! If the miracles which were performed in you had been performed in Sodom, it would still be in existence today! You can be sure that on the Judgment Day God will show more mercy to Sodom than to you!"

Matthew 11: 20-24

> "...God will show more mercy..."

Merciful God

Jesus juxtaposes the very public sins of various towns with God's unlimited mercy and forgiveness. To emphasize his point, he repeats the phrase, "God will show mercy..." twice in this short passage. It would seem that God's mercy can extend to some pretty grim situations.

Recently Serbia was put on trial for genocide – the first time an entire country has been accused of genocide. The list of crimes perpetuated by Serbia against Bosnia's Muslim population is beyond my comprehension. But, if I apply today's reading to this situation, God's mercy and forgiveness are beyond my comprehension, too.

If God's mercy can extend to such extreme situations, why do I hesitate to turn to God when I know my actions have hurt another person?

**Merciful God, may I have the faith
to turn to you for mercy and forgiveness.**

A t that time Jesus said, "Father, Lord of heaven and earth! I thank you because you have shown to the unlearned what you have hidden from the wise and learned. Yes, Father, this was how you were pleased to have it happen. My Father has given me all things. No one knows the Son except the Father, and no one knows the Father except the Son and those to whom the Son chooses to reveal him."

Matthew 11: 25-27

"...what you have hidden from the wise and learned."

A lot to learn

Over the years, I've come up with a lot of ideas about life. If I happen to be smarter than some people, or have more education, then I'm even more convinced my answers are right. But Jesus challenges my settled way of looking at things. He says: Getting ahead isn't important; caring about another human in distress is. Forgive. Put God first. Stop worrying about money: God will take care of your every need. "Come, follow me...."

Jesus teaches me that following the gospel message will make my life complete. But I can't begin to understand that message unless I'm first willing to admit I have a lot to learn.

Lord, teach me to open myself up to the "impossible" message that you give me in your gospel.

" ome to me, all of you who are tired from carrying heavy loads, and I will give you rest. Take my yoke and put it on you, and learn from me, because I am gentle and humble in spirit; and you will find rest. For the yoke I will give you is easy, and the load I will put on you is light."

Matthew 11: 28-30

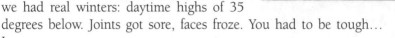

"...learn from me, because I am gentle..."

Embrace life

Life is tough. And you better be tough... I guess. I delivered mail years ago, when we had real winters: daytime highs of 35 degrees below. Joints got sore, faces froze. You had to be tough... I guess.

One carrier, Gordie, was always cheerful, always singing. No matter how cold it was. Never a grim face or word. Never. He was a gentle man. And he knew that the weight of the yoke depends on us, at least in part.

Maybe that's what Jesus was saying in today's reading: think of your life as a gift to share. Treat each person, even the hard ones, as a gift to you. And your yoke will be easy and your load light. Like Gordie's.

Lord, let me not only accept your load. Let me embrace it.

J esus' disciples were hungry, so they began to pick heads of wheat and eat the grain. When the Pharisees saw this, they said, "Look, it is against our Law for your disciples to do this on the Sabbath!"

Jesus answered, "Have you never read what David did that time when he and his men were hungry? He went into the house of God, and he and his men ate the bread offered to God, even though it was against the Law for them to eat it…. Or have you not read in the law of Moses that every Sabbath the priests in the Temple actually break the Sabbath law, yet they are not guilty? I tell you that there is something here greater than the Temple. The scripture says, 'It is kindness that I want, not animal sacrifices.'"
Matthew 12: 1-8

> "The scripture says, 'It is kindness that I want…'"

Wanted: kindness

Last winter, a professional hockey player swung his stick and hit another player with a vicious blow to the head. The debate raged on every TV and radio station: should this be considered a criminal offence? Should the matter be decided by the courts? Should acts of violence be tolerated on the ice? One caller asked, "Would this behaviour be treated differently if it had happened in the arena's parking lot?"

Do our hockey players (read "priests") receive different treatment because they perform in the hockey arena (read "Temple")? Does the Law itself find them "not guilty"?

Jesus says, "It is kindness that I want…." In the Temple or in the wheat fields. In the hockey arena or in the parking lot. What matters most is what's in my heart.

**Lord, when I am tempted to judge a person's actions,
may I try to understand what is in his or her heart.**

The Pharisees made plans to kill Jesus. When Jesus heard about the plot against him, he went away from that place; and large crowds followed him. He healed all the sick and gave them orders not to tell others about him. He did this so as to make come true what God had said through the prophet Isaiah: "Here is my servant, whom I have chosen, the one I love, and with whom I am pleased. I will send my Spirit upon him, and he will announce my judgment to the nations. He will not argue or shout, or make loud speeches in the streets. He will not break off a bent reed, nor put out a flickering lamp. He will persist until he causes justice to triumph, and on him all peoples will put their hope."

Matthew 12: 14-21

"He will persist until he causes justice to triumph…"

A persistent love

The neighbourhood bully preys on the misfit. An aggressive, powerful nation overtakes one that is defenceless and peace-loving. There is a vicious streak within us that finds expression whenever we trample on the vulnerable in an attempt to strengthen ourselves. We are all capable of it at some level – manipulating our family with angry moods, gossiping to defame our neighbour, buying "cheap" and perpetuating economic exploitation of others.

Jesus is clear that this is not his way. He does not despise or reject us for our weakness. Neither does he take advantage of us, forcing us to follow him. Patiently, persistently, he confronts us with his truth until our love ignites, and we freely place our hope in him.

Do we do the same for one another?

**Lord, fill me with your strength when I am weak.
Help me bring your patient love to others when they are weak.**

Y ou are good to us and forgiving,
full of constant love for all who pray to you.
Listen, Lord, to my prayer;
hear my cries for help….
All the nations that you have created
will come and bow down to you;
they will praise your greatness.
You are mighty and do wonderful things;
you alone are God….
But you, O Lord, are a merciful and loving God,
always patient, always kind and faithful.
Turn to me and have mercy on me;
strengthen me and save me,
because I serve you just as my mother did. *Psalm 86: 5-6, 9-10, 15-16*

> "…a merciful and loving God…"

God of mercy

Last winter three homeless people died in Toronto. People die on this city's streets because of unbearable heat, frigid cold, severe malnutrition or diseases such as tuberculosis.

As I read the small mention in the newspaper, I wondered if the dead included the young man on Parliament Street who is trying to kick his heroin habit. Or the woman who sits spastically on the corner of Yonge and Bloor everyday.

I want to think that the God of compassion – in whatever form – was with them as they struggled to live on the streets of Toronto. And as they died there. I want the God of mercy to speak to the powerful – to all of us – so that there will soon be a roof over all our heads.

God, open my heart to your message of love and mercy.
Help me to bring your love, your mercy to others today.

L isten to the Lord's case against Israel. Arise, O Lord, and present your case.... The Lord says, "My people, what have I done to you? How have I been a burden to you? Answer me...."

What shall I bring to the Lord, the God of heaven, when I come to worship him? Shall I bring the best calves to burn as offerings to him? Will the Lord be pleased if I bring him thousands of sheep or endless streams of olive oil? Shall I offer him my first-born child to pay for my sins? No, the Lord has told us what is good. What he requires of us is this: to do what is just, to show constant love, and to live in humble fellowship with our God.

Micah 6: 1-4, 6-8

"...to do what is just, to show constant love..."

Understanding why...

When I first started editing, I studied all the rules of punctuation and grammar. Unfortunately, there were – and still are – more rules about commas alone than any one person could master. I discovered that no rule can cover every possible eventuality. Not in punctuation. Not in life.

One day, a younger but wiser fellow editor did for me what the prophet Micah did for the Jews' 613 laws that covered everything from slavery to washing their hands. Micah cut through the details, and gave the people simple principles to follow.

The editor told me that my job was just to help the reader. That principle didn't tell me what to do, or how to do it. But it helped me understand why I was doing it.

Cutting through the conflicting pressures of daily duties isn't easy, God. Share with me your wisdom.

O God, you are my God,
and I long for you.
My whole being
desires you; like a dry,
worn-out, and waterless land,
my soul is thirsty for you.
Let me see you in the sanctuary;
let me see how mighty and
glorious you are.
Your constant love is better
than life itself,
and so I will praise you.
I will give you thanks
as long as I live;
I will raise my hands to you
in prayer.
My soul will feast and
be satisfied, and I will sing
glad songs of praise to you.
As I lie in bed, I remember you;
all night long I think of you,
because you have always been
my help.
In the shadow of your wings
I sing for joy.
I cling to you,
and your hand keeps me safe.

Psalm 63: 1-8

"My whole being desires you…"

The yearnings of my heart

I know longing. When there is conflict in my family, I long for peace.
When I am feeling lonely, I long for companionship. When I am exhausted, I long for sleep. But how often do I allow myself to feel the
longing in my heart… for God?

When I do feel that disquieting emptiness in my heart, I quickly
rush to fill it with distracting chatter, with frenetic busyness or with
"comfort food." But, I am filling the longing in my heart with all the
wrong things, and my deepest desire remains unfulfilled.

Why am I afraid to listen to this longing? Doesn't God promise
to meet my every need? I need to trust that when I open my heart to
God, I will find the peace and the love that I seek.

**Dear God, may I have the courage to be still,
and to listen to the yearnings of my heart.**

"Once there was a man who went out to sow grain. As he scattered the seed in the field, some of it fell along the path, and the birds came and ate it up. Some of it fell on rocky ground, where there was little soil. The seeds soon sprouted, because the soil wasn't deep. But when the sun came up, it burned the young plants; and because the roots had not grown deep enough, the plants soon dried up. Some of the seed fell among thorn bushes, which grew up and choked the plants. But some seeds fell in good soil, and the plants bore grain: some had one hundred grains, others sixty, and others thirty." Jesus concluded, "Listen, then, if you have ears!"

Matthew 13: 1-9

"But some seeds fell in good soil…"

Seeds of life

When I was a boy, many people sowed grain in the empty field that was my young life. Sometimes the grain was words: of love, of advice, of direction, of admonishment. Sometimes the grain was action: the teacher who loaned me books; the friend who called me every day when I was depressed; the secure home I grew up in.

I know there were times when the ground must have looked pretty rocky. And my parents sometimes wondered whether anything at all would grow.

But, as time passed, some of those seeds took root and grew. I found worthwhile work, love and even became a grain-sowing father. So, to those patient farmers: thanks for your persistence.

Thank you, Lord, for helping others believe in me.

T hen the disciples asked Jesus, "Why do you use parables when you talk to the people?" Jesus answered, "The reason I use parables in talking to them is that they look, but do not see, and they listen, but do not hear or understand. So the prophecy of Isaiah applies to them: 'This people will listen and listen, but not understand; they will look and look, but not see, because their minds are dull, and they have stopped up their ears and have closed their eyes. Otherwise, their eyes would see, their ears would hear, their minds would understand, and they would turn to me, says God, and I would heal them.'

"As for you, how fortunate you are! Your eyes see and your ears hear." *Matthew 13: 10-17*

"Your eyes see and your ears hear."

Listening deeply

I remember how my children loved stories and would ask for the same story over and over again! Through those much read, much loved books they came to understand the message or idea contained in the story.

Jesus' parables are stories – verbal pictures – that illustrate his teaching. But to fully understand Jesus' teaching we need to hear his stories more than once.

Often when I hear a parable I don't give it the time it needs to expand in my heart, to have an impact on my life. But as I hear the same story over and over again, different parts of Jesus' message "sink in." As a verbal image, a parable lets me return to its message, and each time discover something new.

Lord, give me eyes to see and ears to hear your love.
Help me live your message of love today.

We who have this spiritual treasure are like common clay pots, in order to show that the supreme power belongs to God, not to us. We are often troubled, but not crushed; sometimes in doubt, but never in despair; there are many enemies, but we are never without a friend; and though badly hurt at times, we are not destroyed. At all times we carry in our mortal bodies the death of Jesus, so that his life also may be seen in our bodies. Throughout our lives we are always in danger of death for Jesus' sake, in order that his life may be seen in this mortal body of ours. This means that death is at work in us, but life is at work in you....

We know that God, who raised the Lord Jesus to life, will also raise us up with Jesus and take us, together with you, into his presence. *2 Corinthians 4: 7-15*

"...we are always in danger of death..."

Unexplainable strength

My friend is dying. We all know it, including him. He has colon cancer. It spread into his liver, then to his bones. The result is inevitable.

He used to be a big man – big boned, big hearted. He has shrivelled away. I tried to tell him that I cared about what was happening to him. But what came out was, "I'm afraid I may never see you again!" And then I found myself sobbing on his shoulder, as he comforted me.

It should have been the other way around. Those who have accepted their inevitable death seem to gain strength that the able-bodied lack. I wonder, sometimes, if that gave Paul the courage to risk his life for Christ, over and over.

Come live in me, Lord Jesus,
so that your courage may also be my courage.

"**A**s for you, how fortunate you are! Your eyes see and your ears hear. I assure you that many prophets and many of God's people wanted very much to see what you see, but they could not, and to hear what you hear, but they did not."

Matthew 13: 16-17

"...wanted very much to see what you see..."

Trusting the Spirit

During a workshop on spirituality and creativity, a woman asked timidly, "How can I be sure it's the Holy Spirit talking when I'm doing creative work?" I don't think I gave her the answer she was looking for. "What makes you think it isn't?" I asked. "I don't know," she answered. "What if it's just my imagination?"

Sadly, I told her, many people have grown to depend on others to affirm or deny their experiences of God, forgetting that God has historically worked through the imagination of people – just like them.

As I develop tools to discern the quiet voice within, and as I start to trust myself, I can become a vehicle of God's wisdom. Often it begins with the courage to ask a question.

God, help me to trust what you show me through my imagination.

We know that in all things God works for good with those who love him, those whom he has called according to his purpose. Those whom God had already chosen he also set apart to become like his Son, so that the Son could be the first among many believers. And so those whom God set apart, he called; and those he called, he put right with himself, and he shared his glory with them.

In view of all this, what can we say? If God is for us, who can be against us? Certainly not God, who did not even keep back his own Son, but offered him for us all! He gave us his Son – will he not also freely give us all things?

Romans 8: 28-32

"If God is for us, who can be against us?"

If God is for us...

Maitet is working hard to convince financial institutions and governments in the northern hemisphere to forgive the unpayable debts of the poorest countries of the south. She knows firsthand the hardship that debt is causing her people.

Some believe that Maitet is foolish to think anyone will give these poor countries a break. Others believe that she has been set apart to do God's work.

Maitet has witnessed the end of the Cold War, the collapse of apartheid, and the signing of the treaty banning land mines. These events give her confidence. So does her faith. It teaches her that God cares about the poor – and wants us to work on their behalf. If God is for Maitet and her work, who can be against her?

Lord, help me to believe that with you all things are possible.

Jesus told another parable: "The kingdom of heaven is like this. A man takes a mustard seed and sows it in his field. It is the smallest of all seeds, but when it grows up, it is the biggest of all plants. It becomes a tree, so that birds come and make their nests in its branches."

Jesus told them still another parable: "The kingdom of heaven is like this. A woman takes some yeast and mixes it with a bushel of flour until the whole batch of dough rises."

Jesus used parables to tell all these things to the crowds; he would not say a thing to them without using a parable. He did this to make come true what the prophet had said, "I will use parables when I speak to them; I will tell them things unknown since the creation of the world."   *Matthew 13: 31-35*

> "...he would not say a thing to them without using a parable."

The storyteller syndrome

Dave Jones is a brilliant teacher. He's won many awards. One of his students even praised him on a television commercial.

One day he told me his secret: "Never give them the answers," he said. "Give them the exercise. Give them the experience. But they'll remember the point much better if they come up with it themselves."

Dave didn't realize it, but he was copying the Jewish rabbinical method. That was their technique, too. In response to a question, the rabbis told a story. If the hearers remained puzzled, they told another story. And another. Until a little light went on, and they got it.

That's why Jesus told so many parables. He was waiting for that "Aha!" moment to dawn.

**Tell me the old, old stories – and maybe someday
I'll understand their intent a little better.**

A s Jesus and his disciples went on their way, he came to a village where a woman named Martha welcomed him in her home. She had a sister named Mary, who sat down at the feet of the Lord and listened to his teaching. Martha was upset over all the work she had to do, so she came and said, "Lord, don't you care that my sister has left me to do all the work by myself? Tell her to come and help me!"

The Lord answered her, "Martha, Martha! You are worried and troubled over so many things, but just one is needed. Mary has chosen the right thing, and it will not be taken away from her."

Luke 10: 38-42

"You are worried and troubled over so many things…"

God and my messy life

My daughter has a book about an owl who, one night, is delighted to see the moon rising. But when the moon seems to follow him home, Owl gets increasingly alarmed. "You must stay up over the sea, where you look so fine," he says. "You really must not come home with me. My house is small. You would not fit through the door."

I'm a lot like Owl. I am happy for God to stay "up over the sea," or safely in church. But what if God wants to come home with me, into my life? It's a bit of a mess; I'm not ready. I don't have much to offer him.

Like Martha, when I am "troubled over so many things," I can't hear what God is saying.

Lord, silence the voice that says, "I am not good enough."
Help me to listen to your voice instead.

"The kingdom of heaven is like this. A man happens to find a treasure hidden in a field. He covers it up again, and is so happy that he goes and sells everything he has, and then goes back and buys that field.

"Also, the kingdom of heaven is like this. A man is looking for fine pearls, and when he finds one that is unusually fine, he goes and sells everything he has, and buys that pearl."   *Matthew 13: 44-46*

"…sells everything he has, and buys that pearl."

Mindfulness

A colleague of mine commented that she rarely, if ever, sees me sitting still or empty-handed. As we talked, I kept photocopying, sorting and stapling… and I had to agree with her. Like so many people these days, I'm into "multi-tasking." I feel obliged to cram as much as possible into my day, and often end up juggling too much.

I can't imagine acting like the man in this parable. Rarely do I concentrate on one thing. The thought of enthusiastically and joyfully putting all of my resources towards one goal seems almost foolish.

What if I focused on doing one thing in an effort to bring more peace and harmony to my world? Who knows what wonderful things might happen!

**God, help me approach this day
with a focused heart and a glad hand.**

The Lord said to me, "Go down to the potter's house, where I will give you my message." So I went there and saw the potter working at his wheel. Whenever a piece of pottery turned out imperfect, he would take the clay and make it into something else.

Then the Lord said to me, "Don't I have the right to do with you people of Israel what the potter did with the clay? You are in my hands just like clay in the potter's hands."

Jeremiah 18: 1-6

"...like clay in the potter's hands."

Clay with attitude

When I read this text, I can't help but smile and picture myself as clay – clay with attitude! I've been a seminary student, a restaurant worker, a forklift driver, a husband and a graduate student. Right now I'm a single parent/college professor.

It seems that God has started over with me not once, but several times. I don't think that means I keep "getting it wrong." Rather, I see my life as an active, ongoing dialogue with the Potter.

So, as "clay with attitude," my goal is not to work at "getting it right" once and for all. Instead, I need to look for and recognize the Potter's touch in the very ebb and flow of my life's journey.

Potter God, let me see the changes in my life as the dance between my living clay and your loving touch.

Jesus went back to his hometown. He taught in the synagogue, and those who heard him were amazed. "Where did he get such wisdom?" they asked. "And what about his miracles? Isn't he the carpenter's son? Isn't Mary his mother, and aren't James, Joseph, Simon and Judas his brothers? Aren't all his sisters living here? Where did he get all this?" And so they rejected him.

Jesus said to them, "A prophet is respected everywhere except in his hometown and by his own family." Because they did not have faith, he did not perform many miracles there.

Matthew 13:54-58

"...he did not perform many miracles there."

An openness to change

Aileen is an experienced family therapist. "I can often predict how my patients will respond to treatment," she observes. "Some make good progress while others linger for years, stuck in the same old rut. Usually I can tell ahead of time."

How can she know what will happen? "Sometimes I'm wrong, but what I look for are a positive attitude, a willingness to follow instructions and an openness to change. It boils down to faith."

In today's reading, Jesus' power likewise depends on faith. In my naïve imagination, I see Jesus with a magic wand performing special tricks called miracles. But evidently even God can't heal the sick who are too stubborn to recover, the blind who refuse to see, the lame who are afraid to walk.

God, help me to believe.
Only then will I be ready for miracles.

Save me from sinking
in the mud;
keep me safe
from my enemies,
safe from the deep water.
Don't let the flood
come over me;
don't let me drown
in the depths
or sink into the grave....
But I am in pain and despair;
lift me up, O God, and save me!

I will praise God with a song;
I will proclaim his greatness
by giving him thanks.
This will please the Lord
more than offering him cattle,
more than sacrificing
a full-grown bull.
When the oppressed see this,
they will be glad;
those who worship God
will be encouraged.

Psalm 69: 14-15, 29-33

"I will praise God with a song..."

A gift of praise

As I step outside to call my family in for supper, I hear my daughter singing to herself in the garden. I spot her tiny back hunched down among the hostas, and hear her voice as it drifts upon the dappled glow of evening. Deep in concentration she is unaware of my presence. What is she up to?

I take a breath to call her, but catch myself before I break the spell of her singing. Edging closer, I can just make out her words: "Thank you. Thank you. Thank you for the flowers."

Her voice continues, rising and falling. Soon it is lost among the chimes swaying on our cherry tree. I smile. I am sure God has heard this pure gift of praise.

**God, may I always remember to give you thanks and praise –
even when the demands of life threaten to overwhelm me.**

T he Lord says,
"Come, everyone who is thirsty –
here is water!
Come, you that have no money –
buy grain and eat!
Come! Buy wine and milk –
it will cost you nothing!
Why spend money on what does not satisfy?
Why spend your wages and still be hungry?
Listen to me and do what I say,
and you will enjoy the best food of all.
Listen now, my people, and come to me;
come to me, and you will have life."

Isaiah 55: 1-3

> "Why spend money on what does not satisfy?"

Seeking peace

In the months following the start of the U.S. bombing campaign in Afghanistan, a small group gathered by the courthouse every Monday evening. We held candles in silence for a period of thirty minutes, occasionally sharing a thought or a song. We shivered through drizzle and snow; we struggled to keep candles lit against the wind. We appreciated evenings of crisp winter stillness.

We probably looked foolish and impractical to many. But our candles glowed with the lament and the invitation of God. Why spend money – and lives – on pursuits that cannot satisfy us with peace?

We don't have all the answers. But we listen in silence for God's invitation to find our way to a banquet of peace – established through justice, rather than bombs.

God, our world needs people willing to accept your invitation.
Let me find a way to respond – in peace and with justice.

The boat was far out in the lake, tossed about by the waves.... Between three and six o'clock in the morning Jesus came to the disciples, walking on the water. When they saw him, they were terrified. "It's a ghost!" they screamed. Jesus spoke to them at once. "Courage!" he said. "It is I. Don't be afraid!"

Then Peter spoke up. "Lord, if it is really you, order me to come out on the water to you." "Come!" answered Jesus. So Peter got out of the boat and started walking on the water to Jesus. But when he noticed the strong wind, he was afraid and started to sink down in the water. "Save me, Lord!" he cried. Jesus reached out and grabbed hold of him and said, "What little faith you have! Why did you doubt?"

Matthew 14: 22-36

> "It is I. Don't be afraid!"

Peace amid the storm

In my enthusiasm, I tend to overcommit myself to a range of projects. Then I wake up in the middle of the night in a panic: "How am I ever going to do all this?" Like Peter sinking in the water, I feel overwhelmed and afraid.

Last week I had such an episode. Going for a walk with an old friend helped me realize that my fears were about myself: What if I fall apart, have a breakdown? My friend offered me peace and perspective.

I remembered the importance of the projects waiting for me, and the work involved. I'm better off not thinking about the impossibility of it all, but remembering that I can do it – with the help of Jesus.

**Jesus, when I am overwhelmed and afraid,
help me to keep my eyes on you.**

The Lord says
to his people,
"Your wounds
are incurable,
your injuries
cannot be healed....
Complain no more
about your injuries;
there is no cure for you.
I punished you like this
because your sins are many
and your wickedness
is great...."
The Lord says,
"I will restore my people
to their land
and have mercy
on every family....
The people who live there
will sing praise;
they will shout for joy....
They will be my people,
and I will be their God."

Jeremiah 30: 12-22

> "Your wounds are incurable..."

A terrible wound

After the dropping of the atomic bomb on Hiroshima and Nagasaki, Dorothy Day began to refer to the first days of August as "the anniversary of our great shame."

Every year, on that terrible anniversary, Ammon Hennacy, one of the editors of the Catholic Worker newspaper, would fast from food and drink only water. Year after year, he would add one more day to his fast – for each year that passed since the bombs were dropped. By the time of his death, Ammon was fasting twenty-five consecutive days.

Ammon was doing penance for a wound that could not be healed, asking others to do the same.

**Lord, only your forgiveness heals these sores
and restores our joy.**

J esus took with him Peter, James and John and led them up a high mountain where they were alone. As they looked on, a change came over Jesus: his face was shining like the sun, and his clothes were dazzling white. Then the three disciples saw Moses and Elijah talking with Jesus. So Peter said to Jesus, "Lord, how good it is that we are here! If you wish, I will make three tents here, one for you, one for Moses, and one for Elijah." While he was talking, a shining cloud came over them, and a voice from the cloud said, "This is my own dear Son, with whom I am pleased – listen to him!"… Jesus ordered them, "Don't tell anyone about this vision you have seen until the Son of Man has been raised from death."

Matthew 17: 1-9

> "This is my own dear Son,
> with whom I am pleased…"

My own dear child

I had the good fortune to be present at the birth of each of my three children and, I can tell you, it's like no other experience I have ever had.

For nine months, I imagined every change and development and I wondered, "Who is this person?" When the time came and the baby was ready to be born – ah, what a moment that was! This new person whom I already had a relationship with, whom I already loved, emerged into the light. And everything was transformed.

When I saw each child for the first time, the face I'd long imagined seemed to shine like the sun and the baby's body seemed dazzling white. The moment was overwhelming and I had only one response: "This is my own dear child."

**Lord, thank you for the transforming gift of parenthood.
Help me to be a good parent to my children.**

Jesus asked his disciples, "Who do people say the Son of Man is?"

"Some say John the Baptist," they answered. "Others say Elijah, while others say Jeremiah or some other prophet."

"What about you?" he asked them. "Who do you say I am?" Simon Peter answered, "You are the Messiah, the Son of the living God."

"Good for you, Simon son of John!" answered Jesus. "For this truth did not come to you from any human being, but it was given to you directly by my Father in heaven."   *Matthew 16: 13-23*

"Who do you say I am?"

Who are you?

It always comes down to this: me standing uncomfortably with the Twelve. I've done what I can to avoid it. I've tried proclaiming the folly of any religious belief, the irrationality of the Christian message, the hypocrisy of believers. I've tried regular church attendance, theological study, searching for God's presence in the world.

These two paths seem to go in opposite directions, but somehow I always end up at the same place. Right in front of Jesus' insistent question: "Who do you say I am?"

I stand there tongue-tied and frustrated. I don't know the answer and don't like the question. But after fifty years, I guess I have to accept that this question just won't go away.

Lord, tell me: Who are you?

Jesus said to his disciples, "If any of you want to come with me, you must forget yourself, carry your cross, and follow me. For if you want to save your own life, you will lose it; but if you lose your life for my sake, you will find it. Will you gain anything if you win the whole world but lose your life? Of course not! There is nothing you can give to regain your life. For the Son of Man is about to come in the glory of his Father with his angels, and then he will reward each one according to his deeds. I assure you that there are some here who will not die until they have seen the Son of Man come as King."

Matthew 16: 24-28

"…you must forget yourself, carry your cross, and follow me."

True happiness

Good old Jesus: always with the paradox! I'm getting older so perhaps I'm beginning to understand….

A few years ago, I had photographs of our babies framed for our wedding anniversary. The young girl in the framing shop asked how long I'd been married. When I told her, she replied, "That's longer than I've been alive. What's it like?" I answered, "You won't understand until you've lived it: but it's much worse, and infinitely better, than you can ever imagine."

It's strange how I scramble for things to make me happy, when all the time the true happiness lies in nights of lost sleep while walking my baby; shiny, new skates alongside my worn out shoes; a friend saying, "Thanks," and my replying, "No problem."

**Lord, help me to forget myself…
and to remember what's important.**

A man came to Jesus and said, "Sir, have mercy on my son! He is an epileptic and has such terrible attacks that he often falls in the fire or into water. I brought him to your disciples, but they could not heal him."

Jesus answered, "How unbelieving and wrong you people are! How long do I have to put up with you? Bring the boy here to me!" Jesus gave a command to the demon, and it went out of the boy, and at that very moment he was healed.

Then the disciples came to Jesus in private and asked him, "Why couldn't we drive the demon out?"

"It was because you do not have enough faith," answered Jesus. "I assure you that if you have faith as big as a mustard seed, you can say to this hill, 'Go from here to there!' and it will go. You could do anything!"   *Matthew 17: 14-20*

> "…you can say to this hill, 'Go…'"

Moving mountains

Recently a young woman told me that she'd been raped during a war. She lived her pregnancy in constant flight, and the baby was born in the jungle. Many raped girls abandoned their babies because their crying revealed their hiding places, she said. But when she gave birth, she was amazed that although she was thin and starved, there was milk in her breasts, and the baby was healthy. At that moment she had a revelation of God's love for every human being on earth. She looked past the face of her aggressor, and fell in love with her baby. Right there and then she gave him a name: "Magnifique."

A mountain of hate, blown apart by the Spirit, replaced with wonder and love.

**Lord, give me the faith of a mustard seed
and I'll move mountains.**

The Lord spoke, "Elijah, what are you doing here?" He answered, "Lord God Almighty, the people of Israel have broken their covenant with you.... I am the only one left."

"Go out and stand before me on top of the mountain," the Lord said. Then the Lord passed by and sent a furious wind that split the hills and shattered the rocks – but the Lord was not in the wind. The wind stopped blowing, and then there was an earthquake – but the Lord was not in the earthquake. After the earthquake there was a fire – but the Lord was not in the fire. And after the fire there was the soft whisper of a voice. When Elijah heard it, he covered his face with his cloak and went out and stood at the entrance of the cave. A voice said to him, "Elijah, what are you doing here?"   *1 Kings 19: 9-13*

> " ...after the fire there was the soft whisper of a voice."

Finding God

Twenty years ago, on a typical summer's day in Alberta, the sky suddenly turned dark and the temperatures quickly plummeted. A tornado touched down to the south of the city, killing nearly thirty people, injuring hundreds, and destroying trailer homes and a nearby industrial park.

Officials provided all manner of immediate care, and eventually a tornado warning system was put in place. But what I especially remember are the stories of compassion and quiet heroism in the long and often mundane process of recovery and re-building. Throughout the city, people opened their hearts and wallets to total strangers.

Like Elijah, I found God – not in the noise of a storm, but in the eerie yet prayer-filled silence that followed.

Dear God, when disaster strikes,
may I continue to look for you in the silence that follows.

There in Babylonia beside the Chebar River, I heard the Lord speak to me, and I felt his power.... I heard the noise their wings made in flight.... When they stopped flying, they folded their wings, but there was still a sound coming from above the dome over their heads.

Above the dome there was something that looked like a throne made of sapphire, and sitting on the throne was a figure that looked like a human being. The figure seemed to be shining like bronze in the middle of a fire. It shone all over with a bright light that had in it all the colors of the rainbow. This was the dazzling light which shows the presence of the Lord.

Ezekiel 1: 2-5, 24-28

"... shows the presence of the Lord."

A sign of God's presence

Unlike Ezekiel, I haven't seen the heavenly throne – but Renée has. At age four, Renée was clinically dead for several minutes. Years later, she can still describe God's loving presence and the jewelled crown she saw – which God explained would be hers someday, but not yet. She remembers finding herself back in the hospital, sad to leave heaven, but joyfully welcomed by her family and the nurses.

Why did Ezekiel and Renée receive their visions? And what do their visions offer us? I think they show that when the Infinite reaches into finite souls, what is beyond words finds expression in images of absolute beauty and comfort. We may not know more of God and heaven, but we do not know less.

Dear God, thank you for these mysterious glimpses of comfort and love – beyond my imagining.

A t that time the disciples came to Jesus, asking, "Who is the greatest in the kingdom of heaven?" So Jesus called a child to come and stand in front of them, and said, "I assure you that unless you change and become like children, you will never enter the kingdom of heaven. The greatest in the kingdom of heaven is the one who humbles himself and becomes like this child. And whoever welcomes in my name one such child as this, welcomes me.

"See that you don't despise any of these little ones. Their angels in heaven, I tell you, are always in the presence of my Father in heaven."

Matthew 18: 1-5, 10, 12-14

"...unless you change and become like children..."

Childlike wonder

Buddy is a four-month-old Jack Russell ter-rier who nuzzled his way into my heart two months ago. Now I can't imagine life with-out him.

Someday I may write a book entitled *Everything I Needed to Know, I Learned from my Dog.* Why? Because Buddy is helping me to redis-cover my child's heart. Watching him romp and play, I throw adult caution to the wind and join in his fun. Through his explorings and adventures, I realize that every tree, every bush, every blade of grass is magical. Buddy lives in the present moment and revels in each new discovery. He also shows no hesitation when lavishing his love and devotion upon me.

Wonder. Passion. Delight. My child's heart struggles to break free, to live again!

> **God, today, may I rediscover wonder,**
> **delight and magic in my life.**

" If your brother sins against you, go to him and show him his fault. But do it privately, just between yourselves. If he listens to you, you have won your brother back. But if he will not listen to you, take one or two other persons with you, so that 'every accusation may be upheld by the testimony of two or more witnesses,' as the scripture says. And if he will not listen to them, then tell the whole thing to the church. Finally, if he will not listen to the church, treat him as though he were a pagan or a tax collector....

"And I tell you more: whenever two of you on earth agree about anything you pray for, it will be done for you by my Father in heaven. For where two or three come together in my name, I am there with them."

Matthew 18: 15-20

"But if he will not listen to you..."

Truth-telling

I recall a situation when I felt that I'd been "sinned against." I met with the person and told him how his actions had hurt me, causing great damage to our friendship. He listened, but I left wondering if he'd really heard me.

Today's reading prompts me to reconsider how I handled the situation. Why didn't I take the next step of discussing his actions before "two or more witnesses" – friends who cared about both of us? (Taking the third step never even crossed my mind!)

Why? Because I felt that discussing his "sin" in front of other people would have exposed his weakness (and mine!). But my decision to protect him means that the truth of the situation remains hidden, and the opportunity for true reconciliation is lost.

Lord, give me the courage to tell the truth in all situations.

Peter asked, "Lord, if my brother keeps on sinning against me, how many times do I have to forgive him?" Jesus replied....

"Once there was a king who decided to check on his servants' accounts.... One of them was brought in who owed him millions of dollars. The servant did not have enough to pay his debt, so the king ordered him to be sold as a slave, with his wife and his children and all that he had, in order to pay the debt. The servant fell on his knees before the king. 'Be patient with me,' he begged, 'and I will pay you everything!' The king felt sorry for him, so he forgave him the debt and let him go."

Matthew 18: 21 – 19: 1

"...so he forgave him the debt..."

A clean slate

After years of making monthly mortgage payments, I am amazed at how long it actually takes to pay down a debt. Interest rates – no matter how low – keep me from wiping the slate clean!

It occurs to me that, in some of my relationships, my forgiveness includes some hidden "interest rates." On the surface, I try to be forgiving, but I tend to hold onto past debts. My tendency to go over old ground keeps my friends on the hook.

I yearn to be like the king who forgives the whole amount. How hard it is to truly forgive an entire debt, and wipe the slate clean.

God, help me to learn to forgive – totally and fully.

Mary said, "My heart praises the Lord; my soul is glad because of God my Saviour, for he has remembered me, his lowly servant! From now on all people will call me happy, because of the great things the Mighty God has done for me. His name is holy; from one generation to another he shows mercy to those who honour him. He has stretched out his mighty arm and scattered the proud with all their plans. He has brought down mighty kings from their thrones, and lifted up the lowly. He has filled the hungry with good things, and sent the rich away with empty hands. He has kept the promise he made to our ancestors, and has come to the help of his servant Israel. He has remembered to show mercy to Abraham and to all his descendants forever!"

Luke 1: 39-56

> "He has remembered to show mercy…"

Hitchhiker's Magnificat

As my car inched along the icy road, I heard a tap at my window. A pale, waif-like face peered in at me. "Could you give me a ride?" she asked. I don't usually pick up hitchhikers, but these were exceptional circumstances.

She was pregnant. And alone. Estranged from her family. But her child's life would be different, she insisted. Her child would not grow up disadvantaged. She was going back to school, to finish her Grade 12, so that she could get a decent job.

Like Mary, with a baby coming, she saw the world differently. It was now a place where injustice needed to be fought, where relationships mattered, where love became the primary motivation.

And if things were going to improve, she had to do something about it.

God, may I see your face in those I meet,
and may those I meet see your face in me.

The Lord spoke to me and said, "What is this proverb people keep repeating in the land of Israel? 'The parents ate the sour grapes, but the children got the sour taste.'

"As surely as I am the living God," says the Sovereign Lord, "you will not repeat this proverb in Israel any more. The life of every person belongs to me, the life of the parent as well as that of the child. The person who sins is the one who will die....

"I, the Sovereign Lord, am telling you Israelites that I will judge each of you by what you have done.... Give up all the evil you have been doing, and get yourselves new minds and hearts.... Turn away from your sins and live."   *Ezekiel 18: 1-13, 30-32*

> "...I will judge each of you by what you have done."

The gift of free will

When I was a young man and knew everything, I was certain that all my problems were my parents' fault. I was simply the innocent victim of their mistakes, acting out the part they, in their faulty parenting, had created for me.

This was comforting for a while – too long, in fact – but eventually I chafed at it. I wanted to make my own decisions: to mess up or do good, but know that it was I who did it. In short, I wanted to be responsible for my own actions, and breathe the honest, bracing air of freedom.

It wasn't hard, actually. I simply recognized that the cards I had been given in life – and I had been given some pretty good ones – were mine to play and always had been.

Lord, although I am your creature, weak and flawed,
I thank you for the gift of free will.

God, be merciful to us
and bless us;
look on us
with kindness,
so that the whole world
may know your will;
so that all nations
may know your salvation.
May the peoples praise you,
O God;
may all the peoples praise you!
May the nations be glad
and sing for joy,
because you judge the peoples
with justice
and guide every nation
on earth.
May the peoples praise you,
O God;
may all the peoples praise you!
The land has produced its
harvest;
God, our God, has blessed us.
God has blessed us;
may all people everywhere
honour him.

Psalm 67: 1-7

"The land has produced its harvest…"

Gifts from the earth

"Look, Mom! More tomatoes!" My daughter is delighted to find yet another basket of vegetables waiting on our porch. "And look at this zucchini!" She starts swinging it around like a baseball bat. My parents are generous with the harvest from their garden. One-third of their tiny back yard is dedicated to a vegetable patch, yet all summer long it feeds us all. We can hardly keep up!

Today we delight in the richness of this harvest – not only for the taste but also for the parade of colours that dances on our table. During the winter, when pale tomatoes taste like sawdust and zucchini shrink to the size of pickles, I will remember today's gifts from the earth. And I will give thanks.

Thank you, God, for your many gifts from the earth.

Once a man came to Jesus. "Teacher, what good thing must I do to receive eternal life?" "There is only One who is good. Keep the commandments if you want to enter life." "What commandments?" he asked. Jesus answered, "Do not commit murder; do not commit adultery; do not steal; do not accuse anyone falsely; respect your father and your mother; and love your neighbour as you love yourself."

"I have obeyed all these commandments. What else do I need to do?" Jesus said to him, "If you want to be perfect, go and sell all you have and give the money to the poor, and you will have riches in heaven; then come and follow me."

When the young man heard this, he went away sad, because he was very rich. *Matthew 19: 16-22*

"What else do I need to do?"

Rich in love

I lived much of my life believing that I could earn love and happiness by doing the "good" and "right" things. I applied this mathematical approach to my faith, too. I tried to win God's love and my own salvation. A capable "do-er" of many worthwhile things, I hoarded accounts of good deeds. I clung to my record as to an amassed fortune.

But over the years, failure, disappointment, loss and suffering pried me loose. Finally incapable of doing anything more on my own, I experienced God's love in the very depths of my being!

As I learn to be "who I am" for God and others, any good I do is but a joyful response to the rich gifts of love and life I have received.

Lord, fill me with your love, that I may share it with those whose paths will cross mine today.

J esus said, "I assure you: it is much harder for a rich person to enter the kingdom of God than for a camel to go through the eye of a needle." When the disciples heard this, they were completely amazed. "Who, then, can be saved?" they asked. Jesus looked straight at them and answered, "This is impossible for human beings, but for God everything is possible."

Then Peter spoke up. "Look, we have left everything and followed you. What will we have?" Jesus said, "Everyone who has left houses or brothers or sisters or father or mother or children or fields for my sake, will receive a hundred times more and will be given eternal life. But many who now are first will be last, and many who now are last will be first."   *Matthew 19: 23-30*

> "…to go through the eye of a needle."

Wide and narrow

There's a woman who comes to our church who stands out, and not just because she's very tall. She wears a nightgown with a petticoat over the top, a big square hat and a dramatically torn fur coat. She carries a jewel-encrusted gold handbag stuffed with loose bits of paper. She makes me feel like the most boring dresser in the world.

Conversations with her rush off in several directions at once, and sometimes she breaks into song mid-sentence. Just today she called to invite herself for supper, and I said No. Why did I do that? I can't phone her back – she has no phone.

One thing's sure: she may be large and flamboyant, but she'll fit through the eye of that needle long before I will.

Lord, help me see the essentials.
Narrow me down so I can fit through.

The Lord is my shepherd; I have everything I need.
He lets me rest in fields of green grass
and leads me to quiet pools of fresh water.
He gives me new strength.
He guides me in the right paths, as he has promised.
You prepare a banquet for me,
where all my enemies can see me;
you welcome me as an honoured guest and fill my cup to the brim.
I know that your goodness and love
will be with me all my life;
and your house will be my home as long as I live.   *Psalm 23: 1-6*

> "...and your house will be my home..."

Loving care

Today's reading reminds me of a weekend visit with friends whose hospitality mirrors God's promise of loving support.

On a rare get-away weekend from my children, my friends "welcomed me as an honoured guest." They "let me rest" – giving me the opportunity to sleep in! They "prepared a banquet for me" where every meal – even breakfast – was a celebration. They "filled my cup to the brim" with water, juice, tea, wine – whatever I desired. And their "house was my home" as they handed me a front door key so I could come and go as I pleased.

Their hospitality renewed me – "giving me new strength" – to carry on with the often overwhelming responsibilities of parenting alone. Indeed, their "goodness and love will be with me all my life!"

Loving God, thank you for those people through whom your love touches my life. May I give to others in a similar fashion.

Thursday | **AUGUST 21**

Create a pure heart in me,
O God,
and put a new
and loyal spirit in me.
Do not banish me
from your presence;
do not take your holy spirit
away from me.
Give me again the joy that
comes from your salvation,
and make me willing
to obey you.

Then I will teach sinners
your commands,
and they will turn back
to you....
You do not want sacrifices,
or I would offer them;
you are not pleased with burnt
offerings.
My sacrifice is a humble spirit,
O God;
you will not reject a humble
and repentant heart.

Psalm 51: 10-13, 16-17

"Do not banish me from your presence…"

Lost and lonely

Ororoino was the last of his race. For generations, his people had been the priestly class on Easter Island, away out in the Pacific. They, and they alone, knew the technology for carving and moving the great stone statues that have since led the United Nations to declare Easter Island a World Heritage Site.

But they used their knowledge to enslave other people, in an obsession with carving bigger and bigger statues.

The other racial groups rebelled against being taken away from food production. In that civil war, every member of Ororoino's caste was massacred. Only Ororoino survived.

He must have felt terribly isolated, cut off, rejected. I think that he might have understood the mood of today's psalm.

**When I feel lost and lonely, Lord,
please reach out in the darkness and hold my hand.**

242

When the Pharisees heard that Jesus had silenced the Sadducees, they came together, and one of them, a teacher of the Law, tried to trap him with a question. "Teacher," he asked, "which is the greatest commandment in the Law?"

Jesus answered, "'Love the Lord your God with all your heart, with all your soul, and with all your mind.' This is the greatest and the most important commandment. The second most important commandment is like it: 'Love your neighbour as you love yourself.' The whole Law of Moses and the teachings of the prophets depend on these two commandments."

Matthew 22: 34-40

> "...with all your heart, with all your soul, and with all your mind."

Heart, mind and soul

I easily give my heart in love; sometimes too easily! At other times, it's my mind that dominates, cautioning me to be careful. I must admit that, when it comes to love, my soul takes the back seat!

Similarly, I find that it's easy to love others, to attend to their needs, while forgetting to take care of my own needs. And often, when I try to please God, I realize that I have ignored the needs of others in the process.

It's not a checklist: Heart – Mind – Soul. God – Others – Self. If my love is to be genuine and integrated, I first need to experience God's love for me. Rooted in that love, I have the courage to live and to love freely, passionately and responsibly.

Loving God, help me love deeply with my heart, mind and soul. Guide me with your love.

I am listening to what the Lord God is saying;
he promises peace to us, his own people,
if we do not go back to our foolish ways.
Surely he is ready to save those who honour him,
and his saving presence will remain in our land.
Love and faithfulness will meet;
righteousness and peace will embrace.
Human loyalty will reach up from the earth,
and God's righteousness will look down from heaven.
The Lord will make us prosperous,
and our land will produce rich harvests.
Righteousness will go before the Lord
and prepare the path for him.

Psalm 85: 8-13

"…if we do not go back to our foolish ways."

Daily choices

Over the past few years, mad cow disease and toxic salmon have challenged our food production and consumption habits. Genetically engineered food and irresponsible water use have become concerns for our global community. Procuring and protecting oil and diamonds have caused violence and even war. So many "justice" issues are linked to the choices we make daily.

I need to look at how I interact with my world: what food do I buy, and where? When I am at the market this weekend, am I willing to pay a little more for locally grown vegetables? Am I willing to ride my bike to the farmers' market, or do I drive my family van to the big-box grocery store instead?

**Lord, help me bring about peace and justice
– starting with my own behaviour.**

O the depth of the riches and wisdom and knowledge of God! How unsearchable are his judgments and how inscrutable his ways! "For who has known the mind of the Lord? Or who has been his counsellor?" "Or who has given a gift to him, to receive a gift in return?" For from him and through him and to him are all things. To God be the glory forever! Amen.

Romans 11: 33-36

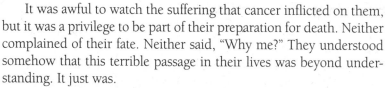

"To God be the glory forever! Amen."

Glory to God

The worst time of my life was when both my parents were diagnosed with terminal cancer and my sisters and I, and our families, became their main caregivers.

It was awful to watch the suffering that cancer inflicted on them, but it was a privilege to be part of their preparation for death. Neither complained of their fate. Neither said, "Why me?" They understood somehow that this terrible passage in their lives was beyond understanding. It just was.

As the weeks passed and more and more of their life was taken from them, the little that remained seemed to grow deeper and richer. At the end what was left was the sheer wonder, mystery, and, yes, joy of being alive – their final gift to their family.

**Lord, your ways are beyond my understanding.
Help me always to be thankful for the gift of my life.**

"How terrible for you, teachers of the Law and Pharisees! You hypocrites! You lock the door to the kingdom of heaven in people's faces, but you yourselves don't go in, nor do you allow in those who are trying to enter!

"How terrible for you, teachers of the Law and Pharisees! You hypocrites! You sail the seas and cross whole countries to win one convert; and when you succeed, you make him twice as deserving of going to hell as you yourselves are!

"How terrible for you, blind guides! You teach, 'If someone swears by the Temple, he isn't bound by his vow; but if he swears by the gold in the Temple, he is bound.' Blind fools! Which is more important, the gold or the Temple which makes the gold holy?"

Matthew 23: 13-22

"You hypocrites!"

Hypocrisy and humility

This is not the calm, cool, collected Jesus I'm used to hearing about in the gospels. He's on quite a roll here!

Hypocrisy is a hard one – because I'm as guilty of it as anyone. It's an occupational hazard for me as a parent, and as a teacher who is in the business of "training" children.

Where I teach I've seen students suspended for swearing in class, and then gone into the staff room only to hear teachers swearing! I've seen kids being "reamed out" in the hall for being late for class by a teacher who takes days off to catch up on marking.

There are days when I would love to scream "hypocrite!" – just as Jesus did. But instead, I think I'll work on practising what I preach.

**Lord, help me to practise what I preach
and remain humble about my own righteousness.**

"How terrible for you, teachers of the Law and Pharisees! You hypocrites! You give to God one tenth even of the seasoning herbs, such as mint, dill, and cumin, but you neglect to obey the really important teachings of the Law, such as justice and mercy and honesty. These you should practise, without neglecting the others. Blind guides! You strain a fly out of your drink, but swallow a camel!

"How terrible for you, teachers of the Law and Pharisees! You hypocrites! You clean the outside of your cup and plate, while the inside is full of what you have gotten by violence and selfishness. Blind Pharisee! Clean what is inside the cup first, and then the outside will be clean too!"

Matthew 23: 23-26

"Clean what is inside the cup first..."

Pause before judging

Alex and I went to the same high school. He smoked too much, swore... that sort of thing. He was held up as an example to other students of how not to behave.

Late one night, a bunch of us were heading into an all-night café. On the sidewalk there was a woman, a "working girl," as it were. She was a little drunk, probably having finished for the night. The remarks started – from the ones who were the "good" boys, I'm ashamed to admit. Alex, however, asked her, "Want a coffee?" She came in and he bought her a coffee and something to eat, and talked to her. When she left, he said, "Take care of yourself."

Whose cup was cleanest on the inside?

God, may I remember to look within
before judging someone else.

"How terrible for you, teachers of the Law and Pharisees! You hypocrites! You are like whitewashed tombs, which look fine on the outside but are full of bones and decaying corpses on the inside. In the same way, on the outside you appear good to everybody, but inside you are full of hypocrisy and sins.

"How terrible for you, teachers of the Law and Pharisees! You hypocrites! You make fine tombs for the prophets and decorate the monuments of those who lived good lives; and you claim that if you had lived during the time of your ancestors, you would not have done what they did and killed the prophets. So you actually admit that you are the descendants of those who murdered the prophets! Go on, then, and finish up what your ancestors started!" *Matthew 23: 27-32*

"…but inside you are full of hypocrisy and sins."

My own hypocrisy

Before I visited Rwanda, I felt very superior to the Africans who had been slaughtering each other in senseless tribal warfare. I would never do that, I thought.

But when I met people who had risked their lives to save others, I heard amazing stories of true heroism. The stories of thousands of anonymous Rwandan martyrs will never be told. Would I be that brave? I have never been tested.

Back in the west again, I so quickly settle into my comfortable world of cars and computers and weapons of mass destruction. How I am one of those hypocrites or "whitewashed tombs"! I can feel quite innocent, even smug, while on my behalf people far away are refused asylum, enslaved to debt, or poisoned by my waste.

God, open my heart so that I can see the suffering of others, and my own part in it.

From Paul, who was called by the will of God to be an apostle of Christ Jesus, and from our brother Sosthenes.

To the church of God that is in Corinth, to all who are called to be God's holy people, who belong to him in union with Christ Jesus, together with all people everywhere who worship our Lord Jesus Christ, their Lord and ours:

May God our Father and the Lord Jesus Christ give you grace and peace.

I always give thanks to my God for you because of the grace he has given you through Christ Jesus. For in union with Christ you have become rich in all things…. God is to be trusted, the God who called you to have fellowship with his Son Jesus Christ, our Lord.

1 Corinthians 1: 1-9

> "To the church of God that is in Corinth…"

The beauty of letters

Letter-writing has become a lost art.

My mother was the letter-writer in our family. Once a week, every week, she wrote to her two sisters in Ireland. Every second week, she wrote to her closest friends. And when she got letters from those sisters, those friends, she read them aloud to her own family.

Those letters took weeks to get delivered. But when we visited Ireland, even though we had been separated for years, we felt instantly in touch. We already shared their successes and failures, their joys and sorrows.

Like Paul's letters, my mother's letters kept us in touch. Telephone calls may be more direct, and e-mail more instant, but we don't share ourselves the way we used to in letters.

Lord, thank you for letter-writers like Paul. And thank you for those who had the wisdom to preserve those letters.

Herod had John tied up and put in prison. Herod did this because of Herodias, whom he had married, even though she was the wife of his brother Philip. John the Baptist kept telling Herod, "It isn't right for you to marry your brother's wife!"

Herodias held a grudge against John…. Finally Herodias got her chance. It was on Herod's birthday, when he gave a feast…. The daughter of Herodias came in and danced, and pleased Herod and his guests. So the king said to the girl, "What would you like to have? I will give you anything you want…."

So the girl went out and asked her mother, "What shall I ask for?"

"The head of John the Baptist," she answered….

This made the king very sad, but he could not refuse her because of the vows he had made in front of all his guests. So he sent off a guard at once with orders to bring John's head.   *Mark 6: 17-29*

> "This made the king very sad…"

Second thoughts

Think first, talk second, eh, Herod! It's a lesson that I imagine we've all learned sometime in our lives. And another man loses his head.

I know it's a stretch: I've never cost anyone their head. But how often have I, blinded by my own wants, said or done something that has cost someone else? When I was a child, it was more obvious. You know, teasing the kid everyone teased. Having the words come out, knowing they shouldn't have. And now? The hurtful words spoken when I'm tired, words that I can't take back. Or the little negative comments that may change a person's attitude about someone else.

All of those things that can never be taken back. I wonder what Herod thought, in the years that followed.

Lord, may I think before I speak.
Help me say things I can live with later.

Now remember what you were, my friends, when God called you. From the human point of view few of you were wise or powerful or of high social standing. God purposely chose what the world considers nonsense in order to shame the wise, and he chose what the world considers weak in order to shame the powerful. He chose what the world looks down on and despises and thinks is nothing, in order to destroy what the world thinks is important. This means that no one can boast in God's presence. But… God has made Christ to be our wisdom. By him we are put right with God; we become God's holy people and are set free. So then, as the scripture says, "Whoever wants to boast must boast of what the Lord has done."

I Corinthians 1: 26-31

> "…we become God's holy people and are set free…"

A missed opportunity

"I can't see my stop!" cries an elderly lady at the front of the bus. The windows are all misted over. The other passengers are deep in conversation, lost in a magazine or quietly dozing. One talks on a cell phone, while many stare blankly out the window. No one, me included, makes a move. Then, a frail lady with a cane crosses the aisle and takes the woman's hand. "Tell me where you are going, and I'll tell you when we get there," she says.

They eventually fall into conversation. And I understand exactly what Paul is getting at in today's reading: how the weak continue to shame the powerful – not in the abstract, but in our everyday encounters with each other, in tiny moments of our missed opportunities.

Dear God, shake me out of my self-involvement so I can open up to those around me.

O God, you are my God,
and I long for you.
My whole being
desires you;
like a dry, worn-out,
and waterless land,
my soul is thirsty for you....
Your constant love
is better than life itself,
and so I will praise you.
I will give you thanks
as long as I live;
I will raise my hands to you
in prayer.

My soul will feast
and be satisfied,
and I will sing glad songs
of praise to you.
As I lie in bed, I remember you;
all night long I think of you,
because you have always
been my help.
In the shadow of your wings
I sing for joy.
I cling to you,
and your hand keeps me safe.

Psalm 63: 1-8

"...my soul is thirsty for you."

Thirsty for God

One of our neighbourhood gardens is a study in neglect. Though lovingly tended in the spring, the owners usually leave for a three-week vacation at the hottest time of the year. They return to find their garden wilted from the sun and overgrown with weeds. I wonder what it would take for neighbours to come together to care for the garden?

My soul can be like this garden: thirsty for God yet suffering from neglect. I fail to tend to my own spiritual needs with tenderness and attention. Or I feel abandoned by those who might offer the nourishment I need during the dry spells.

Tending a garden takes time and tenderness. The same can be said for the soul.

Loving God, help me lovingly tend to my soul.

Jesus went to Nazareth… and on the Sabbath he went as usual to the synagogue. He stood up to read the Scriptures and was handed the book of the prophet Isaiah. "The Spirit of the Lord is upon me, because he has chosen me to bring good news to the poor. He has sent me to proclaim liberty to the captives and recovery of sight to the blind, to set free the oppressed and announce that the time has come when the Lord will save his people." Jesus rolled up the scroll, gave it back to the attendant, and sat down. "This passage of scripture has come true today, as you heard it being read."

When the people heard this, they were filled with anger.

Luke 4: 16-30

"He has sent me to proclaim liberty to captives."

True courage

Ever stood up for what was right, no matter what? Ever been possessed with the raw courage to speak out clearly to an act of injustice? I work in a high school where that courage is shown every day. Inevitably when people gang up on someone who is weak, a voice will dare to speak up and say, "Hang on now. That isn't right!" It happens all the time.

Wow! Courage breaks through even in the face of the verbal assaults sure to follow! "Who are you to tell us what to do?" they'll scream. "You're just…." But the young prophet delivers the word, and its power is undeniable. No one can misunderstand the challenge.

Youth know the prophetic ways of Jesus. It's in their blood.

**O God, create within me a heart of courage
to speak your word today in a world that longs for truth.**

In the synagogue was a man who had the spirit of an evil demon in him; he screamed out in a loud voice, "Ah! What do you want with us, Jesus of Nazareth? Are you here to destroy us? I know who you are: you are God's holy messenger!"

Jesus ordered the spirit, "Be quiet and come out of the man!" The demon threw the man down in front of them and went out of him without doing him any harm.

The people were all amazed and said to one another, "What kind of words are these? With authority and power this man gives orders to the evil spirits, and they come out!"   *Luke 4: 31-37*

"...who had the spirit of an evil demon..."

Inner demons

The American psychologist Kay Jamison writes about "possession" from a unique perspective. Early in her professional career she was felled by a sudden series of breakdowns. These were eventually diagnosed as chronic manic-depression or bipolar disorder. She writes about her own experiences to help others understand this condition, and how we might be more tolerant when we encounter anyone struggling with such powerful inner demons.

Jamison shares with Jesus the understanding that the voice of the demon often possesses an amazing ability to tell an uncomfortable truth, albeit in an unconventional way. Rendered safe by Jesus – or, in her case, by medicine – Jamison reminds me that this is a temporary measure. Demons return.

Lord, when I encounter troubled "crazies" on the street, help me not to judge too quickly.

J esus went to Simon's home. Simon's mother-in-law was sick with a high fever, and they spoke to Jesus about her. He went and stood at her bedside and ordered the fever to leave her. The fever left her, and she got up at once and began to wait on them.

After sunset all who had friends who were sick with various diseases brought them to Jesus; he placed his hands on every one of them and healed them all. Demons also went out from many people, screaming, "You are the Son of God!"

Jesus gave the demons an order and would not let them speak, because they knew he was the Messiah.

Luke 4: 38-44

> "Simon's mother-in-law was sick…"

Women in ministry

Occasionally I am asked to preach in other churches. My wife, Joan, gets quite upset when the people make a fuss over me, the visiting preacher, but completely ignore her.

Wives get short shrift in the gospels. Without this reference to Simon's mother-in-law, we would never have known any of the disciples were married.

When I was younger, I got a distinct impression that I should approve of the disciples for leaving their nets and their jobs to follow Jesus. But now I realize they also left their wives.

Perhaps some of those wives were among the women who ministered to Jesus, who stood by him at the cross, who came to anoint him on Easter morning. But you'd never know it from the gospel writers.

**Dear God, sometimes I get too preoccupied
with my own concerns. Keep me from ignoring those I love.**

Jesus was standing on the shore of Lake Gennesaret while the people pushed their way up to him to listen to the word of God. He saw two boats pulled up on the beach.... Jesus got into one of the boats – it belonged to Simon – and asked him to push off a little from the shore. Jesus sat in the boat and taught the crowd.

When he finished speaking, he said to Simon, "Push the boat out further to the deep water, and you and your partners let down your nets for a catch."

"Master," Simon answered, "we worked hard all night long and caught nothing. But if you say so, I will let down the nets." They let them down and caught such a large number of fish that the nets were about to break.

Luke 5: 1-11

> "...let down your nets for a catch."

Seeing in a new way

"Well, instead of clearing the drain, I've made it worse." "So try the plunger," piped up my son. "Plungers are for toilets!" "Just try it!" *Et voilà*: the tub now drains.

Why is it so hard for me to take advice from someone who doesn't have my knowledge or experience? I assume they can't possibly help, yet quite often they do help by getting me to see the problem in a new way.

Why do the disciples listen to Jesus? He is just a carpenter's son. What could he know about fishing? Yet they don't hesitate to follow him. Jesus says, "Don't be afraid." They are rewarded for their openness: Jesus calls them to a life of taking chances, of seeing in a new way.

Lord, give me the courage to take chances:
to follow my heart and not just my head.

You should think of us as Christ's servants, who have been put in charge of God's secret truths. The one thing required of such servants is that they be faithful to their master. Now, I am not at all concerned about being judged by you or by any human standard…. My conscience is clear, but that does not prove that I am really innocent. The Lord is the one who passes judgment on me. So you should not pass judgment on anyone before the right time comes. Final judgment must wait until the Lord comes; he will bring to light the dark secrets and expose the hidden purposes of people's minds. And then all will receive from God the praise they deserve.

I Corinthians 4: 1-5

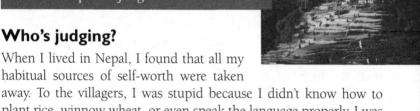

"The Lord is the one
who passes judgment on me."

Who's judging?

When I lived in Nepal, I found that all my habitual sources of self-worth were taken away. To the villagers, I was stupid because I didn't know how to plant rice, winnow wheat, or even speak the language properly. I was ugly because I was thin – a sign of poverty and low status, and my hair was brown – a sign of malnutrition. I was a loser because I had no children. But they accepted me, something that I couldn't control or even understand. Abandoning myself to their acceptance was an experience of pure grace.

If worthiness can be so different from one culture to another, imagine how differently God judges me and others – from the way I judge myself and them!

Lord, root out all the judgments I pass on myself and others.

Jesus was walking through some wheat fields on a Sabbath. His disciples began to pick the heads of wheat, rub them in their hands, and eat the grain. Some Pharisees asked, "Why are you doing what our Law says you cannot do on the Sabbath?"

Jesus answered them, "Haven't you read what David did when he and his men were hungry? He went into the house of God, took the bread offered to God, ate it, and gave it also to his men. Yet it is against our Law for anyone except the priests to eat that bread."

And Jesus concluded, "The Son of Man is Lord of the Sabbath."

Luke 6: 1-5

"The Son of Man is Lord of the Sabbath."

Who's right?

Shel Silverstein, in his poem "Ma and God," highlights some of the conflicts between Ma's rules and the God-given joys of childhood: preferring fingers to forks, splashing in puddles, petting strange dogs, and getting dirty beyond measure. His poem concludes, "There's one thing for certain – either Ma's wrong, or else God is."

Jesus' words to the Pharisees hold a similar ring to them. At its best, the Law reflects God's will that human life flourish; at its worst, it can set obedience to rules in direct competition with the flourishing of life.

In these moments, as Silverstein suggests, "Either the law's wrong, or else God is."

**Jesus, when rules collide, let me place my trust
in your word so that life may flourish.**

" If your brother sins against you, go to him and show him his fault. But do it privately, just between yourselves. If he listens to you, you have won your brother back. But if he will not listen to you, take one or two other persons with you, so that 'every accusation may be upheld by the testimony of two or more witnesses,' as the scripture says. And if he will not listen to them, then tell the whole thing to the church. Finally, if he will not listen to the church, treat him as though he were a pagan or a tax collector.

"And so I tell all of you: what you prohibit on earth will be prohibited in heaven, and what you permit on earth will be permitted in heaven."   *Matthew 18: 15-20*

> "…treat him as though he were a tax collector."

Consistent where it counts

Jesus, sometimes you confuse me. You're so frustratingly human: one day you eat with tax collectors and prostitutes; the next, you say if someone doesn't listen to the church, treat him like a tax collector. No wonder the disciples were sometimes left scratching their heads.

So maybe I can forgive myself my own inconsistencies. The other day, I had to reprimand my class – a little more that usual – for talking instead of working. One of the braver ones asked, "Do you have a migraine today, sir?" "Why?" "Well, you're not usually so crabby." Maybe all one can be, as a human, is consistently inconsistent.

What is consistent, Jesus, is your passionate concern and fierce commitment to the two great commandments. Make it so for me.

**Dear God, as I waver this way and that,
keep me centred on the true path.**

rely on your constant love;
I will be glad, because you will rescue me.
I will sing to you, O Lord,
because you have been good to me.

Psalm 13: 5-6

"I rely on your constant love…"

A child's trust

When my kids were very young, I was like a god to them.

Don't misunderstand. They certainly didn't think I was all-powerful or all-wise. No. Their belief in my god-like powers was about something else. When they looked at me, I could tell they were absolutely certain they were safe and that as long as I was there, nothing could go wrong.

It was unnerving. I knew very well my own weaknesses and the uncertainty of the world we live in. But it was deeply moving at the same time. I learned a lot about trust in those moments.

This simple prayer recalls those times, as I, too old to believe in certainty but too human not to long for it, try to put my faith in God.

**Lord, in my weakness and uncertainty,
help me trust in your never-ending goodness.**

Jesus went up a hill to pray and spent the whole night there praying to God. When day came, he called his disciples to him and chose twelve of them, whom he named apostles....

When Jesus had come down from the hill with the apostles, he stood on a level place with a large number of his disciples. A large crowd of people was there from all over Judea and from Jerusalem and from the coast cities of Tyre and Sidon; they had come to hear him and to be healed of their diseases. Those who were troubled by evil spirits also came and were healed. All the people tried to touch him, for power was going out from him and healing them all.

Luke 6: 12-19

"Jesus went up a hill to pray..."

The sound of silence

When I was young, my life had a sound-
track to it. Bach for times I wanted to think.
Rock and roll for getting my energy moving.
Bob Dylan or Paul Simon for stirring me up. My friends were the same, although they had different selections for their soundtracks.

Back then, I didn't care much for silence and solitude. They made me jittery and uncomfortable. The thought of going to some deserted place alone, and talking to God all night, would have sent me round the bend.

Things are different now. I've learned I need the stillness and quiet that Jesus found on that hill. Without them, I can't hear myself, let alone God. And then how would I know how to live my life?

Lord, help me hear your voice in the stillness.

J esus said, "Happy are you poor; the kingdom of God is yours! Happy are you who are hungry now; you will be filled! Happy are you who weep now; you will laugh! Happy are you when people hate you, reject you, insult you, and say that you are evil, all because of the Son of Man! Be glad when that happens and dance for joy, because a great reward is kept for you in heaven....

"But how terrible for you who are rich now; you have had your easy life! How terrible for you who are full now; you will go hungry! How terrible for you who laugh now; you will mourn and weep! How terrible when all people speak well of you; their ancestors said the very same things about the false prophets."

Luke 6: 20-26

"Happy are you who weep now;
you will laugh!"

Glimpses of the truth

I can't really understand today's reading. It's like looking at a very faint, distant star: you catch a glimpse from the corner of your eye, but when you look right at it, it seems to disappear. But maybe I've had glimpses....

I met a man once. He'd lost his wife and only daughter in a fire. He drank himself almost to death. He'd even had the pills in his hand, ready to swallow them. But he chose to live. After his horrific loss, he says he has learned to take joy in small things. "I used to think my house wasn't big enough! Imagine!" And he smiled.

OK for him, yet I'm left wondering about his wife and daughter, and how to "make sense" of their deaths. Like I said, glimpses....

**Dear God, let me find joy
and meaning in every moment of today.**

L ord, you have examined me and you know me.
You know everything I do;
from far away you understand all my thoughts.
You see me, whether I am working or resting;
you know all my actions....
You created every part of me;
you put me together in my mother's womb.
I praise you because you are to be feared;
all you do is strange and wonderful.
I know it with all my heart....
Examine me, O God, and know my mind;
test me, and discover my thoughts.
Find out if there is any evil in me
and guide me in the everlasting way.

Psalm 139: 1-3, 13-14, 23-24

"...you put me together..."

The mirror

Have you ever watched toddlers looking at themselves in the mirror? Sometimes scientists, they simply explore their features, trying to figure out just exactly how their faces work. At other times clowns, they delight in the silliest expressions they can make. They love looking at themselves and easily accept who they are.

Having just turned forty, I have started to look in the mirror with a critical eye. I see wrinkles and imperfections that I would like to change. What a different attitude from those toddlers!

When did I stop looking in the mirror with wonder and acceptance? When did I start seeing myself as a candidate for an extreme makeover – instead an example of God's handiwork?

God, help me to recognize your work in myself and in others.

J esus told this parable: "One blind man cannot lead another one; if he does, both will fall into a ditch. No pupils are greater than their teacher; but all pupils, when they have completed their training, will be like their teacher.

"Why do you look at the speck in your brother's eye, but pay no attention to the log in your own eye? How can you say to your brother, 'Please, brother, let me take that speck out of your eye,' yet cannot even see the log in your own eye? You hypocrite! First take the log out of your own eye, and then you will be able to see clearly to take the speck out of your brother's eye."

Luke 6: 39-42

"First take the log out of your own eye..."

The blind leading the blind

I'm smiling and nodding: Jesus sure told them this time! Then a picture comes to mind, and a memory. In fact, a pair of memories.

In the first, my teenage daughter has made a comment about "my" music. She has hurt my feelings, offended my sensibilities, and I'm lecturing her about respecting other people's tastes.

In the next, "her" music is on the car radio and I'm saying to my friend, "If they had this music a thousand years ago, do you think they'd have needed water torture?" My daughter hears, and her face clouds over.

I hope you're wrong, Jesus. I hope the blind can lead the blind. Because I'm blind, I know. And I suspect we all are.

Lord, help me think before I speak.

"**A** healthy tree does not bear bad fruit, nor does a poor tree bear good fruit. Every tree is known by the fruit it bears; you do not pick figs from thorn bushes or gather grapes from bramble bushes. A good person brings good out of the treasure of good things in his heart; a bad person brings bad out of his treasure of bad things. For the mouth speaks what the heart is full of."

Luke 6: 43-49

"Every tree is known by the fruit it bears…"

God's cherry tree

Over fifteen years ago, we were given a small cherry tree sapling as a house-warming present. That sapling, which now towers over the house, has blessed us with its bounty ever since.

It gives us not just cherries to eat, wonderful though they are, but also beautiful white blossoms in spring, shade on hot summer days, the pleasure of watching visiting birds that stop by to dine, and mischievous squirrels that use it as a playground all year long. Like a dutiful sentinel, it has watched my children grow up as they pass almost daily under its generous, spreading branches.

I see it now as a constant witness to the goodness of creation, and the caring presence of God.

Thank you, Lord, for the many blessings you have given me.

The Israelites left Mount Hor… in order to go around the territory of Edom. But on the way the people lost their patience and spoke against God and Moses. They complained, "Why did you bring us out of Egypt to die in this desert, where there is no food or water?" Then the Lord sent poisonous snakes among the people, and many Israelites were bitten and died. The people came to Moses and said, "We sinned when we spoke against the Lord and against you. Now pray to the Lord to take these snakes away." So Moses prayed for the people. Then the Lord told Moses to make a metal snake and put it on a pole, so that anyone who was bitten could look at it and be healed. So Moses made a bronze snake and put it on a pole. Anyone who had been bitten would look at the bronze snake and be healed.

Numbers 21: 4-9

"Anyone… could look at it and be healed."

Schools of medicine

The Greeks called him Asclepios, the Romans Aesculapius. He was a priest/physician practising in Greece around 1200 B.C. His daughters, Hygiea and Panaceia, were also healers. From them, we inherit hygiene and panacea. Temples and shrines were dedicated to him, called asclepions. People flocked to them for healing and for prayer. Asclepios is linked to snakes because it's thought he used mixtures of venom in creating medicines.

The images of a priest/healer and temples for healing are at the very core of medical tradition. They echo Moses and the healing bronze snake on a pole.

Healing also requires us to learn about disease. Perhaps that's why libraries in the ancient world were also known as houses of healing for the soul.

**Dear God, may your healing love
envelop me in my times of sickness and need.**

The child's father and mother were amazed at the things Simeon said about him. Simeon blessed them and said to Mary, his mother, "This child is chosen by God for the destruction and the salvation of many in Israel. He will be a sign from God which many people will speak against and so reveal their secret thoughts. And sorrow, like a sharp sword, will break your own heart."

Luke 2: 33-35

> "Sorrow... will break your own heart."

Living with sorrow

How could Mary continue? To watch her own child move away from her, out into the world. To see him rejected, mocked, tortured and crucified. How could she survive this horror? How could she carry so much hurt and still have room in her broken heart for the pain of other people?

And as we live and suffer, how can we become wise and loving, not hardened and bitter?

My friend lost her husband and raised the family alone. Her laughter was infectious, her generosity boundless and her tears real when others were in grief. Her life enriched us all. Perhaps, if I do not turn from my own pain, I can feel the pain of others and touch them in their sorrow.

Dear God, help me to live with my own sorrow, so that I can help ease the sorrow of others.

J ust as [Jesus] arrived at the gate of the town, a funeral procession was coming out. The dead man was the only son of a woman who was a widow, and a large crowd from the town was with her. When the Lord saw her, his heart was filled with pity for her, and he said to her, "Don't cry." Then he walked over and touched the coffin, and the men carrying it stopped. Jesus said, "Young man! Get up, I tell you!" The dead man sat up and began to talk, and Jesus gave him back to his mother.

They all were filled with fear and praised God. "A great prophet has appeared among us!" they said; "God has come to save his people!" This news about Jesus went out through all the country and the surrounding territory. *Luke 7: 11-17*

"God has come to save his people!"

God's presence

"The man who laughs/Has simply not yet had/The terrible news" wrote one of my favourite playwrights in a time of war. Filled with contradictory characters and paradoxical extremes, his work echoes realities in my own world.

I recall times when I've felt like the widow in today's reading: lost and quite alone. When I think that nothing could make things worse, inevitably the other shoe falls: a contract is lost, a diagnosis is confirmed.

But then, in the most surprising ways, I am lifted from my self-concern. Not by dramatic miracles, but by "envelopes of light" as a songwriter describes them – by a surprise phone call, a breathtaking sunrise, a sudden smile, a piece of music that says gently, "Don't cry, I am here."

**When I need you most, Lord, may I recognize
your grace-filled presence in the details of my life.**

Love is patient and kind; it is not jealous or conceited or proud; love is not ill-mannered or selfish or irritable; love does not keep a record of wrongs; love is not happy with evil, but is happy with the truth. Love never gives up; and its faith, hope and patience never fail.

When I was a child, my speech, feelings, and thinking were all those of a child; now that I am an adult, I have no more use for childish ways. What we see now is like a dim image in a mirror; then we shall see face-to-face. What I know now is only partial; then it will be complete – as complete as God's knowledge of me. Meanwhile these three remain: faith, hope and love; and the greatest of these is love.

1 Corinthians 12: 31 – 13: 13

"Love never gives up…"

Choosing to love

I had to pass an examination to get a driver's licence. I went through extensive interviews before I got a job. My spouse and I took counselling before we married. But there are no requirements to meet at all for bringing a child into the world. Why?

Perhaps because parenting is too complex for any test. There are no rehearsals to prepare parents for when a daughter falls in with the wrong crowd, or a son has an accident….

Someone told me once, "Love opens your heart to be hurt."

Joan and I didn't know what we were doing when we had children. But we did our best. Even when it hurt. Because we loved them. And we always will. No matter what….

Love is never easy, God.
But you know this much better than I do.

A Pharisee invited Jesus to have dinner with him…. In that town was a woman who lived a sinful life. She heard that Jesus was eating in the Pharisee's house, so she brought an alabaster jar full of perfume and stood behind Jesus, by his feet, crying and wetting his feet with her tears. Then she dried his feet with her hair, kissed them, and poured the perfume on them. When the Pharisee saw this, he said to himself, "If this man really were a prophet, he would know who this woman is who is touching him; he would know what kind of sinful life she lives!"

Jesus said, "Simon, do you see this woman? I tell you, the great love she has shown proves that her many sins have been forgiven. But whoever has been forgiven little shows only a little love."

Luke 7: 36-50

"…who lived a sinful life."

Lovable and loving

I know a woman who, years ago, chose to have an abortion. And I know how she's struggled because of how her decision affected her relationships with her friends and family.

I once asked her if her decision also affected her relationship with God. She explained how, at first, she felt that if she'd asked, God would have told her she was "a sinful woman." So she didn't talk with God, not for a long time.

Time passed, and gradually my friend allowed God to break through her silence. And, as she listened, she heard God say that she was lovable. And capable of loving others. Now, with the understanding that comes from experience, my friend finds herself reaching out to those who are feeling confused and alone.

**Lord, when I want to judge others,
may I pause and consider how you never stop loving me.**

Some time later Jesus travelled through towns and villages, preaching the Good News about the kingdom of God. The twelve disciples went with him, and so did some women who had been healed of evil spirits and diseases: Mary (who was called Magdalene), from whom seven demons had been driven out; Joanna, whose husband Chuza was an officer in Herod's court; and Susanna, and many other women who used their own resources to help Jesus and his disciples.

Luke 8: 1-3

"…women who used their own resources to help Jesus…"

Health and healing

In her mid-thirties, Nicole – doctor, mother, wife and friend – was diagnosed with an aggressive breast cancer. Everyone would have understood had she turned her energies inward – to care for her own health and for the needs of her young family.

Instead, Nicole chose, time after time, to place her many talents and resources at the service of the community. Convinced that pesticides were at the root of her cancer, she initiated a movement that resulted in a total ban of pesticides in our community. She travelled far and wide – to other towns and villages, even countries – sharing the results of her research.

Like the women in today's reading, Nicole's action helped bring health and healing to the many lives that she touched.

**Loving God, help me to choose to put my resources
at your service.**

Someone will ask, "How can the dead be raised to life? What kind of body will they have?" You fool! When you plant a seed in the ground, it does not sprout to life unless it dies. And what you plant is a bare seed, perhaps a grain of wheat or some other grain, not the full-bodied plant that will later grow up....

This is how it will be when the dead are raised to life. When the body is buried, it is mortal; when raised, it will be immortal. When buried, it is ugly and weak; when raised, it will be beautiful and strong. When buried, it is a physical body; when raised, it will be a spiritual body.... Those who belong to the earth are like the one who was made of earth; those who are of heaven are like the one who came from heaven.

1 Corinthians 15: 35-37, 42-50

"...it does not sprout to life unless it dies."

Transformation

I slap a lump of ordinary grayish material on my wheel, centre it and pull up the sides to make a bowl. After the new shape is fired in an electric kiln, the clay turns hard and white. I cover it with a dull, chalky substance and place it in an outdoor raku kiln. When the kiln reaches the appropriate temperature, I pull out the vessel, still red hot, and place it in a nest of leaves and papers that immediately catch fire. Changes in temperature cause the glaze to crackle as smoke from the fire turns the pattern black. It is then plunged into cold water and the soot is rubbed away to reveal a beautiful bowl.

Transformation can be painful and unsettling, but sometimes the results can't be achieved any other way.

God, help me to trust the transformations in my life.

"When evening came, the owner told his foreman, 'Call the workers and pay them their wages....' The men who had begun to work at five o'clock were paid a silver coin each. So when the men who were the first to be hired came to be paid, they thought they would get more; but they too were given a silver coin each. They started grumbling against the employer. 'These men who were hired last worked only one hour,' they said, 'while we put up with a whole day's work in the hot sun – yet you paid them the same as you paid us!' 'Listen, friend,' the owner answered one of them, 'I have not cheated you. After all, you agreed to do a day's work for one silver coin.... Don't I have the right to do as I wish with my own money?'"

Matthew 20: 1-16

"They started grumbling…"

Watching and waiting

At first glance, the owner of this vineyard seems somewhat strange. Certainly, his workers think his method of payment is unfair. And, if he continued paying his workers like this, who'd ever come to work before noon?

I worked in a factory with a man who had an attitude like that of the early workers. He watched constantly: who was doing less than he was? And when he talked, it was about whose house was bigger, who had an easier life. He was a good man; he was always good to me. But he also watched to see who was doing less than I did.

Watching, always watching. But that man didn't laugh. He counted the minutes of each day. I think he watched his life away.

Lord, let me look for what I have, rather than what I have not.

"No one lights a lamp and covers it with a bowl or puts it under a bed. Instead, it is put on the lampstand, so that people will see the light as they come in.

"Whatever is hidden away will be brought out into the open, and whatever is covered up will be found and brought to light.

"Be careful, then, how you listen; because those who have something will be given more, but whoever has nothing will have taken away from them even the little they think they have."

Luke 8: 16-18

"…so that people will see the light as they come in."

A shining light

I come into my daughter's daycare and sit down to wait while Lucie, her caregiver, finishes playing airplane. She passes out light refreshments to the two rows of children seated in the corridor of her apartment, then expertly pilots the plane down to earth.

Lucie is taking our children around the world, even though she's been in a real airplane only once, and never out of the province. She is poorly paid and has low social status, but she has not hidden her light under a bushel and sought a more lucrative career. She radiates the joy of living to the full.

As more parents come in and sit to watch, we learn from her about being patient, imaginative, respectful and loving with our children.

Lord, give me the courage to use my gifts to the full so that through them people can see you.

J esus' mother and brothers came to him, but were unable to join him because of the crowd. Someone said to Jesus, "Your mother and brothers are standing outside and want to see you."

Jesus said to them all, "My mother and brothers are those who hear the word of God and obey it."

Luke 8: 19-21

"Your mother and brothers are standing outside…"

Redefining family

This story used to make me squirm: "Gentle Jesus, meek and mild" more or less dismissing his family – and not because they've done anything wrong. After all, they simply want to see him. His words seem harsh and unfair.

But I'm a parent now whose children are closer to independent adult life than to the dependent life of a child. The time is coming when they will go.

Today I hear no anger in Jesus' voice. Maybe there is even a little sadness as he speaks. Now I think the story is simply telling us that we all grow up. Children have to leave home and make their own way in the world and families have to redefine themselves. That's the nature of human life.

**Lord, I have held my children close.
Help me to let them go.**

J esus called the twelve disciples together and gave them power and authority to drive out all demons and to cure diseases. Then he sent them out to preach the kingdom of God and to heal the sick, after saying to them, "Take nothing with you for the trip: no walking stick, no beggar's bag, no food, no money, not even an extra shirt. Wherever you are welcomed, stay in the same house until you leave that town; wherever people don't welcome you, leave that town and shake the dust off your feet as a warning to them."

The disciples left and travelled through all the villages, preaching the Good News and healing people everywhere. *Luke 9: 1-6*

"Take nothing with you for the trip…"

False security

I think about Jesus' words whenever my wife and I start packing the van for our vacation with our three children. We know we won't use half of what we pack. But every year we over-pack again.

I think of how I travel every day with excess baggage. I recognize how I rely upon the security provided by my professional degrees, my possessions and the people I know.

I have a friend who teaches troubled teenagers. It is intimidating to enter her classroom. In her students' eyes, degrees and possessions mean nothing. And yet, my friend stands before them in complete trust and openness. I marvel at her: she needs no props. Her trust is in the relationship alone.

Lord, help me to cast off my reliance on crutches and supports so that I may trust in you completely.

Generations come and generations go, but the world stays just the same. The sun still rises, and it still goes down, going wearily back to where it must start all over again. The wind blows south, the wind blows north – round and round and back again. Every river flows into the sea, but the sea is not yet full. The water returns to where the rivers began, and starts all over again. Everything leads to weariness – a weariness too great for words. Our eyes can never see enough to be satisfied; our ears can never hear enough. What has happened before will happen again. What has been done before will be done again. There is nothing new in the whole world. "Look," they say, "here is something new!" But no, it has all happened before, long before we were born.   *Ecclesiastes 1: 2-11*

"There is nothing new in the whole world."

What's new?

Recently I accompanied my son's school band to a music camp. The camp was held at an outdoor centre and involved both music work-shops and outdoor activities.

The camp ended with a concert held in the dining hall where picture windows overlook a lake surrounded by pine forest. As dusk fell, a family of ducks swam into the cove. The moment was beauti-ful, peaceful. Then, as the band played, it became magical: the music seemed to reflect the progression of a thunderstorm moving across the lake.

At that moment, I thought, "This is what we bring – our appre-ciation. Perhaps our music says 'thank you' on behalf of the world." That's what is new: each of us sees – with new eyes – the unspeakable beauty that surrounds us.

**Lord, help me to experience your creation
with new eyes and ears today.**

One of the elders asked me, "Who are these people dressed in white robes, and where do they come from?" "I don't know, sir. You do," I answered.

He said, "These are the people who have come safely through the terrible persecution. They have washed their robes and made them white with the blood of the Lamb. That is why they stand before God's throne and serve him day and night in his temple. He who sits on the throne will protect them with his presence. Never again will they hunger or thirst; neither sun nor any scorching heat will burn them, because the Lamb, who is in the centre of the throne, will be their shepherd, and he will guide them to springs of life-giving water. And God will wipe away every tear from their eyes."

Revelation 7: 9-17

> "And God will wipe away every tear from their eyes."

We all cry

"And God will wipe away every tear from their eyes." People of every race, tribe and nation: what do we have in common? I guess one answer is that we all cry. In a lifetime, we cry so many tears.

Tears of laughter, of pain, of joy, of loneliness. Tears for newborn babies, tears for dead sons. Tears for new brides, tears for spouses left alone. Tears for old friends we'll never see again.

Arabs cry and Jews. Serbs cry, too, and Croats. Children cry and mothers. And so do fathers cry, on cold winter nights, alone at kitchen tables. Even Jesus cried, we are told, for his friend Lazarus.

When others cry, I'll try to remember they're just like me – a child of God, in need of God's healing touch.

Dear God, help me dry the tears from others' eyes.

Young people, enjoy your youth. Be happy while you are still young. Do what you want to do, and follow your heart's desire. But remember that God is going to judge you for whatever you do….

So remember your Creator while you are still young, before those dismal days and years come when you will say, "I don't enjoy life…."

We are going to our final resting place, and then there will be mourning in the streets. The silver chain will snap, and the golden lamp will fall and break; the rope at the well will break, and the water jar will be shattered. Our bodies will return to the dust of the earth, and the breath of life will go back to God, who gave it to us.

Useless, useless, said the Philosopher. It is all useless.

Ecclesiastes 11:9 – 12:8

"Useless, useless, said the Philosopher."

The gift of life

Today's reading talks of youth, and of death… at the end of one's life. But what of the senseless deaths of those who die young?

I find myself reeling from the recent tragedies within my community: an eight-year-old dies when his family's car flips over. A thirty-year-old mother fights breast cancer… for the second time. A mother and her son are trapped and die in a house fire. A forty-year-old man battles leukemia. A teenage girl dies in a traffic accident. What chance did they have to "enjoy their youth"? I find myself raging at the injustice of it all.

"Useless…. It is all useless." Yes, but somewhere within the very agony of our loss – somehow – we find a reason to go on living.

**God, life is so fleeting. May I savour the gift of life,
and be alive to every moment of every day.**

"There was once a man who had two sons. He went to the older one and said, 'Son, go and work in the vineyard today.' 'I don't want to,' he answered, but later he changed his mind and went. Then the father went to the other son and said the same thing. 'Yes, sir,' he answered, but he did not go. Which one of the two did what his father wanted?" "The older one," they answered. So Jesus said to them, "I tell you: the tax collectors and the prostitutes are going into the kingdom of God ahead of you. For John the Baptist came to you showing you the right path to take, and you would not believe him; but the tax collectors and the prostitutes believed him."

Matthew 21: 28-32

"...the tax collectors and the prostitutes believed..."

Judged and found wanting

It is surprising to hear Jesus praise the prostitutes and tax collectors for their faith and their openness to the word of God. After all, these people were the most unworthy characters in Israel, weren't they?

But whom have I judged as unworthy today? A colleague? A neighbour? A politician? How often have I been comfortable in my own righteousness?

Faced with those whom I judge to be unworthy, why is it easier for me to condemn them before taking a moment to reflect on my own failings? There is a saying – when I point a finger at others to criticize, three fingers point back at myself. Today I hope to remember to contemplate my own need for growth before I criticize others.

Loving God, help me to fold my hands in prayer before pointing my finger at others.

When Jesus saw Nathanael coming to him, he said about him, "Here is a real Israelite; there is nothing false in him!" Nathanael asked him, "How do you know me?" Jesus answered, "I saw you when you were under the fig tree before Philip called you."

"Teacher," answered Nathanael, "you are the Son of God! You are the King of Israel!" Jesus said, "Do you believe just because I told you I saw you when you were under the fig tree? You will see much greater things than this!" And he said to them, "I am telling you the truth: you will see heaven open and God's angels going up and coming down on the Son of Man."

John 1: 47-51

"...there is nothing false in him!"

The straight goods

It was a big occasion and I had to make a speech on a podium. I had no idea what to wear – did I want to appear as this kind of person, or that kind of person? Finally, I stood still in the middle of the room, clothes strewn around me in heaps, and realized that I just had to be myself. Then it was easy; I knew exactly what to wear.

The minute Jesus caught sight of Nathaniel he saw right through him. Nathaniel saw through Jesus pretty fast, too. Neither was trying to project an image; they were living in the middle of the truth. Only in that truth can God and I meet and delight in each other the way Jesus and Nathaniel did.

Lord, I want to be true and to touch the truth in others.

Finally Job broke the silence
and cursed the day on which he had been born.
God, put a curse on the day I was born;
put a curse on the night when I was conceived….
I wish I had died in my mother's womb
or died the moment I was born….
If I had died then, I would be at rest now….
Why let people go on living in misery?
Why give light to those in grief?
They wait for death, but it never comes;
they prefer a grave to any treasure.

Job 3: 1-3, 11-17, 20-23

"Why let people go on living in misery?"

Depths of darkness

Sometimes, it's so hard to hope, so hard to go on. Sometimes, it's almost unbearable. She's sitting there, telling me why she's been absent from class. The mornings, she says, are the worst. Or maybe the nights when she's afraid to sleep. The days aren't much better.

Violence in the family, repeated through father and stepfather. Caring for siblings. Struggling in school and, unable to master the work, abandoning a dream. It's just become too much. "Sir," she says, "I feel like I'm going insane. Sometimes, I think I should just…." She shakes her head, forcing back tears. I take a breath. We talk. She will get help.

Sometimes, the voyage to light begins in the depths of darkness.

**Lord, help me bring your light into the darkness
of those who suffer.**

A s they went on their way, a man said to Jesus, "I will follow you wherever you go." Jesus said to him, "Foxes have holes, and birds have nests, but the Son of Man has no place to lie down and rest." He said to another man, "Follow me." But that man said, "Sir, first let me go back and bury my father." Jesus answered, "Let the dead bury their own dead. You go and proclaim the kingdom of God."

Someone else said, "I will follow you, sir; but first let me go and say good-bye to my family." Jesus said to him, "Anyone who starts to plow and then keeps looking back is of no use for the kingdom of God." *Luke 9: 57-62*

"I will follow you wherever you go."

"Yes, my love!"

One of my children asks me to come and play. "Not yet, hon," I say. Another wants to talk to me about something. "In a little while," I say, "when I finish this work." God comes knocking on my door every day through my children, and I respond with a tepid "Not yet!"

What if I changed? What if I made responding wholeheartedly to God my number one priority? Indeed the only priority! God is willing to do that for me. No questions asked.

Living in the past, building my security, or getting ready for a distant "right time" to act isn't enough. An audible, "Yes, my love," is needed. See God and respond. Now is the only moment.

**God, create in me a desire to respond to you,
wherever and whenever you show yourself to me.**

A t that time the disciples came to Jesus, asking, "Who is the greatest in the kingdom of heaven?" So Jesus called a child to come and stand in front of them, and said, "I assure you that unless you change and become like children, you will never enter the kingdom of heaven. The greatest in the kingdom of heaven is the one who humbles himself and becomes like this child. And whoever welcomes in my name one such child as this, welcomes me....

"See that you don't despise any of these little ones. Their angels in heaven, I tell you, are always in the presence of my Father in heaven."

Matthew 18: 1-5, 10

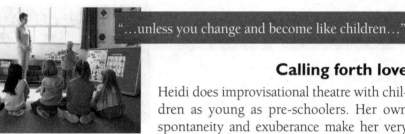

"...unless you change and become like children..."

Calling forth love

Heidi does improvisational theatre with children as young as pre-schoolers. Her own spontaneity and exuberance make her very good at what she does. She models for the kids what she asks of them.

Part of Heidi's success is her confidence in the kids themselves. She knows that by age three or four, they already have everything they need: trust, energy and imagination. She just needs to call these gifts forth.

When Heidi invites the children to join her on stage, she reminds me of today's reading. The kingdom of God is a lot like improvisational theatre. It unfolds in our midst – when our trust, energy and imagination come together at God's invitation.

**God, give me the trust, energy and imagination
to improvise love in my world.**

L ord, you have examined
me and you know me.
You know everything I do;
from far away you understand
all my thoughts.
You see me, whether I am
working or resting;
you know all my actions....
Where could I go
to escape from you?
Where could I get away
from your presence?
If I went up to heaven,
you would be there;
if I lay down in the world of
the dead, you would be there.
If I flew away beyond the east
or lived in the farthest place
in the west,
you would be there
to lead me....
You created every part of me;
you put me together
in my mother's womb.
I praise you because
you are to be feared;
all you do is strange
and wonderful.
I know it with all my heart.

Psalm 139: 1-3, 7-10, 13-14

"...you put me together..."

Cut and paste

My six-year-old daughter struggles to complete the finishing touches
on a paper scarecrow for our front door. Our work table is scattered
with glue and string, paper and felt. Getting the straw hair into place
and gluing it down is no easy task. I resist the temptation to jump in
and do it for her.

With exasperation, she abandons the glue and drops her forehead into her hands. "I sure hope God had an easier time putting me
together," she scowls.

She snuggles her way onto my lap. "You certainly were worth the
trouble," I assure her. "All children are."

**Creator God, may all children know that they are made
by your loving hands.**

J esus was filled with joy by the Holy Spirit and said, "Father, Lord of heaven and earth! I thank you because you have shown to the unlearned what you have hidden from the wise and learned. Yes, Father, this was how you were pleased to have it happen.

"My Father has given me all things. No one knows who the Son is except the Father, and no one knows who the Father is except the Son and those to whom the Son chooses to reveal him."

Then Jesus turned to the disciples and said to them, "How fortunate you are to see the things you see! I tell you that many prophets and kings wanted to see what you see, but they could not, and to hear what you hear, but they did not." *Luke 10: 17-24*

"…this was how you were pleased to have it happen."

Trusting in God's gift

Tensely I watched as my daughter began riding her first two-wheeler. Personally, I had grown to rely on those little training wheels, and was reluctant to let them go. "Whoa, a little wobbly there, honey… Ooops, don't go too fast now." She, on the other hand, was much more brash about the outcome of this whole experience. "Don't hold me, Daddy! I'm okay. Let go!"

How I wish I could! Like many self-appointed "wise and learned" types, I'm bound by my fears. My little one, having conquered her fear of the dark, of "boogie-men," and now of falling, was once again utterly determined to ride on freely. Her trust in God's gift of life was as solid as a rock.

"Wise and learned" – indeed.

**God, renew me and help me to see the world again –
with a child's wild passion and love of life.**

Don't worry about anything, but in all your prayers ask God for what you need, always asking him with a thankful heart. And God's peace, which is far beyond human understanding, will keep your hearts and minds safe in union with Christ Jesus.

In conclusion, my friends, fill your minds with those things that are good and that deserve praise: things that are true, noble, right, pure, lovely and honourable. Put into practice what you learned and received from me, both from my words and from my actions. And the God who gives us peace will be with you.

Philippians 4: 6-9

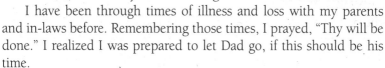

"Don't worry about anything…"

Time with Dad

Last week, my Dad went into the hospital with symptoms of heart failure. As I sat beside his bed, I found myself wondering what the week would hold.

I have been through times of illness and loss with my parents and in-laws before. Remembering those times, I prayed, "Thy will be done." I realized I was prepared to let Dad go, if this should be his time.

Then I did something I'd never done before. I reached for the lotion on his bedside table. I gently placed Dad's hand in mine, and began to massage his weathered skin. He was surprised, I think, by this act of intimacy, but smiled, and continued to reminisce with me.

Our little corner of the hospital room seemed quite holy.

**Gentle God, guide my hands to put into practice
what I have received from you.**

"There was once a man who was going down from Jerusalem to Jericho when robbers attacked him, stripped him, and beat him up, leaving him half dead. It so happened that a priest was going down that road; but when he saw the man, he walked on by on the other side. In the same way a Levite also came there, went over and looked at the man, and then walked on by on the other side. But a Samaritan who was travelling that way came upon the man, and when he saw him, his heart was filled with pity. He went over to him, poured oil and wine on his wounds and bandaged them; then he put the man on his own animal and took him to an inn, where he took care of him...." And Jesus concluded, "In your opinion, which one of these three acted like a neighbour toward the man attacked by the robbers?" The teacher of the Law answered, "The one who was kind to him." Jesus replied, "You go, then, and do the same."

Luke 10: 25-37

"You go, then, and do the same."

Taking care of...?

The past two days have left me somewhat uneasy. As I walk from my hotel to my meetings, I pass some panhandlers. One young woman in shabby black dress kneels, holding a cup against her forehead. A cardboard sign in front of her asks for money for her three children.

Around the corner a heavyset man lies sleeping, sprawled on a sleeping bag on top of the vent for the subway, where the warm air heats a whole city block. To his side, a large black dog sits motionless; between them, a paper cup with some coins in it.

The more I look around, the more I realize how I have distanced myself from "going and doing the same."

Dear God, I tend to observe life while avoiding full participation in the world around me. Give me a rude awakening.

Lord, you have examined me and you know me.
You know everything I do;
from far away you understand all my thoughts.
You see me, whether I am working or resting;
you know all my actions....
I praise you because you are to be feared;
all you do is strange and wonderful.
I know it with all my heart.
When my bones were being formed,
carefully put together in my mother's womb,
when I was growing there in secret,
you knew that I was there –
you saw me before I was born.

Psalm 139: 1-3, 13-16

"You know everything I do..."

Known as I am

Henri Nouwen was a well-known writer and university professor when he arrived at L'Arche Daybreak. People appreciated him for his books and lectures. But at Daybreak, the people with learning disabilities didn't know anything about his books or lectures. They simply wanted him to spend time with them and to be their friend.

This was quite disconcerting for Henri. But with time, he found freedom to simply be himself and discovered a profound sense of home at Daybreak.

Prayer is like that for me. It can be disconcerting to realize that God knows me so well. Ultimately, prayer frees me to be my truest self, to find my home in God's intimate love for me.

**Lord, may I find rest in your intimate knowledge
of and love for me.**

One day Jesus was praying in a certain place. When he had finished, one of his disciples said to him, "Lord, teach us to pray, just as John taught his disciples."

Jesus said to them, "When you pray, say this: 'Father: May your holy name be honoured; may your kingdom come. Give us day by day the food we need. Forgive us our sins, for we forgive everyone who does us wrong. And do not bring us to hard testing.'"

Luke 11: 1-4

"When you pray, say this…"

Searching for the right words

The poet Tennyson has given me an insight into the risks of reading Scripture. He wrote: "Words, like Nature, half reveal/And half conceal the Soul within." Today's reading both reveals and conceals my understanding of God.

When I think of God, I don't think of my "father." Now don't get me wrong, I loved and respected my father. And, surprisingly, I speak of him more now after his death than I did when he was alive.

But when I pray, I struggle to find the right words with which to address God. God is rarely the "Dad" of my quirky family story. God is certainly present – caring and accessible as my dad was. Yet God also remains a soul-challenging, word-defying mystery.

**Dear God, may I always search for ways
to communicate with you.**

Jesus said to his disciples, "Suppose one of you should go to a friend's house at midnight and say, 'Friend, let me borrow three loaves of bread....' And suppose your friend should answer from inside, 'Don't bother me! The door is already locked, and my children and I are in bed. I can't get up and give you anything.' Well, what then? I tell you that even if he will not get up and give you the bread because you are his friend, yet he will get up and give you everything you need because you are not ashamed to keep on asking. And so I say to you: Ask, and you will receive; seek, and you will find; knock, and the door will be opened to you."

Luke 11:5-13

"Ask, and you will receive..."

Good neighbours

When we first moved to our small street in Toronto, I couldn't know that we were to be blessed with wonderful neighbours. I'd grown up thinking that it was important to be self-sufficient. I was reluctant to be a bother, so I rarely asked for anything.

Over the years, I have learned that asking for help is part of the glue that holds our community together. I have wandered across the driveway to ask for everything from butter to antifreeze!

What strikes me is how my neighbours always meet my requests with such generosity. They have taught me something far greater than self-sufficiency. Through them I have learned how to ask, and receive, with grace.

Lord, give me the courage to ask for help when I need it.

Friday | OCTOBER 10

Consider the experience of Abraham; as the scripture says, "He believed God, and because of his faith God accepted him as righteous." You should realize, then, that the real descendants of Abraham are the people who have faith. The scripture predicted that God would put the Gentiles right with himself through faith. And so the scripture announced the Good News to Abraham: "Through you God will bless all people." Abraham believed and was blessed; so all who believe are blessed as he was.   *Galatians 3: 6-14*

"…the real descendants of Abraham are the people who have faith."

Family ties

Our genetic line is coming to an end. Neither my wife nor I have any brothers or sisters. We have only one child, and she is unable to have children – and believe me, she has tried!

Recently, our daughter applied for an international adoption. If she's successful, our grandchild-to-be will probably have brown skin and come from a gene pool far removed from our Scottish/Irish/Scandinavian mix.

But I take heart from Paul. True descendants, he says, are not necessarily blood-linked. They're faith-linked. In a culture that traced its roots by family connections, that claim was a huge break with tradition. It gives me more confidence that our family has a future, too.

**All who believe in the same God
are my brothers and sisters in faith.**

B efore the time for faith came, the Law kept us all locked up as prisoners until this coming faith should be revealed. And so the Law was in charge of us until Christ came, in order that we might then be put right with God through faith. Now that the time for faith is here, the Law is no longer in charge of us.

It is through faith that all of you are God's children in union with Christ Jesus. You were baptized into union with Christ, and now you are clothed, so to speak, with the life of Christ himself. So there is no difference between Jews and Gentiles, between slaves and free people, between men and women; you are all one in union with Christ Jesus... and will receive what God has promised.   *Galatians 3: 22-29*

> "...the Law is no longer in charge of us."

Loving what is

I've always been a person who likes order. As a child, I was recognized for my neat handwriting at school. At home I was scrupulous when scrubbing sinks, sweeping floors and shovelling snow. When I left home, I went to university, got married, bought a house and had children. Life was as it should be.

Then my husband was diagnosed with cancer and was given six to twelve months to live. I had to face the fact that we wouldn't grow old together. My children wouldn't know their father. Suddenly life was *not* as it should be.

I sympathize with the Pharisees who liked the security the Law provided – with its strict rules and rigid categories. Like them, I'm challenged to discover God in life, with its upheavals and challenges.

Lord, give me the courage to put aside my neat categories and expectations. Open my eyes to see life as it is.

The Lord is my shepherd; I have everything I need.
He lets me rest in fields of green grass
and leads me to quiet pools of fresh water.
He gives me new strength.
He guides me in the right paths, as he has promised.
Even if I go through the deepest darkness,
I will not be afraid, Lord,
for you are with me.
Your shepherd's rod and staff protect me....
I know that your goodness and love will be with me all my life;
and your house will be my home as long as I live.   *Psalm 23: 1-6*

> "The Lord is my shepherd..."

Modern shepherds

Not long ago, a big wind ripped up the lake, tearing apart log booms. The morning after, logs littered the lakeshore, extending farther out than I could throw a rock.

That afternoon, company boats began rounding up the loose bundles. They drove their boats the way cowboys drive horses. They circled the straying logs, rounding them up. They herded the gathered logs together and raced to lasso errant logs drifting farther up the lake.

Very few of us know sheep personally, which makes shepherding an unfamiliar experience. We know something about it, but it's not something we imagine ourselves doing. And yet we could see shepherding going on all around us, *if* we weren't so attached to a single image.

**I love the psalm about your shepherd care, God.
Help me to see you in other contexts, too.**

"How evil are the people of this day! They ask for a miracle, but none will be given them except the miracle of Jonah. In the same way that the prophet Jonah was a sign for the people of Nineveh, so the Son of Man will be a sign for the people of this day. On the Judgment Day the Queen of Sheba will stand up and accuse the people of today, because she travelled all the way from her country to listen to King Solomon's wise teaching; and there is something here, I tell you, greater than Solomon. On the Judgment Day the people of Nineveh will stand up and accuse you, because they turned from their sins when they heard Jonah preach; and I assure you that there is something here greater than Jonah!" *Luke 11: 29-32*

"They ask for a miracle..."

Everyday miracles

Miracles happen every day – at least, if you believe the advertising industry. Sales pitches regularly offer "miraculous" remedies for every possible ailment – from insomnia to baldness to financial woes. If only life's problems could be so easily solved!

Miracles *do* happen, however. Sometimes it's just that I'm too busy, too bored or too depressed to notice.

In my first year of university there was a student from Malaysia in our residence. The first snowfall that autumn scarcely registered with most of us jaded Canadians. But Pui-Lin had never in her life seen snow! Wide-eyed wonder turned to delighted laughter as she ran outside to touch and taste this mysterious new substance. To Pui-Lin, clearly, that snowfall was a miracle!

God of wonder, open my eyes to the daily miracles, great and small, that reveal your presence in the world.

When Jesus finished speaking, a Pharisee invited him to eat with him; so he went in and sat down to eat. The Pharisee was surprised when he noticed that Jesus had not washed before eating. So the Lord said to him, "Now then, you Pharisees clean the outside of your cup and plate, but inside you are full of violence and evil. Fools! Did not God, who made the outside, also make the inside? But give what is in your cups and plates to the poor, and everything will be ritually clean for you."

Luke 11: 37-41

"…you clean the outside of your cup and plate…"

Appearances are deceiving

Imagine a person who didn't care about appearances. I'm lucky to have known such a person. He was a junk man who wore green clothes, usually had three days' growth of beard, and an ever-present "roll-your-own" stuck to his lower lip. He was thoroughly wonderful, kind and gentle; a great storyteller.

After my mother's funeral, Harry and his family came back to our house. Soon, everyone was listening to Harry's stories – as he knocked his ashes into the cuff of his pants, too polite to ask for the ashtray we had forgotten to offer. He brought life that day – as always, with grace.

Many people saw him, with his old clothes and five o'clock shadow, and didn't know they were looking at a king.

Dear God, let me not worry about what is on the outside – of me, or of those I meet.

"How terrible for you Pharisees! You give to God one tenth of the seasoning herbs, such as mint and rue and all the other herbs, but you neglect justice and love for God. These you should practise, without neglecting the others.

"How terrible for you Pharisees! You love the reserved seats in the synagogues and to be greeted with respect in the marketplaces. How terrible for you! You are like unmarked graves which people walk on without knowing it."

One of the teachers of the Law said to him, "Teacher, when you say this, you insult us, too!" Jesus answered, "How terrible also for you teachers of the Law! You put onto people's backs loads which are hard to carry, but you yourselves will not stretch out a finger to help them carry those loads."   *Luke 11: 42-46*

> "How terrible for you Pharisees!"

Speaking the truth

Friends come in many varieties: the person you want to go out and have fun with might not be the same person you call when you have a problem. What I most value, though, is the friend who tells me the truth.

Mary and I have been friends all of our adult lives and have seen each other at our best and worst. As a result, there is a real freedom in our exchanges. She can tell me things about myself that I would not want to hear from family members or other friends.

We all need someone brave and caring enough in our lives to speak the truth – because the truth is we all have a little bit of the Pharisee in us.

Forgive me, Lord, for being smug and self-satisfied.
Fill my heart with your everlasting truth.

S ing a new song to the Lord;
he has done wonderful things!
By his own power and holy strength
he has won the victory....
He kept his promise to the people of Israel
with loyalty and constant love for them.
All people everywhere have seen the victory of our God.
Sing for joy to the Lord, all the earth;
praise him with songs and shouts of joy!
Sing praises to the Lord!
Play music on the harps!
Blow trumpets and horns,
and shout for joy to the Lord, our king.

Psalm 98: 1-6

"Sing for joy to the Lord, all the earth…"

Joyful noise!

It's easy to forget "joy." Easier to remember "obligation" and "respon-sibility" – good things to remember, certainly. Even when there's time to rest, a sigh of relief comes easier to my lips than a joyful noise. It's so easy to be focused on what I have to do tomorrow.

That's where "joyful noise" comes in. It roots me in the present, in the beauty of the moment. These days my joyful noise comes from teenagers with guitars, amps and drums in my basement. Noise? Sure, but it's joyful! And it reminds me that while tomorrow will come soon enough, there's joy in the moment.

When I think of Jesus, I imagine he might feel at home in my kitchen, surrounded by the joyful noise of God's children at play.

**Lord, remind me to make my joyful noise
as I thank you for the gift of my life!**

J esus said, "Be on guard against the yeast of the Pharisees – I mean their hypocrisy. Whatever is covered up will be uncovered, and every secret will be made known. So then, whatever you have said in the dark will be heard in broad daylight, and whatever you have whispered in private in a closed room will be shouted from the housetops.

"I tell you, my friends, do not be afraid of those who kill the body but cannot afterward do anything worse. I will show you whom to fear: fear God, who, after killing, has the authority to throw into hell. Believe me, he is the one you must fear!

"Aren't five sparrows sold for two pennies? Yet not one sparrow is forgotten by God. Even the hairs of your head have all been counted. So do not be afraid; you are worth much more than many sparrows!"   *Luke 12: 1-7*

"Yet not one sparrow is forgotten by God."

Forgotten

Sometimes I think the sparrows of this world are having a better time than the people. Sparrows aren't as cruel to one another when they fight. And if they need to get away, they can cross borders freely; they don't need to fake documents or depend on leaky, overloaded boats.

It's almost easier for me to believe that God cares about the sparrows than about the nearly ten million refugees in the world, living in those overcrowded, unsafe and filthy refugee camps we see on TV. From my privileged life, in this complacent first-world bubble, I ask myself, If God hasn't forgotten them, why are they there? Then I realize it's me who has forgotten them… as soon as the next ad comes on.

Lord, let me show with my life that you forget no one.

The Lord chose another seventy-two men and sent them out two by two, to go ahead of him to every town and place where he himself was about to go. He said to them… "Go! I am sending you like lambs among wolves. Don't take a purse or a beggar's bag or shoes…. Whenever you go into a house, first say, 'Peace be with this house.' If someone who is peace-loving lives there, let your greeting of peace remain on that person; if not, take back your greeting of peace. Stay in that same house, eating and drinking whatever they offer you, for workers should be given their pay. Don't move around from one house to another. Whenever you go into a town and are made welcome, eat what is set before you, heal the sick in that town, and say to the people there, 'The kingdom of God has come near you.'"

Luke 10: 1-9

"Whenever you go into a house…"

Open to others

Jesus tells the disciples to go into a person's home and to decide if the person there is peace-loving or not. Spending time getting to know someone implies an openness, a vulnerability – and the possibility of getting hurt. But that's the risk that Jesus asks of his disciples. And of me.

Most of my friends would agree that I am too trusting. I meet people with an open heart, and with a willingness to get to know them, and to be known by them.

There have been occasions when I've been hurt in my relationships. Yes, I know I could have been less trusting, and protected myself more. But getting to know others has helped me learn more about myself – and to become capable of loving more fully.

**Loving God, teach me to remain open to others –
in order to learn how to give more deeply of myself.**

The Pharisees went off and made a plan to trap Jesus with questions.... "Teacher," they said, "we know that you tell the truth. You teach the truth about God's will for people, without worrying about what others think, because you pay no attention to anyone's status. Tell us, then, what do you think? Is it against our Law to pay taxes to the Roman Emperor, or not?"

Jesus, however, was aware of their evil plan, and so he said, "You hypocrites! Why are you trying to trap me? Show me the coin for paying the tax!" He asked them, "Whose face and name are these?" "The Emperor's," they answered. So Jesus said to them, "Well, then, pay to the Emperor what belongs to the Emperor, and pay to God what belongs to God."

Matthew 22: 15-21

"Why are you trying to trap me?"

Questions that reveal

I'm often tempted to compare one of my sons to the Pharisees in today's reading. He's constantly pushing at the limits I've established as a parent. He's very articulate so his questions (and objections) can be quite a challenge!

With some insight from books on parent-child relationships, I've begun to see that my son's questions are not meant to "trap" me. They are his attempt to understand what's negotiable and what's not. He wants me to identify which values are important to me.

The Pharisees' questions often illustrate for us what Jesus believed. In the same way, my son's questions make me clarify what I hold to be true. Only then can I answer him with conviction – and help him in his own search for the truth.

**God, help me use the questions I encounter today
to clarify what I hold to be true and loving.**

"There was once a rich man…. He began to think to himself, 'I don't have a place to keep all my crops. What can I do? This is what I will do,' he told himself; 'I will tear down my barns and build bigger ones, where I will store the grain and all my other goods. Then I will say to myself, Lucky man! You have all the good things you need for many years. Take life easy, eat, drink, and enjoy yourself!' But God said to him, 'You fool! This very night you will have to give up your life; then who will get all these things you have kept for yourself?'"

Jesus concluded, "This is how it is with those who pile up riches for themselves but are not rich in God's sight."

Luke 12: 13-21

> "…rich in God's sight."

True riches

We have a big family and a small house. It's funny how some people react when they come to visit. They are astounded and even appalled that we can live like this. They think we're fools.

I have to admit that sometimes I dream of a bigger house with fancy furniture and lots of extras. But does bigger equal happier? Will lots of closets make me say to myself, "lucky woman"? Am I blind to the richness in my small home?

Today's gospel reminds me that possessions aren't what is important in life. Rather it's the love of my husband and children that makes me rich. Now, if I can just keep this in mind when we all need the bathroom at once!

Lord, please keep me focused on what's really important, so I can become rich in your sight.

" **B**e ready for whatever comes, dressed for action and with your lamps lit, like servants who are waiting for their master to come back from a wedding feast. When he comes and knocks, they will open the door for him at once. How happy are those servants whose master finds them awake and ready when he returns! I tell you, he will take off his coat, have them sit down, and will wait on them. How happy they are if he finds them ready, even if he should come at midnight or even later!"

Luke 12: 35-38

"Be ready for whatever comes…"

Live the moment

Being ready for whatever comes is easier said than done! I think of the servants *waiting* for their master's return – while still *doing* all their daily tasks and responsibilities.

And myself: trying to be ready for the next life while I'm so wrapped up in this one. Exams to write, projects to finish, a mortgage to pay, and, yes, meditations to write!

Perhaps, if I try to remember that today is special – possibly my last – then I won't leave the important things for tomorrow. I'll tell the people closest to me that I love them. I'll make peace with those I've hurt. I'll try to take care of my responsibilities without letting them possess me. I'll appreciate the beauty that surrounds me.

Lord, let me be in the world, but not of it.
Help me live so that I am "ready for whatever comes."

was made a servant of the gospel by God's special gift.... I am less than the least of all God's people; yet God gave me this privilege of taking to the Gentiles the Good News about the infinite riches of Christ, and of making all people see how God's secret plan is to be put into effect. God, who is the Creator of all things, kept his secret hidden through all the past ages, in order that at the present time, the angelic rulers and powers in the heavenly world might learn of his wisdom in all its different forms. God did this according to his eternal purpose, which he achieved through Christ Jesus our Lord. In union with Christ and through our faith in him we have the boldness to go into God's presence with all confidence.

Ephesians 3: 1-12

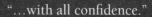

"...with all confidence."

God's special gift

Henri Nouwen tells this story: While living and working within a community of mentally handicapped adults, he was invited to speak at a national conference on the meaning of ministry. Bob, a member of Henri's community, travelled with him to the conference, as he sometimes did.

At the end of Henri's talk, Bob unexpectedly joined Henri at the podium and made a short, impromptu presentation of his own. It was not eloquent or profound by most people's measures, but it said more about the meaning of ministry than all of Henri's well-crafted words.

Bob's boldness was the clearest witness possible to the welcome he felt, both from Henri and from God. Indeed, he brought the Good News of Christ to the conference participants that day!

God, may I help one person today discover the confidence that comes from experiencing your love.

ask God to give you power through his Spirit to be strong in your inner selves, and I pray that Christ will make his home in your hearts through faith. I pray that you may have your roots and foundation in love, so that you, together with all God's people, may have the power to understand how broad and long, how high and deep, is Christ's love. Yes, may you come to know his love – although it can never be fully known – and so be completely filled with the very nature of God.

To him who by means of his power working in us is able to do so much more than we can ever ask for, or even think of: to God be the glory in the church and in Christ Jesus for all time, forever and ever! Amen.

Ephesians 3: 13-21

> "...have your roots and foundation in love..."

Rooted in love

When asked *how* I became interested in spirituality, I paused, then replied, "Through my parents." And I explained how we'd pick lily-of-the-valley to place before the statue of Mary each May. And during Advent the little stable that my father built stood empty, waiting for each wooden figure to arrive in turn. Epiphany was celebrated with a special pie: the one who found the dried pea would be "king" for the evening! Easter meant hot-cross buns and special treats.

But beneath all these "traditions," one memory stands out. Every evening my mother would sit on our beds and read from the Bible. Her love for the scriptures has shaped my own search for meaning – helping me discover the height and the breadth of God's love.

Thank you, God, for those who have shown, and who continue to reveal, your love for our world. May I do the same for others.

J esus said, "When you see a cloud coming up in the west, at once you say that it is going to rain – and it does. And when you feel the south wind blowing, you say that it is going to get hot – and it does. Hypocrites! You can look at the earth and the sky and predict the weather; why, then, don't you know the meaning of this present time?

"Why do you not judge for yourselves the right thing to do? If someone brings a lawsuit against you, do your best to settle the dispute before you get to court. If you don't, you will be dragged before the judge, who will hand you over to the police, and you will be put in jail."   *Luke 12: 54-59*

> "...don't you know the meaning of this present time?"

The signs of the times

Our world is hurting; are we listening to its cries?

An ecological activist committed suicide – he felt he wasn't making enough of a difference. A leading thinker in climate change is predicting a worldwide grain shortage – long-term droughts induced by global warming are said to be the culprit. Russian scientists studying global warming on a permanent ice floe had to be rescued – their ice station was breaking up!

How committed am I in my recycling efforts? Do I choose to ride my bike rather than drive my van? Am I willing to pay extra for fair trade products and organically grown produce? I try, but how the hypocrite label stings!

Lord, the environmental prophets have spoken.
Help me to respond through the choices I make.

Jesus told them this parable: "There was once a man who had a fig tree growing in his vineyard. He went looking for figs on it but found none. So he said to his gardener, 'Look, for three years I have been coming here looking for figs on this fig tree, and I haven't found any. Cut it down! Why should it go on using up the soil?' But the gardener answered, 'Leave it alone, sir, just one more year; I will dig around it and put in some fertilizer. Then if the tree bears figs next year, so much the better; if not, then you can have it cut down.'"

Luke 13: 1-9

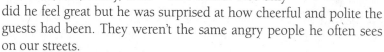

"There was once a man who had a fig tree…"

Into new life

Earlier this year, my eldest son worked in our church's soup kitchen. This was his first direct encounter with the homeless. He came home after his first shift, hot, sticky, tired – and elated. Not only did he feel great but he was surprised at how cheerful and polite the guests had been. They weren't the same angry people he often sees on our streets.

We all flourish if we are fed and watered. In the soup kitchen, my son received more than he gave. He also learned that we are all fig trees, perhaps sad and neglected ones, that can be loved back to fruitfulness. God is ready to coax and nurture each one of us, without exception, into new life.

**Today, may I look at others with God's eyes,
and see not their failings, but the promise of new growth.**

When the Pharisees heard that Jesus had silenced the Sadducees, they came together, and one of them, a teacher of the Law, tried to trap him with a question. "Teacher," he asked, "which is the greatest commandment in the Law?" Jesus answered, "'Love the Lord your God with all your heart, with all your soul, and with all your mind.' This is the greatest and the most important commandment. The second most important commandment is like it: 'Love your neighbour as you love yourself.' The whole Law of Moses and the teachings of the prophets depend on these two commandments."

Matthew 22: 34-40

"Love your neighbour as you love yourself."

Loving my neighbour

Jesus' answer – to the lawyer trying to trap him – tells me everything that I need to know about God's law. Yet, sometimes when I'm behind the wheel of my car, I forget all about my neighbour's rights – and needs. Running late for an appointment, I rush to get through a traffic light and cut off a driver who has been waiting patiently. To save a few minutes, I refuse to yield to someone who wants to change lanes. Why do I behave this way?

I tend to forget that God's law puts as much emphasis on the second commandment as it does on the first. I need to remember that I show my love for God in how I treat my neighbour every moment of every day.

**God, help me to show my love for you
in my concern for others.**

B e kind and tender-hearted to one another, and forgive one another, as God has forgiven you through Christ.

Since you are God's dear children, you must try to be like him. Your life must be controlled by love, just as Christ loved us and gave his life for us as a sweet-smelling offering and sacrifice that pleases God....

Do not let anyone deceive you with foolish words; it is because of these very things that God's anger will come upon those who do not obey him. So have nothing at all to do with such people. You yourselves used to be in the darkness, but since you have become the Lord's people, you are in the light. So you must live like people who belong to the light. *Ephesians 4: 32 – 5: 8*

> "Be kind and tender-hearted to one another..."

Kind and tender-hearted

"Everyone here is so kind!" exclaimed my son. Just days into our summer holidays on Prince Edward Island, he'd noticed how gentle and polite people were with one another. The Island – with its rolling hills, spectacular ocean views and slower pace of life – seemed to work its magic on me, too. Within days I'd noticed that I was treating others with greater kindness and consideration also!

Back from our holidays, I easily slipped into the pressure-cooker of work deadlines and sports schedules, homework and music lessons. Now, as we approach the shorter, darker days of winter, I recall the healing brought by the sea, the sunshine and the Islanders' kindness. And I hope I can bring healing to others by being kinder and more tender-hearted today.

**Lord, heal my heart so I can bring your healing love
to those who live in darkness.**

H ow clearly the sky reveals God's glory!
How plainly it shows what he has done!
Each day announces it to the following day;
each night repeats it to the next.
No speech or words are used,
no sound is heard;
yet their message goes out to all the world
and is heard to the ends of the earth.
God made a home in the sky for the sun.

Psalm 19: 1-4

"No speech or words are used…"

Night sky

On a recent family vacation, I saw the northern lights for the first time in my life. There are no words to fully describe the experience. In the North, the sky itself is a wonder – a treat for a city dweller who rarely sees an unobstructed view of the heavens.

I was gazing into the vault of darkness when the slightest hint of colour shimmered across the sky. Even my six-year-old daughter (whose running commentary on life could rival the most eloquent tour guide) fell silent.

As we drifted off to sleep that night, she couldn't help but comment, "God sure did a good one with that sky tonight." I could see her smile in the darkness. And I'm sure God did, too.

Thank you, God, for the gift of your magnificent skies.

S omeone asked [Jesus], "Sir, will just a few people be saved?" He answered, "Do your best to go in through the narrow door; because many people will surely try to go in but will not be able. The master of the house will get up and close the door; then when you stand outside and begin to knock on the door, and say, 'Open the door for us, sir!' he will answer you, 'I don't know where you come from!' Then you will answer, 'We ate and drank with you; you taught in our town!' But he will say again, 'I don't know where you come from. Get away from me, all you wicked people...!' Then those who are now last will be first, and those who are now first will be last."

Luke 13: 22-30

> "Do your best to go in through the narrow door…"

The last will be first

The squeegee kid walked up to my car and offered to clean the windshield. I'd just had it done at the last red light so I shook my head. He shrugged and smiled. "Have a good day anyway," he called as he moved on. Just then the light turned green, and the guy in an expensive car behind me leaned on his horn.

Why was the affluent man so angry about a second's delay? Why was the kid, who had so little of the world's goods, content to take my shake of the head and offer back a smile?

The first shall be last. The self-important often miss out on ordinary human contact. The last shall be first. Those who don't take themselves too seriously can share their humanity with others.

**Lord, help me to avoid self-importance,
to see everyone with your perspective.**

A t that same time some Pharisees came to Jesus and said to him, "You must get out of here and go somewhere else, because Herod wants to kill you."

Jesus answered them, "Go and tell that fox: 'I am driving out demons and performing cures today and tomorrow, and on the third day I shall finish my work.' Yet I must be on my way today, tomorrow, and the next day; it is not right for a prophet to be killed anywhere except in Jerusalem.

"Jerusalem, Jerusalem! You kill the prophets, you stone the messengers God has sent you! How many times I wanted to put my arms around all your people, just as a hen gathers her chicks under her wings, but you would not let me!"   *Luke 13: 31-35*

"You must get out of here..."

My true self

Halloween is a day for disguises and costumes, for wearing masks that hide the real self. Children will be out on the street, pretending to be what they are not. But it's always easy to see through them.

Today's reading also shows the real face behind the false one. I always think of Pharisees as hypocrites at best, or dangerous enemies of Jesus at worst. But when a real threat appears, it's Pharisees who come to warn Jesus, urging him to escape.

I find this surprising, but not as much as I find it encouraging. After all, if Pharisees can drop their facade, then maybe I, who can successfully wear my disguise of modern, up-to-date sophisticate, can reveal my true self, too.

**Lord, help me find the courage to show the person
behind the mask.**

One Sabbath Jesus went to eat a meal at the home of one of the leading Pharisees; and people were watching Jesus closely. A man whose legs and arms were swollen came to Jesus, and Jesus spoke up and asked the teachers of the Law and the Pharisees, "Does our Law allow healing on the Sabbath or not?"

But they would not say a thing. Jesus took the man, healed him, and sent him away. Then he said to them, "If any one of you had a child or an ox that happened to fall in a well on a Sabbath, would you not pull it out at once on the Sabbath itself?"

But they were not able to answer him about this.

Luke 14: 1-6

> "...on the Sabbath itself?"

Sabbath time

Every day Gloria is haunted by what happened. Her daughter, Cindy, had come home late one Saturday night, and had been drinking. The family always went to mass together, but that time Cindy wanted to sleep in. Gloria was not going to let her 'get away' with that. "If you are going to live in our house, you will do what I tell you," she said as she stormed off to mass.

When Gloria returned home, Cindy had packed her bag and was gone. That was three years ago; since then, her brief phone calls come from all over the country.

Oh, if only she could take those words back. There is scarcely an hour of the day she does not pray for her little girl. She meant well, but....

God, help me to remember that you love mercy
more than the law.

"**H**appy are those who know they are spiritually poor; the kingdom of heaven belongs to them! Happy are those who mourn; God will comfort them! Happy are those who are humble; they will receive what God has promised! Happy are those whose greatest desire is to do what God requires; God will satisfy them fully! Happy are those who are merciful to others; God will be merciful to them! Happy are the pure in heart; they will see God! Happy are those who work for peace; God will call them his children! Happy are those who are persecuted because they do what God requires; the kingdom of heaven belongs to them! Happy are you when people insult you and persecute you…. Be happy and glad, for a great reward is kept for you in heaven." *Matthew 5: 1-12*

"Happy are the pure in heart…"

A wake-up call

I work in a busy downtown high school where tensions often run high. I tend to see my job, and sometimes my whole life, as a series of "tasks" to accomplish: responsibilities at work, coaching duties, my elderly parents' illness, my children's swimming lessons. I get frustrated when I compare the daily balancing act in my life to the lot of those whose lives seem calm and stress-free.

The beatitudes are my wake-up call. They help me recognize what is important. I particularly like the one that reads, "Happy are the pure in heart; they will see God!" It reminds me to keep my focus on the still, quiet centre where I meet the One who gives purpose to all my activities.

Lord, help me to be single-hearted in all that I do.

The Lord is merciful and loving,
      slow to become angry and full of constant love....
      As a father is kind to his children,
so the Lord is kind to those who honour him.
He knows what we are made of;
he remembers that we are dust.
As for us, our life is like grass.
We grow and flourish like a wild flower;
then the wind blows on it, and it is gone –
no one sees it again.
But for those who honour the Lord,
his love lasts forever,
and his goodness endures for all generations.   *Psalm 103: 8-18*

"He knows what we are made of…"

An everlasting love

I put it down to middle age: I'm much more observant of the natural world than I was before. Though I haven't felt compelled to learn their botanical names, I find I'm more aware of vibrant colours of petals, the pattern of trees in stark silhouette, or the determined shoots forcing their way through cracks in paved pathways. I now feel the total inadequacy of the word "golden" to describe the last of the leaves as they tumble and spin in autumn gusts.

Although today's psalm underlines the relative shortness of life, I find it strangely comforting. I'm reminded that God's love is neither increased nor diminished by my particular failures or successes. Like the wind carrying autumn leaves, God's love will continue to carry me – now, and in times to come.

**Dear God, help me discover the mystery of your love
hidden in the wonder of your creation.**

L ord, I have given up my pride
and turned away from my arrogance.
I am not concerned with great matters
or with subjects too difficult for me.
Instead, I am content and at peace.
As a child lies quietly in its mother's arms,
so my heart is quiet within me.
Israel, trust in the Lord
now and forever!

Psalm 131: 1-3

"As a child lies quietly in its mother's arms..."

Giving over

What a lovely feeling it is to have a child fall asleep in my arms. My girls are too big for that now, so it's a pleasure to spend time with my neighbour's one-year-old son for the afternoon. We play together far past nap time. Then, without warning, his tiny arms circle my neck and he doesn't let go. His head nuzzles its way onto my shoulder. Within moments, he is asleep.

It is a pleasure to share this sudden stillness. I feel blessed by this moment of unexpected tranquility. I wonder if God yearns to hold me this way?

Today I will try to quiet my soul, to let go of the worries of the moment, and to give myself over to the possibility of peace.

**Loving God, help me let go of my worries
to find a place of rest with you.**

I n the full assembly I will praise you for what you have done;
in the presence of those who worship you
I will offer the sacrifices I promised.
The poor will eat as much as they want;
those who come to the Lord will praise him.
May they prosper forever!
All nations will remember the Lord.
From every part of the world they will turn to him;
all races will worship him.
The Lord is king,
and he rules the nations.
All proud people will bow down to him;
all mortals will bow down before him.   *Psalm 22: 25-31*

"The poor will eat as much as they want…"

An end to hunger

Today's psalm represents a world where the poor will get to eat their fill.

A few years ago, in Vancouver, delegates to the United Nations' Third World Urban Forum learned that one billion people – roughly one-third of the world's urban population – live in slums. This is nearly the same percentage – but now a greater number – of people living in urban slums and squatter communities when the same group met in Vancouver in 1976.

What has changed in thirty years? Today, the rich countries are richer, and the poor are poorer. What can I do to help move my world to become one where "the poor will eat as much as they want"?

**Lord, help those who work for justice not to lose hope
in their efforts to build a world that shares its wealth.**

"Those who come to me cannot be my disciples unless they love me more than they love father and mother, wife and children, brothers and sisters, and themselves as well. Those who do not carry their own cross and come after me cannot be my disciples. If one of you is planning to build a tower, you sit down first and figure out what it will cost, to see if you have enough money to finish the job. If you don't, you will not be able to finish the tower after laying the foundation; and all who see what happened will make fun of you. 'You began to build but can't finish the job!'

"In the same way," concluded Jesus, "none of you can be my disciple unless you give up everything you have." *Luke 14: 25-33*

"...unless you give up everything you have."

Letting go

I remember when my little brother took his first step. He let go of my hand and tottered towards another pair of outstretched hands. It was a day of celebration!

Learning to swim, I was afraid to take my feet off the bottom, but one day I suddenly did. What a joy to discover my body was buoyant!

This letting go of what gives me security – to discover new freedom – is a lifelong invitation. Jesus challenges me to let go of everything that prevents me from growing in relationship with God – a particular friendship, my need to be in control, my comfortable routine.

Change will be painful. It will "cost," but ultimately it will lead me to new freedom and joy.

Lord, still my heart. May I recognize where you are calling me to greater freedom today.

The Pharisees and the teachers of the Law started grumbling, "This man welcomes outcasts and even eats with them!" So Jesus told them this parable:

"Suppose one of you has a hundred sheep and loses one of them – what do you do? You leave the other ninety-nine sheep in the pasture and go looking for the one that got lost…. When you find it, you are so happy that you put it on your shoulders and carry it back home. Then you call your friends and neighbours together and say to them, 'I am so happy I found my lost sheep. Let us celebrate!' In the same way, I tell you, there will be more joy in heaven over one sinner who repents than over ninety-nine respectable people who do not need to repent."

Luke 15: 1-10

"I am so happy, I found my lost sheep."

Calling out to God

"Mommy! Where are you?" While out walking, my husband and I hear a young boy's sobs. His cries become more intense the longer he is lost. Fortunately, and to our great relief, we turn the corner to see his mother tucking him safely into her arms.

As time passes, how unfortunate that I hesitate before calling out for guidance. Unlike the little boy, I wear myself out trying to do things on my own. Then, as a last resort, I call out to God for help.

How thankful I am that God cares enough to come looking for me. Yet, in a world that stresses self-sufficiency, do I have the dependence of a child? God knows my voice. Will I call out in times of need?

**Lord, help me call out to you,
rather than relying on my own strength.**

Keep on imitating me, my friends. Pay attention to those who follow the right example that we have set for you. I have told you this many times before, and now I repeat it with tears: there are many whose lives make them enemies of Christ's death on the cross. They are going to end up in hell.... They are proud of what they should be ashamed of, and they think only of things that belong to this world. We, however, are citizens of heaven, and we eagerly wait for our Saviour, the Lord Jesus Christ, to come from heaven....

So then, my friends, how dear you are to me and how I miss you! How happy you make me, and how proud I am of you! – this, dear friends, is how you should stand firm in your life in the Lord.

Philippians 3: 17-21; 4: 1

"Keep on imitating me, my friends."

Be like me?

Would I actually encourage others to imitate me? As a parent, if I ask my children to imitate me, what traits should they imitate? Should they imitate my disorganization, or the way I make the same mistakes, over and over again? Should they imitate the way I unfairly snap at others when I'm overtired? The way I lose my temper when I've cut the board the wrong length?

What behaviours, what attitudes do I want my children to imitate? Well, perhaps these: when someone needs help, I try to be there. When I fall down, I get back up and try again. And when I see others fall, I realize they're just like me.

If my children can learn these lessons by imitating me, maybe I've done well.

Dear Lord, help me be a person whom my children can emulate.

"**A**nd so I tell you: make friends for yourselves with worldly wealth, so that when it gives out, you will be welcomed in the eternal home. Whoever is faithful in small matters will be faithful in large ones; whoever is dishonest in small matters will be dishonest in large ones. If, then, you have not been faithful in handling worldly wealth, how can you be trusted with true wealth? And if you have not been faithful with what belongs to someone else, who will give you what belongs to you?

"No servant can be the slave of two masters; such a slave will hate one and love the other or will be loyal to one and despise the other. You cannot serve both God and money."

Luke 16: 9-15

"You cannot serve both God and money."

Which master?

Here we are in our consumption-driven culture: get the big house, get the satellite, get the SUV. Don't forget the condo in Florida. Meanwhile, the spouse has become a stranger, and the kids are left adrift. No one can serve two masters.

My friend's daughter started to fall off the rails: marks falling, unhappy, directionless. She was losing her.

So the mother quit her job. Sold the house, and took her daughter to Asia. Showed her poverty, people's desperate struggle to live.

The daughter is now studying medicine in order to go back. The laughter returned; the meaning returned.

No one can serve two masters. This woman served the right one. There's a lesson in that for me.

**Dear God, help me search for what's important,
and to know to ignore what's not.**

The man led me back to the entrance of the Temple. Water was coming out from under the entrance and flowing east, the direction the Temple faced.... He said to me, "This water flows through the land to the east and down into the Jordan Valley and to the Dead Sea. When it flows into the Dead Sea, it replaces the salt water of that sea with fresh water. Wherever the stream flows, there will be all kinds of animals and fish. The stream will make the water of the Dead Sea fresh, and wherever it flows, it will bring life.... On each bank of the stream all kinds of trees will grow to provide food. Their leaves will never wither, and they will never stop bearing fruit... because they are watered by the stream that flows from the Temple." *Ezekiel 47: 1-2, 8-9, 12*

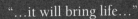

"...it will bring life..."

Faced with loss

A few summers ago I stood on a hill high above the village of Quidi Vidi in my native Newfoundland. Everything was still under the blue sky: the small boats, the piles of nets, the water itself.

My chest heaved as I remembered busier, noisier, happier times when cod nourished our bodies and nurtured our souls. I thought of my cousins Jim, Steve and Jerry, men with calloused hands who knew every rock and underwater ledge, but who will never fish again. Then I felt like the loss was unbearable.

I've mourned in this way every summer for a decade now. Looking at the Atlantic Ocean, I want to cling to hope, but it's very hard in the face of such stillness.

God, help me to remember that you are with your earth, your water and your people at all times.

Jesus said to his disciples, "Things that make people fall into sin are bound to happen, but how terrible for the one who makes them happen! It would be better for him if he were thrown into the sea than for him to cause one of these little ones to sin....

"If your brother sins, rebuke him, and if he repents, forgive him. If he sins against you seven times in one day, and each time he comes to you saying, 'I repent,' you must forgive him."

The apostles said to the Lord, "Make our faith greater." The Lord answered, "If you had faith as big as a mustard seed, you could say to this mulberry tree, 'Pull yourself up by the roots and plant yourself in the sea!' and it would obey you."

Luke 17: 1-6

> "...and if he repents, forgive him."

Learning to forgive

Forgive someone seven times in one day? You must be kidding! That's hardly fair! My obnoxious relative/colleague/neighbour needs to be taught a lesson! I don't want to be seen as a doormat!

So often my children are my best teachers. My twelve-year-old daughter has a friend who frequently provokes arguments or leaves in a huff when the game isn't turning out in her favour. Inevitably, the next day she's back on our doorstep, wanting to "be friends" again. And, sometimes to my considerable amazement, Sarah never fails to welcome her back ungrudgingly. She clearly values their underlying friendship enough to overlook her friend's faults.

Would that I were always so accepting and forgiving of the faults in others!

**O Lord, whose forgiveness is beyond measure,
help me to see others through your eyes.**

"Suppose one of you has a servant who is plowing or looking after the sheep. When he comes in from the field, do you tell him to hurry along and eat his meal? Of course not! Instead, you say to him, 'Get my supper ready, then put on your apron and wait on me while I eat and drink; after that you may have your meal.' The servant does not deserve thanks for obeying orders, does he? It is the same with you; when you have done all you have been told to do, say, 'We are ordinary servants; we have only done our duty.'"

Luke 17:7-10

> "...we have only done our duty."

Our duty

At school, when I ask a student to do some small job – carrying a set of books back to the book room, taking a note to the office, stapling some papers – it is not uncommon to hear, "What will you give me?" or "What's in it for me?"

I know parents who say to their children, "If you're good, we'll go to McDonald's." After my son's soccer game, he expects me to buy him a treat. Why does there always have to be a tangible reward?

When I tell my children or my students that "Virtue is its own reward," they stare at me blankly. What, no pizza party, no ice cream? "Duty" has become a dirty word, but is it not my duty to love and serve others – without expecting a reward?

Lord, let me do something for someone else today, expecting no reward.

Jesus was going into a village when he was met by ten men suffering from a dreaded skin disease. They stood at a distance and shouted, "Jesus! Master! Have pity on us!"

Jesus saw them and said to them, "Go and let the priests examine you." On the way they were made clean. When one of them saw that he was healed, he came back, praising God in a loud voice. He threw himself to the ground at Jesus' feet and thanked him. The man was a Samaritan. Jesus spoke up, "There were ten who were healed; where are the other nine? Why is this foreigner the only one who came back to give thanks to God?" And Jesus said to him, "Get up and go; your faith has made you well."

Luke 17: 11-19

> "...he came back, praising God in a loud voice."

Giving thanks

I have four children who take me for granted. As I tend to their needs, my efforts, though appreciated, are unacknowledged. Yet occasionally, in the middle of a meal, my four-year old will say, "Thank you, Mom, for making this meal!" It is a grace-filled moment for me – as he offers his pure and simple gratitude, and I respond to his thanks with a smile and a hug.

Jesus must have felt taken for granted, too. He was expected to heal the sick, and he did so. Yet the one who returned had a gift for Jesus. His gratitude touched Jesus, who was moved to praise him.

Remembering to give thanks is a way I can touch the heart of others.

**Lord, create in me a grateful heart,
both as I offer thanks and as I receive it.**

The Lord always keeps his promises;
he judges in favour of the oppressed
and gives food to the hungry.
The Lord sets prisoners free
and gives sight to the blind.
He lifts those who have fallen;
he loves his righteous people.
He protects the strangers who live in our land;
he helps widows and orphans,
but takes the wicked to their ruin.
The Lord is king forever.
Your God, O Zion, will reign for all time.

Psalm 146: 6-10

"The Lord always keep his promises…"

Broken promises

Today's psalm makes me nervous. As a U.S. citizen, I know that we have broken every promise made to our Native American brothers and sisters. Today, too many are hungry and lack adequate health care – in this land of plenty.

And, unlike God, we seem determined *not* to set prisoners free, labelling them 'enemy combatants' and imprisoning them without any right to appeal. We debate immigration reform – less interested in "protecting the strangers in our land" than in blaming them for having the same aspirations we do. We cut social programs, often leaving today's "widows and orphans" in peril. Yet, as a nation we, even our leaders, often take pride in worshipping God.

Reading today's psalm, I worry that maybe we're worshipping some god other than this God.

God, let my actions, privately and publicly, reflect the God you are.

"As it was in the time of Noah so shall it be in the days of the Son of Man. Everybody kept on eating and drinking, and men and women married, up to the very day Noah went into the boat and the flood came and killed them all. It will be as it was in the time of Lot. Everybody kept on eating and drinking, buying and selling, planting and building. On the day Lot left Sodom, fire and sulphur rained down from heaven and killed them all. That is how it will be on the day the Son of Man is revealed.

"On that day someone who is on the roof of a house must not go down into the house to get any belongings; in the same way anyone who is out in the field must not go back to the house. Those who try to save their own life will lose it; those who lose their life will save it."

Luke 17: 26-37

"...on the day the Son of Man is revealed."

Opportunity knocks

Eating and drinking are good. So is marrying. Buying and selling, planting and building are all necessary aspects of life. But it's so easy to get caught up in my everyday busyness and forget what really matters in life.

Usually it takes a crisis to get my attention. In today's reading, the floodwaters and the rainstorm of fire and sulphur got people's attention. For me, my husband's death made me search for meaning. A prolonged period of illness has slowed me down, making me consider the choices I was making.

Whatever the crisis, it's often an opportunity that I'm being offered. And, in that opportunity, I can discover the deeper truth revealed in Jesus – albeit in a challenging way.

Dear God, may I learn that what I perceive as crisis is, in fact, an opportunity to discover your love in a new way.

327

Jesus told his disciples a parable to teach them that they should always pray and never become discouraged. "In a certain town there was a judge who neither feared God nor respected people. And there was a widow in that same town who kept coming to him and pleading for her rights. For a long time the judge refused to act, but at last he said to himself, 'Because of all the trouble this widow is giving me, I will see to it that she gets her rights. If I don't, she will keep on coming and finally wear me out!'"

And the Lord continued, "Now, will God not judge in favour of his own people who cry to him day and night for help?"

Luke 18: 1-8

> "I will see to it that she gets her rights."

Gutsy determination

In biblical times, "widows and orphans" were understood to be the vulnerable ones, those needing care and protection by others (usually males) in society. But here, in today's reading, a widow stands up for her rights and her request is met by a corrupt (male) judge! What an example of gutsy determination!

I think of the women who have spoken up for their rights and for the rights of others. Not for what they might want or need – but for their *rights*. The right to vote. The right to walk on city streets in safety. The right for them and their children to live without fear of abuse in their homes. The right to be full, contributing members of their church communities.

I hope to learn from their example.

**Dear God, give me the courage to ask –
not for my needs or wants – but that my rights be met.**

There is no need to write you, friends, about the times and occasions when these things will happen. For you yourselves know very well that the Day of the Lord will come as a thief comes at night. When people say, "Everything is quiet and safe," then suddenly destruction will hit them! It will come as suddenly as the pains that come upon a woman in labour, and people will not escape. But you, friends, are not in the darkness, and the Day should not take you by surprise like a thief. All of you are people who belong to the light, who belong to the day. We do not belong to the night or to the darkness. So then, we should not be sleeping like the others; we should be awake and sober.

I Thessalonians 5: 1-6

"...will come as a thief comes at night."

When death comes

At age thirty-six my husband was told he had a brain tumour and had six to twelve months to live. While the actual moment of death would come "like a thief in the night," he knew that he had only a few months left with his family.

He could have spent that time being angry; instead he spent it *preparing* for the time when he would no longer be with us. Among other house-related projects, he arranged to have the foundation mended and the roof re-shingled!

As the end drew near, my husband helped with the funeral arrangements: planning the funeral liturgy, even choosing the gravesite and headstone with me. Knowing death was near made him want to do whatever he could to make life easier for others.

**Loving God, help me to live each moment of my life
with love and compassion – as if it were my last.**

A s Jesus was coming near Jericho, there was a blind man sitting by the road. When he heard the crowd passing by, he asked, "What is this?"

"Jesus of Nazareth," they told him. He cried out, "Jesus! Son of David! Have mercy on me!" The people told him to be quiet. But he shouted even more loudly, "Son of David! Have mercy on me!" So Jesus ordered the blind man to be brought to him. When he came near, Jesus asked him, "What do you want me to do for you?"

"Sir," he answered, "I want to see again." Jesus said to him, "Then see! Your faith has made you well." At once he was able to see, and he followed Jesus, giving thanks to God. When the crowd saw it, they all praised God. *Luke 18: 35-43*

"Your faith has made you well."

A healing faith

If it's possible, Jessa's prayers were even more startling than this blind man's persistent cries. Last spring, during her junior year in college, Jessa died of cystic fibrosis. She knew death was coming – and sooner rather than later. Like the blind man, Jessa, too, called out to Jesus.

At the campus memorial service, several friends offered remembrances of her. Two of them read prayers written in Jessa's journal just months before she died. I was amazed. Jessa did not pray to be miraculously healed. She sought a deeper miracle: to see life through eyes of hope and gratitude.

As I listened to all who shared memories of her, I knew that Jessa, too, had heard Jesus say to her, "Your faith has made you well."

**Jesus, shape my prayers so that I, too,
long for what will truly make me well.**

Th
here was a chief tax collector named Zacchaeus.... He was trying to see who Jesus was, but he was a little man and could not see Jesus because of the crowd. So he ran ahead and climbed a sycamore tree to see Jesus.... When Jesus came to that place, he looked up and said, "Hurry down, Zacchaeus, because I must stay in your house today."

Zacchaeus hurried down and welcomed him with great joy. The people started grumbling, "This man has gone as a guest to the home of a sinner!" Zacchaeus said to the Lord, "Listen, sir! I will give half my belongings to the poor, and if I have cheated anyone, I will pay back four times as much."

Jesus said, "The Son of Man came to seek and to save the lost."

Luke 19: 1-10

"...I must stay in your house today."

There's hope for me, too

It's hard not to love Zacchaeus, the little guy up in the tree, surprised by grace. "Hurry down, Zacchaeus, because I must stay in your house today."

And yet, as far as his people were concerned, Zacchaeus was a traitor, an enemy collaborator. He collected taxes for the hated oppressors.

Zacchaeus gives me hope. Even if I've failed people who depended on me, even if I've cheated and betrayed them the way Zacchaeus did – even then I can be surprised by God's grace. I believe that if I keep trying to catch a glimpse of Jesus, God will reach out to me. I will find that the Lord has come to stay, and my life will never be the same again.

Lord, come and stay with me today.
I believe that you will transform my life.

Praise the Lord!
Praise God in his Temple!
Praise his strength in heaven!
Praise him for the mighty things he has done.
Praise his supreme greatness.
Praise him with trumpets.
Praise him with harps and lyres.
Praise him with drums and dancing.
Praise him with harps and flutes.
Praise him with cymbals.
Praise him with loud cymbals.
Praise the Lord, all living creatures!
Praise the Lord!

Psalm 150: 1-6

> "Praise the Lord, all living creatures!"

Praise the Lord!

Today's psalm describes a celebration of praise that is so good, even the animals join in with the musicians. It sounds like a Narnian party!

But when we take the time to notice it, we see that the animals are always praising God. They can't help it. An animal's praise is extinguished only when a species is extinguished.

Today, conservative estimates of the effects of global warming on animals suggest a loss of between 15 and 37 per cent of all species.

That's losing a lot of praise if we don't take the first steps to care for our world. What would it take, for example, to live up to the minimum requirements of the Kyoto accord? To surpass them?

Lord, give me the wisdom and the courage to accept responsibility for creation.

Thursday | NOVEMBER 20

Jesus came closer to the city, and when he saw it, he wept over it, saying, "If you only knew today what is needed for peace! But now you cannot see it! The time will come when your enemies will surround you with barricades, blockade you, and close in on you from every side. They will completely destroy you and the people within your walls; not a single stone will they leave in its place, because you did not recognize the time when God came to save you!"

Luke 19: 41-44

"If you only knew today what is needed for peace!"

A fragile peace

The headlines scream with the daily litanies of violence. Each newscast keeps score of the number of Palestinians and Israelis injured and killed. As yet another plan for peace evolves, it is likely to be exploded by a suicide bomber or intercepted with a volley of shots from a helicopter gunship.

Jesus offered a dire warning to the people of Jerusalem. What he said then, remains a timeless plea *today* as we search for ways to change. He challenged his followers to look for the hand of God amid the violence and the rhetoric, the rubble and the bloodstains.

And, as a would-be disciple today, I am equally responsible for nurturing this fragile, yet essential, peace.

Inspired by Saint Francis, may I become an instrument of peace – in this time of uncertainty and violence.

Jesus went into the Temple and began to drive out the merchants, saying to them, "It is written in the Scriptures that God said, 'My Temple will be a house of prayer.' But you have turned it into a hideout for thieves!"

Every day Jesus taught in the Temple. The chief priests, the teachers of the Law, and the leaders of the people wanted to kill him, but they could not find a way to do it, because all the people kept listening to him, not wanting to miss a single word.

Luke 19: 45-48

"Every day Jesus taught in the Temple."

Religion and politics

We had a guest preacher at our church one morning. His sermon blasted the provincial government's process of negotiating a treaty with the province's native bands. After the service a number of people were visibly angry.

"He shouldn't mix religion and politics," they said. I wonder if they read the same Bible as I do. Jesus overturned the traders' tables in the Temple. And it wasn't just a hit-and-run protest. "Every day," Luke says, "Jesus taught in the Temple."

For sheer political audacity, a comparison today would be someone going to Afghanistan, while the Taliban still had supreme power, to stand in a public square and openly accuse them of wrongdoing. Such a prophet probably wouldn't last long. Neither did Jesus.

God, give me the courage to say what you call me to say, regardless of personal risk.

Some Sadducees, who say that people will not rise from death, came to Jesus....

Jesus said to them, "The men and women of this age marry, but the men and women who are worthy to rise from death and live in the age to come will not then marry. They will be like angels and cannot die. They are the children of God, because they have risen from death. And Moses clearly proves that the dead are raised to life. In the passage about the burning bush he speaks of the Lord as 'the God of Abraham, the God of Isaac, and the God of Jacob.' He is the God of the living, not of the dead, for to him all are alive."

Some of the teachers of the Law spoke up, "A good answer, Teacher!"

Luke 20: 27-40

"He is the God of the living, not of the dead..."

God of the living

For a while after my parents died, my youngest child would sometimes ask me what they were doing.

I have puzzled over the meaning of death and agonized over its silent mystery for years. But I had no hesitation or uncertainty when I answered him: "I don't know everything, but I do know they are watching over you. They see you every day and look on you with love and pride. They are still part of your life."

These words comforted him, I know. But they were not empty words meant to make a young boy feel less sad. I felt them to be true in a way I could not really understand myself. His grandparents were not dead and gone. They were living and here.

Lord, the life you have given is an unfathomable mystery. Help me live fully each day.

"The King will say, 'Come, you that are blessed by my Father! Come and possess the kingdom.... I was hungry and you fed me, thirsty and you gave me a drink; I was a stranger and you received me in your homes, naked and you clothed me; I was sick and you took care of me, in prison and you visited me.' The righteous will then answer him, 'When, Lord, did we ever see you hungry and feed you, or thirsty and give you a drink? When did we ever see you a stranger and welcome you in our homes, or naked and clothe you? When did we ever see you sick or in prison, and visit you?' The King will reply, 'I tell you, whenever you did this for one of the least important of these followers of mine, you did it for me.'"

Matthew 25: 31-46

> "When did we ever see you a stranger...?"

Habits of the heart

Sometimes people don't see the good they do. Maybe the habit of love becomes so ingrained, they don't even know they're being good anymore.

Growing up, I never noticed it in my mother. Like the people in today's reading, I imagine her saying: "Lord, when did we ever see you hungry...?" Yet, when someone died, she'd be making egg salad sandwiches. If a neighbour's spouse walked, they'd be sitting at our kitchen table. If the husband of the woman down the street drank the grocery money, she'd say: "Here's a little something until payday."

If someone complimented her, she'd reply: "I'm only doing what I'm supposed to do." Her favourite prayer: "Oh Lord, I am not worthy...." Guess what, Mom? I disagree; I think you were very worthy.

**Lord, help me give of myself in little ways,
so helping others becomes a habit.**

J esus looked around and saw rich people dropping their gifts in the Temple treasury, and he also saw a very poor widow dropping in two little copper coins. He said, "I tell you that this poor widow put in more than all the others. For the others offered their gifts from what they had to spare of their riches; but she, poor as she is, gave all she had to live on."

Luke 21: 1-4

"...she, poor as she is, gave all she had to live on."

Give till it hurts

I have a friend, a now-retired bicycle racer, who knows about giving every ounce. John is a man of faith, although not a religious man.

He once had a dream to have a traditional brick oven in his yard, and he set about building it. When half-finished, he said to me, "There's a reason I'm building this. I don't know what it is yet, but it's there." The oven is now the centre of the neighbourhood.

Like the widow who followed the call to give, John follows his call. And like her, he is rich in ways the world does not understand. He teaches me that when we give everything, be it money or effort, we are truly, truly alive.

Lord, help me to give till it hurts.

Some of the disciples were talking about the Temple, how beautiful it looked with its fine stones and the gifts offered to God. Jesus said, "All this you see – the time will come when not a single stone here will be left in its place; every one will be thrown down."

"Teacher," they asked, "when will this be? And what will happen in order to show that the time has come for it to take place?"

Jesus said, "Watch out; don't be fooled. Many men, claiming to speak for me, will come and say, 'I am he!' and, 'The time has come!' But don't follow them. Don't be afraid when you hear of wars and revolutions; such things must happen first, but they do not mean that the end is near."

Luke 21: 5-11

"...not a single stone here will be left in its place."

Seeking the eternal

Recently my son and I went to a museum of science and technology. There were the predictable "old" things: steam engines, the first cars, old telephones. But when I came to the display on the history of computers, I saw a Commodore 64 under glass! The Commodore 64 was one of the first PCs – 20 million were made, and the company no longer exists.

As I get older, I begin to see things that were once important passing away or being destroyed, and I am left wondering: What never passes away? What is eternal?

The disciples heard that the stones of the Temple would someday "be thrown down." Today's throw-away world is even more vulnerable to collapse and decay, and so I seek what is eternal.

**Dear Lord, in this rapidly changing world,
help me hold onto what is eternal.**

S ing a new song to the Lord;
   he has done wonderful things!
   By his own power and holy strength
he has won the victory.
The Lord announced his victory;
he made his saving power known to the nations.
He kept his promise to the people of Israel
with loyalty and constant love for them....
Roar, sea, and every creature in you;
sing, earth, and all who live on you!
Clap your hands, you rivers;
you hills, sing together with joy before the Lord,
because he comes to rule the earth.   *Psalm 98: 1-3, 7-9*

"Roar, sea, and every creature in you..."

Speaking from the heart

"Today's lesson is on the importance of finding your voice. This is important for all writers in order that their work be authentic...."

Often I go through stages of trying on other people's voices. While this is an interesting exercise, until I find my own way of expressing myself, my writing lacks heart and cannot touch others as it might.

I feel the same way about prayer. I am very good at reciting prayers that others have written. I appreciate the work that has gone into them, and I recognize the comfort and insight that come from them. However, I need to be comfortable and confident in talking to God heart-to-heart – in my own voice.

**Dear God, help me to find a way to tell you
all that is in my heart.**

"When you see Jerusalem surrounded by armies, then you will know that it will soon be destroyed…. Terrible distress will come upon this land, and God's punishment will fall on this people….

"There will be strange things happening to the sun, the moon, and the stars. On earth whole countries will be in despair, afraid of the roar of the sea and the raging tides. People will faint from fear as they wait for what is coming over the whole earth, for the powers in space will be driven from their courses. Then the Son of Man will appear, coming in a cloud with great power and glory. When these things begin to happen, stand up and raise your heads, because your salvation is near."

Luke 21: 20-28

> "…stand up and raise your heads…"

Facing death

When I saw the blockbuster movie *Titanic*, I marvelled at the cinematography and special effects. But what stirred my emotions most deeply was sharing the final moments of people's lives.

Faced with imminent death, I wonder how I would react. Would I curl up in despair, or be moved by compassion for others? Would I faint with fear, race into frenzied panic, or calmly stand and await my fate?

Perhaps it depends on my behaviour throughout my whole life. Have I waited for others to rescue me? Have I used my energy and intelligence to advance only my own interests? Have I cared deeply for others and placed my faith in God's saving power? The answers may predict how I would act in a crisis.

**Lord of Life, teach me to live today
as if it were my last day on earth.**

d them this parable: "Think of the fig tree and all
es. When you see their leaves beginning to ap-
ow that summer is near. In the same way, when
happening, you will know that the kingdom of
e. Remember that all these things will take place
v living have all died. Heaven and earth will pass
vill never pass away."

Luke 21: 29-33

vill never pass away."

Recently a friend introduced me to *Paradise
Lost* by John Milton. Writing over 300 years
ago, the poet grapples with the reality of good and evil and tries to
understand "the ways of God."

I was struck by the fact that the questions Milton asks are questions we continue to ask today – questions of life's meaning, of love,
of justice. Why do these questions endure? Similarly, why will Jesus'
words never pass away?

I stop and consider the questions I ask and the words I use. And
I wonder, after I die, what will my friends and family remember? Will
they remember words of love and encouragement, or words of anger
and criticism? What words of mine "will never pass away"?

**Lord, may I strain to hear your words of love. May they shape
the words I speak and the decisions I make today.**

T he angel showed me the river of the water of life, sparkling like crystal, and coming from the throne of God and of the Lamb and flowing down the middle of the city's street. On each side of the river was the tree of life, which bears fruit twelve times a year… and its leaves are for the healing of the nations. Nothing that is under God's curse will be found in the city.

The throne of God and of the Lamb will be in the city, and his servants will worship him. They will see his face, and his name will be written on their foreheads. There shall be no more night, and they will not need lamps or sunlight, because the Lord God will be their light, and they will rule as kings forever and ever.   *Revelation 22: 1-7*

"…the Lord God will be their light…"

God's light

Do you know what real darkness is like? When I was very small, we had no electricity on our farm. On long winter nights we depended on coal oil lamps and a gas lantern for light. There was barely enough light for cleaning eggs, or darning socks, or doing homework at the kitchen table.

And if I needed something from my bedroom, I ascended the stairs into true darkness – the kind where unknown forces lurked under beds and monsters waited in the closets.

As a grown-up, I've had to face new monsters: loneliness, financial problems, ill-health. What if I accepted God's bright light and let it shine upstairs and downstairs, under the bed and into the closets of my life, to help dispel my fears?

Lord, let your light shine in my life. Let me see clearly.

"**H**eaven and earth will pass away, but my words will never pass away. No one knows, however, when that day or hour will come – neither the angels in heaven, nor the Son…. Be on watch, be alert, for you do not know when the time will come. It will be like a man who goes away from home on a trip and leaves his servants in charge, after giving to each one his own work to do and after telling the doorkeeper to keep watch. Watch, then, because you do not know when the master of the house is coming – it might be in the evening or at midnight or before dawn or at sunrise. If he comes suddenly, he must not find you asleep. What I say to you, then, I say to all: Watch!"   *Mark 13: 31-37*

> "…you do not know when the time will come."

Choose life… today

When Frances learned she had cancer and had only a few months to live, the news changed her life. She let go of activities and possessions and took time for relationships. She now realized they were the most important things in her life. I visited her in hospital, after she had outlived the doctor's prediction. "These are gift days," she said with a bright smile.

Frances taught me a lot about being expectant and alert, as Jesus counsels me to be in today's reading.

If this were the last day of my life, I would want to take time for relationships, treating people more kindly, giving thanks for this day as a gift and being alert for signs of God's coming. What's stopping me from doing that today?

**Lord, help me awaken to the reality of your love
and the gift of my life today.**

When Jesus entered Capernaum, a Roman officer met him and begged for help: "Sir, my servant is sick in bed at home, unable to move and suffering terribly."

"I will go and make him well," Jesus said.

"Oh no, sir," answered the officer. "I do not deserve to have you come into my house. Just give the order, and my servant will get well. I, too, am a man under the authority of superior officers, and I have soldiers under me. I order this one, 'Go!' and he goes...."

When Jesus heard this, he was surprised and said to the people following him, "I tell you, I have never found anyone in Israel with faith like this...." Jesus said to the officer, "Go home, and what you believe will be done for you." *Matthew 8: 5-11, 13*

"I do not deserve to have you come into my house."

Beyond divisions

This story, a couple of millennia later, strikes me as rather charming. But think of it: the officer belongs to the occupying force; he's the enemy. Now he's asking the local prophet for a favour. And, *voilà!* It's done for him. What does this say about "us" and "them"?

Years ago, I got into a fight with a kid who was the outsider. After that fight, we seemed to get along, but I found myself criticized by my friends for talking to him. After all, he was "the enemy."

We like it that way: us and them. Good guys and bad. It's a hard thing Jesus asks of me – to go beyond these divisions, to love my enemies. A very hard thing.

**Lord, help me be open to all people,
even when they've hurt me.**

J esus was filled with joy by the Holy Spirit and said, "Father, Lord of heaven and earth! I thank you because you have shown to the unlearned what you have hidden from the wise and learned. Yes, Father, this was how you were pleased to have it happen.

"My Father has given me all things. No one knows who the Son is except the Father, and no one knows who the Father is except the Son and those to whom the Son chooses to reveal him."

Then Jesus turned to the disciples and said to them privately, "How fortunate you are to see the things you see! I tell you that many prophets and kings wanted to see what you see, but they could not, and to hear what you hear, but they did not."

Luke 10: 21-24

"…because you have shown to the unlearned…"

From the heart

At a L'Arche farm, George lived with Gord, a man with a developmental disability. George saved his money to buy a handsome pair of leather boots which he left by the door to wear to church.

One Sunday morning he was dismayed to discover the boots had disappeared, and he was furious to find Gord at work in the chicken pen – wearing his boots! Gord was very sorry. "Say it's okay, George," he pleaded. But George was too angry.

After several days, Gord became morose and despondent. George had never met anyone who so simply asked for forgiveness and so visibly suffered from his refusal to give it. Finally George softened: "It's okay, Gord." In Gord he had discovered a teacher of the heart.

God, help me to be open to the wisdom of those who are often rejected by our world.

J esus said, "I feel sorry for these people, because they have been with me for three days and now have nothing to eat. I don't want to send them away without feeding them, for they might faint on their way home." The disciples asked, "Where will we find enough food in this desert to feed this crowd?"

"How much bread do you have?" Jesus asked. "Seven loaves," they answered, "and a few small fish." Jesus took the seven loaves and the fish, gave thanks to God, broke them, and gave them to the disciples; and the disciples gave them to the people. They all ate and had enough. Then the disciples took up seven baskets full of pieces left over.

Matthew 15: 29-37

"How much bread do you have?"

God will provide

I really don't know what to think about miracles, but today's reading reminds me of my buddy, Riaz. I teach with him; I think he invented math and physics. He's a great guy, very generous.

Riaz is from Pakistan. I told him it's an irony that the best Christian in the place is a Muslim. Whenever anyone needs something, Riaz looks skyward and says, "He will provide."

One day, I had no lunch and Riaz insisted that I take half his sandwich. "Riaz, I don't want to take your lunch!" I protested. "He will provide!" replied Riaz.

The next thing I know, someone doesn't want their salad and someone else gives us fries. We had more food than anyone!

Riaz fed us both on one, little sandwich.

**Lord, let me be as faithful and as generous
as my dear friend, Riaz.**

A day is coming
when the people
will sing this song
in the land of Judah:
Our city is strong!
God himself defends its walls!
Open the city gates
and let the faithful nation enter,
the nation whose people
do what is right.
You, Lord, give perfect peace
to those who keep
their purpose firm
and put their trust in you.
Trust in the Lord forever;
he will always protect us.
He has humbled those
who were proud;
he destroyed the strong city
they lived in,
and sent its walls
crashing into the dust.
Those who were oppressed
walk over it now
and trample it under their feet.

Isaiah 26: 1-6

"… he destroyed the strong city they lived in…"

In times of war

Born in the years following the Second World War, I grew up believing that my generation had managed to escape war. War was scratchy black-and-white films and ever-smaller parades each November 11th.

But Vietnam, the Gulf War and Iraq have forced me to reassess. Each conflict brought sharper, more urgent imagery, culminating in CNN who turned war into prime-time programming with night-vision cameras following lines of bullets tracing the green night sky.

Today's reading, a prayer for divine deliverance in a time of great conflict, is hard to reconcile with the events of this past year. I cannot forget the lines of wounded civilians outside a hospital with no medical equipment, a city in ruins, the little boy without limbs. God, help us indeed when we drag you into our conflicts.

**Dear God, may I find the courage to never defend
the indefensible by invoking your name.**

J esus left that place, and as he walked along, two blind men started following him. "Have mercy on us, Son of David!" they shouted.

When Jesus had gone indoors, the two blind men came to him, and he asked them, "Do you believe that I can heal you?"

"Yes, sir!" they answered.

Then Jesus touched their eyes and said, "Let it happen, then, just as you believe!" – and their sight was restored. Jesus spoke sternly to them, "Don't tell this to anyone!"

But they left and spread the news about Jesus all over that part of the country.   *Matthew 9: 27-31*

"Do you believe that I can heal you?"

Hurt and healing

How did these two men know it was Jesus who was walking by? They couldn't see with their eyes… but they could see with their hearts! Often when we've been hurt – physically or emotionally – we develop a heightened capacity in some other aspect of our selves. Our woundedness makes us aware of the hurts other people are experiencing in their lives.

From within their woundedness, these two men made a choice: they reached out and asked for help. And Jesus responded to their request. He touched their eyes and their sight was restored.

When another person touches us – in love – our hurts are healed. We know ourselves loved and we are made whole. How do I, in my everyday choices, make the world a place of love and healing?

In my woundedness, Lord, help me open myself to your healing touch. Help me to reach out to others who are in pain.

A s Jesus saw the crowds, his heart was filled with pity…. "The harvest is large, but there are few workers to gather it in. Pray to the owner that he will send out workers to gather in his harvest."

Jesus called his twelve disciples together and gave them authority to drive out evil spirits and to heal every disease and every sickness. They were sent out with the following instructions: "Do not go to any Gentile territory or any Samaritan towns. Instead, you are to go to the lost sheep of the people of Israel. Go and preach, 'The kingdom of heaven is near!' Heal the sick, bring the dead back to life, heal those who suffer from dreaded skin diseases, and drive out demons. You have received without paying, so give without being paid."

Matthew 9: 35 – 10: 8

"You have received without paying…"

The Christmas spirit

For several weeks now, I've seen and heard the advertisements. If my family and I are to have the merriest Christmas ever, then I'd better get out there and shop! How our commercial culture has turned the Christmas feast into a beguiling celebration of what money can buy!

Matthew's story releases the Christmas story from its commercial captivity. We hear Jesus reminding the disciples to reach out to others – by sharing of themselves.

In the midst of this Christmas-buying bonanza, what is my gift that I can share with others? A fun day spent with my children – with no distracting errands to run; a couple of hours babysitting for the couple next door; a smile of reassurance to a worried student I pass in the hallway.

God, help me to appreciate your generosity. Grant me the courage and the creativity to share my gifts with others.

I am listening to what
the Lord God is saying;
he promises peace to us,
his own people,
if we do not go back
to our foolish ways.
Surely he is ready to save
those who honour him,
and his saving presence
will remain in our land.
Love and faithfulness will meet;
righteousness and peace
will embrace.
Human loyalty will reach up
from the earth,
and God's righteousness
will look down from heaven.
The Lord will make us
prosperous,
and our land will produce
rich harvests.
Righteousness will go before
the Lord
and prepare the path for him.

Psalm 85: 8-13

"…righteousness and peace will embrace."

A promise of peace

She grew up in fear of being found out. Her "crime"? Being Jewish. Her father, fearing another anti-Semitic backlash, sent her to a Catholic school. He valiantly tried to hide his family's "true" identity, insisting that the children keep a dangerous secret. That was the plan. But the truth will out, and often in the most painful of circumstances.

Years later, when she had written a play about her childhood experiences, we arranged for a performance for the church community in which she grew up and the synagogue community her family could never face. The result was a cathartic emotional release for all concerned.

We used today's psalm in our publicity materials, to remind us of God's unqualified promise of a saving presence, no matter what.

**Dear God, when darkness overwhelms me,
let me always remember your promise of peace.**

God sent the angel Gabriel to a town in Galilee named Nazareth. He had a message for a young woman [whose] name was Mary…. The angel said, "Peace be with you! The Lord is with you!"

Mary was deeply troubled by the angel's message, and she wondered what his words meant. The angel said, "Don't be afraid, Mary; God has been gracious to you. You will become pregnant and give birth to a son, and you will name him Jesus. He will be great and will be called the Son of the Most High God…."

Mary said, "I am a virgin. How, then, can this be?" The angel answered, "The Holy Spirit will come on you, and God's power will rest upon you. For this reason the holy child will be called the Son of God."

Luke 1: 26-38

"Mary was deeply troubled by the angel's message…"

The voice of an angel

Angels! Mary is visited by an angel with a message that is so very clear. And when Mary asks questions, she gets clear answers. But what of me? Where are my clear answers? It is often difficult to hear the voice of God or to see God's hand at work in my life.

This is the great challenge of our secular age. In the cold of winter, amidst global economic turmoil and bombarded by images of violence, can I hear the voice of an angel – in the laughter shared with a friend, in the offer of help from a colleague, in the hand of a child reaching out to hold mine?

And more, can I be the clear voice of the angel in my dealings with others?

Lord, help me see your hand at work in my life.
Help me choose to be a part of that work.

"What do you think a man does who has one hundred sheep and one of them gets lost? He will leave the other ninety-nine grazing on the hillside and go and look for the lost sheep. When he finds it, I tell you, he feels far happier over this one sheep than over the ninety-nine that did not get lost. In just the same way your Father in heaven does not want any of these little ones to be lost."

Matthew 18: 12-14

"...does not want any of these little ones to be lost."

These little ones

A few years ago, a friend agreed to take in foster children. It has been a real blessing, not only for the children whom she has loved and nurtured, but for many people in the community. One group raised money to build more rooms to accommodate the children; a retired man donated his time to work as a carpenter; others have offered to baby-sit.

As I listen to the stories of some of these "little ones," I find it hard to imagine the pain that they have experienced in their short lives. But, living in this loving environment, many of them blossom and thrive.

Some have remained only a short time; even so, I know that the loving care they have received has made a difference in their lives.

**God, show me where you need your word spoken,
your love shown.**

"Come to me, all of you who are tired from carrying heavy loads, and I will give you rest. Take my yoke and put it on you, and learn from me, because I am gentle and humble in spirit; and you will find rest. For the yoke I will give you is easy, and the load I will put on you is light."

Matthew 11: 28-30

"Come to me, all of you who are tired…"

Heavy burdens

I was at a farm auction once where an old, well-worn yoke came up for bid. I was overcome by a strong feeling of empathy for the farmer – as I imagined him carrying his heavy loads, day in and day out.

Despite all my modern conveniences, I feel like I carry huge loads every day: invisible loads of stress and anxiety. Others carry similar invisible burdens: depression, unreasonable expectations, guilt, remorse. "You look like you're carrying the weight of the world on your shoulders." "I thought I was hiding it pretty well."

That's the part that makes the burden even heavier – trying so hard to appear as though I'm walking light-footed through the world. If only I would stop and hand the burden over to Christ.

Help me with my burden, Lord. Help me to accept your yoke.

" I assure you that John the Baptist is greater than anyone who has ever lived. But the one who is least in the kingdom of heaven is greater than John. From the time John preached his message until this very day the kingdom of heaven has suffered violent attacks, and violent men try to seize it. Until the time of John all the prophets and the Law of Moses spoke about the kingdom; and if you are willing to believe their message, John is Elijah, whose coming was predicted. Listen, then, if you have ears!"   *Matthew 11: 11-15*

"From the time John preached his message..."

Waiting

In one of his children's books, Dr. Seuss describes a waiting place where people are "waiting perhaps for their Uncle Jake or a pot to boil, or a Better Break...." I always seem to be waiting... for rest from the relentless demands of being a single parent, for a phone call from a friend to cheer me up, for reconciliation with members of my family.

John upset people by telling them to stop waiting for the kingdom – it had already arrived! But they didn't want to listen; they might be called to look at their lives and perhaps change the way they were living.

Each year I await the birth of Jesus. How easy it is to forget that he is already here. How hard it is to stop waiting and to start living... now.

Lord, give me the courage to believe that you are with me here, and to live the truth of your kingdom now.

God sent the angel Gabriel to… a young woman promised in marriage to a man named Joseph…. The angel said to Mary, "Peace be with you! The Lord is with you and has greatly blessed you!"

Mary was deeply troubled by the angel's message, and she wondered what his words meant. The angel said, "Don't be afraid, Mary; God has been gracious to you. You will become pregnant and give birth to a son, and you will name him Jesus…." Mary said, "I am a virgin. How, then, can this be?" The angel answered, "The Holy Spirit will come on you, and God's power will rest upon you. For this reason the holy child will be called the Son of God…."

"I am the Lord's servant," said Mary; "may it happen to me as you have said."

Luke 1: 26-38

"…she wondered what his words meant."

A still point

Hidden among the folds of the Christmas narrative are significant moments that I often overlook. I tend to be drawn to the more dramatic events of the story: the splendour of the singing angels and the pageantry of the three kings.

In today's reading, however, there is a moment of silence (a rare thing in my own rush towards Christmas). After a remarkable visit from the angel, I imagine Mary suddenly finding herself alone – and yet not alone. Did she take a deep breath? Did she hear her own heart beating?

This moment – when Mary commits herself to this journey with God – holds the gift of stillness. And it reminds me to pause for a still point on my own hectic path towards Christmas.

**Jesus, I will take a moment of stillness
to hear my own "Yes" alongside that of Mary's.**

Listen to us, O Shepherd of Israel;
    hear us, leader of your flock....
    Look down from heaven at us;
come and save your people!
Come and save this grapevine that you planted,
this young vine you made grow so strong!
Our enemies have set it on fire and cut it down;
look at them in anger and destroy them!
Preserve and protect the people you have chosen,
the nation you made so strong.
We will never turn away from you again;
keep us alive, and we will praise you.

Psalm 80: 1-2, 14-18

> "Come and save this grapevine that you planted..."

A tender shoot

Fifteen years ago, their differences didn't seem to matter at all. They met at a meeting, and they were attracted by the kinds of questions the other asked. They began dating, fell in love, and married. The fact that he was Muslim and she was Catholic wasn't insurmountable. In fact, they were amazed at how much they had in common: so much of the scriptures and a love for their own traditions.

But this year, Ramadan and Christmas have become very painful. Cruel, vicious taunts leave their children in tears and hating to go to school. Although Muslims are a small minority, they are feared and misunderstood.

They seek comfort in their own religious traditions and tell themselves that theirs is a tender shoot which the Lord has planted.

God, you have created a world of great diversity.
Help me be aware of the variety in your garden.

Be joyful always, pray at all times, be thankful in all circumstances. This is what God wants from you in your life in union with Christ Jesus.

Do not restrain the Holy Spirit; do not despise inspired messages. Put all things to the test: keep what is good and avoid every kind of evil.

May the God who gives us peace make you holy in every way and keep your whole being – spirit, soul, and body – free from every fault at the coming of our Lord Jesus Christ. He who calls you will do it, because he is faithful.

1 Thessalonians 5: 16-24

"...be thankful in all circumstances."

Counting my blessings

Right about now I begin worrying that Christmas might get away from me... again.

Instead of feeling blessed by the season, I start down the familiar path of self-criticism: Whom did I overlook? (I knew I should have sent them a card!) Why do I try to pack so much in? (Okay, three commitments on Christmas Day might be too much.) How could I have forgotten? (What distant cousin showed up last year with presents for all my kids?)

Enough! This season holds many blessings. It was nice to get a card from that old friend. The kids will have a great time on Christmas Day. And our gift will be our presence – warmly given. Yes, this year I will head in a new direction, with thanks.

Thank you, God, for the many blessings of this season: people.

The chief priests and the elders came to Jesus and asked, "What right do you have to do these things? Who gave you such right?"

Jesus answered them, "I will ask you just one question, and if you give me an answer, I will tell you what right I have to do these things. Where did John's right to baptize come from...?" "What shall we say? If we answer, 'From God,' he will say to us, 'Why, then, did you not believe John?' But if we say, 'From human beings,' we are afraid of what the people might do, because they are all convinced that John was a prophet." So they answered Jesus, "We don't know." And he said to them, "Neither will I tell you, then, by what right I do these things." *Matthew 21:23-27*

"Who gave you such right?"

True authority

Because I grew up in the rebellious 1960s, I instinctively don't like being bossed around or being told what to do. So I can understand the resentment the chief priests and elders felt at Jesus' authority, and can easily imagine the anger in their voices: "Who put you in charge?"

It can be hard to accept authority – even true authority, the kind that comes from within rather than from a job title. Maybe especially true authority. If authority is assigned, then it's only accidental or temporary, and not fundamental. That's how the chief priests, so modern in their attitude, want to understand Jesus' authority.

Accepting true authority requires humility and a willingness to follow. And who among us is happy to do that?

Lord, help me to follow you with patience and a willing heart.

"There was once a man who had two sons. He went to the older one and said, 'Son, go and work in the vineyard today.' 'I don't want to,' he answered, but later he changed his mind and went. Then the father went to the other son and said the same thing. 'Yes, sir,' he answered, but he did not go. Which of the two did what his father wanted?"

"The older one," they answered. So Jesus said, "I tell you: the tax collectors and the prostitutes are going into the kingdom of God ahead of you. For John the Baptist came to you showing you the right path to take, and you would not believe him; but the tax collectors and the prostitutes believed him. Even when you saw this, you did not later change your minds and believe him."   *Matthew 21: 28-32*

> "Which of the two did what his father wanted?"

Words and actions

Our two children had very different personalities. Our daughter was bubbly, effervescent, always willing to help. Our son, by contrast, was serious, solemn, and often withdrawn.

One day we had some yard work to do: leaves to rake, shrubs to prune, weeds to pull. "Do you two feel like helping?" we asked, as we went outside. "Not me," said our son. "I've got homework to do."

"Sure," said our daughter. "I'll be glad to help." But she never did. The phone rang; a friend mentioned the magic word, "party." Our daughter disappeared out the front door. My wife and I were bundling up the prunings when we realized we had a third person working with us. It was our son.

Jesus' parables aren't stories that happened long ago. They're still happening today.

**My professions of faith aren't worth much, God,
if I merely express them with words.**

Thﬁis is the list of the ancestors of Jesus Christ, a descendant of David, who was a descendant of Abraham. From Abraham to King David: Abraham, Isaac, Jacob, Judah and his brothers; then Perez and Zerah (their mother was Tamar), Hezron, Ram, Amminadab, Nahshon, Salmon, Boaz (his mother was Rahab), Obed (his mother was Ruth), Jesse, and King David. From David to the time when the people of Israel were taken into exile in Babylon: David, Solomon (his mother was the woman who had been Uriah's wife), Rehoboam, Abijah, Asa, Jehoshaphat, Jehoram, Uzziah, Jotham, Ahaz, Hezekiah, Manasseh, Amon, Josiah, and Jehoiachin and his brothers. From the time after the exile in Babylon to the birth of Jesus: Jehoiachin, Shealtiel, Zerubbabel, Abiud, Eliakim, Azor, Zadok, Achim, Eliud, Eleazar, Matthan, Jacob, and Joseph, who married Mary, the mother of Jesus, who was called the Messiah.   *Matthew 1: 1-17*

> "This is the list of the ancestors of Jesus Christ..."

Connections

Family trees give us pause. Last summer I went to a family reunion and met many cousins I'd never known while growing up. The reason we never knew each other was because of a perceived slight that happened at my grandmother's wake – sixty-three years ago! Many families will recognize this severing of family ties.

What happens in families happens in neighbourhoods, races and countries, too. And, in every case, we're the worse for it. The story of Jesus' lineage is a poetic attempt at providing connections. The names themselves read like poetry. I think we, too, need that same poetry of connections in our own lives. Not necessarily back to kings, but to our own kin – both living and dead.

Lord, give me the patience, love and respect for others that allow me to stay connected.

This was how the birth of Jesus Christ took place. His mother Mary was engaged to Joseph, but before they were married, she found out that she was going to have a baby by the Holy Spirit. Joseph was a man who always did what was right, but he did not want to disgrace Mary publicly; so he made plans to break the engagement privately. While he was thinking about this, an angel of the Lord appeared to him in a dream and said, "Joseph, descendant of David, do not be afraid to take Mary to be your wife. For it is by the Holy Spirit that she has conceived...."

Now all this happened in order to make come true what the Lord had said through the prophet, "A virgin will become pregnant and have a son, and he will be called Immanuel" (which means, "God is with us").   *Matthew 1: 18-24*

> "...who always did what was right..."

God-with-us

An unexpected pregnancy. With no committed relationship within which to raise the child. She agonizes over what to do. Throughout her life she has always tried to do "what is right." She considers her future – living either as a single mother or as a woman who has had an abortion. And she doesn't know what is "right" anymore.

Where is God's comforting presence in this time of fear, of confusion? She desperately wants to believe that God is with her – and will always be with her. She struggles, given her family and religious background. Will she be "disgraced" regardless of which path she chooses?

She strains to hear God's promise – made real in Jesus – to be-with-her always.

God, be with me when I struggle to find my way through the dark times of uncertainty and fear.

One day Zechariah was doing his work as a priest in the Temple, taking his turn in the daily service.... An angel of the Lord appeared to him, and said to him, "Don't be afraid, Zechariah! God has heard your prayer, and your wife Elizabeth will bear you a son. You are to name him John...."

Zechariah said to the angel, "How shall I know if this is so? I am an old man, and my wife is old also." "I am Gabriel," the angel answered.... "Because you have not believed, you will be unable to speak; you will remain silent until the day my promise to you comes true."

The people were waiting for Zechariah. When he came out, he could not speak to them, and so they knew that he had seen a vision in the Temple. Unable to say a word, he made signs to them with his hands.
Luke 1: 5-25

"Unable to say a word, he made signs to them..."

Silence and wonder

Today's reading calls me to silence. In the pre-Christmas rush, so many different messages vie for my attention. But hearing Zechariah's story, I find my heart drawn to stillness. With him, I feel moved to a silent awe which seeks to be attentive to the mysterious working of God.

Zechariah had no choice. He had to wait – in silence – for a birth that was beyond his rational understanding. Within all the clamour of the season, can I allow myself a few moments of silence to wait for the simple birth of Jesus?

God's decision that Jesus enter our world as a helpless infant goes beyond my understanding. Instead, given quiet space, it calls me to an attitude of profound wonder.

**God, prepare my heart in silence
for the coming mystery of your birth.**

The Lord sent another message to Ahaz: "Ask the Lord your God to give you a sign. It can be from deep in the world of the dead or high up in heaven." Ahaz answered, "I will not ask for a sign. I refuse to put the Lord to the test."

To that Isaiah replied, "Listen, now, descendants of King David. It's bad enough for you to wear out the patience of people – do you have to wear out God's patience too? Well, then, the Lord himself will give you a sign: a young woman who is pregnant will have a son and will name him 'Immanuel.'" (This name in Hebrew means "God is with us.")

Make your plans! But they will never succeed. Talk all you want to! But it is all useless, because God is with us.

Isaiah 7: 10-14, 8: 10

> "...the Lord himself will give you a sign..."

A fierce love

Nearly six years ago my seven-year-old son and I had a terrible scene: a great stubborn match over bath time. As I finally picked him up and carried him to the tub, he screamed and beat my shoulders with his fists.

In my own anger I responded, "Ben, if you really want to hurt me, just hit me in the face." To my shame he just kept on wailing and said, "No!" "Why?" I challenged. "Because I love you!" he screamed in reply.

I did not know such a fierce love existed that could restrain itself, proclaim itself, in the midst of a temper tantrum. At this low point in my fathering, God's presence showed up as a sign unasked for, but given anyway.

Holy Spirit, keep me open to those signs you send me, especially when I am not looking for them.

I n the sixth month of Elizabeth's pregnancy God sent the angel Gabriel to... a young woman promised in marriage to a man named Joseph. Her name was Mary. The angel came to her and said... "Don't be afraid, Mary; God has been gracious to you. You will become pregnant and give birth to a son, and you will name him Jesus...." Mary said to the angel, "I am a virgin. How, then, can this be?" The angel answered, "The Holy Spirit will come on you, and God's power will rest upon you. For this reason the holy child will be called the Son of God. Remember your relative Elizabeth. It is said that she cannot have children, but she herself is now six months pregnant, even though she is very old. For there is nothing that God cannot do."

"I am the Lord's servant," said Mary; "may it happen to me as you have said."   *Luke 1: 26-38*

"...may it happen to me as you have said."

Anything is possible

As I write this reflection, my daughter (her name is Elizabeth) is undergoing another round of treatments to enable her to have a baby. By the time this reflection is published, we will have had an answer. Maybe during these last days of Advent, my daughter, her husband and all who love them will be rejoicing with Mary and Elizabeth, marvelling at God's power. Or maybe, once again, we will be trying to submit graciously to God's mysterious will.

Although I'm praying for a successful outcome, my most fervent prayer is that my daughter's trust in God not be shaken by these experiences. I pray that she can embrace the outcome, as Mary did, from the bottom of her heart. Only then will she be truly happy.

Lord, there is no peace without accepting your will.
Help me to see this.

M ary said, "My heart praises the Lord; my soul is glad because of God my Saviour, for he has remembered me, his lowly servant! From now on all people will call me happy, because of the great things the Mighty God has done for me. His name is holy; from one generation to another he shows mercy to those who honour him. He has stretched out his mighty arm and scattered the proud with all their plans. He has brought down mighty kings from their thrones, and lifted up the lowly. He has filled the hungry with good things, and sent the rich away with empty hands. He has kept the promise he made to our ancestors, and has come to the help of his servant Israel. He has remembered to show mercy to Abraham and to all his descendants forever!" *Luke 1: 46-56*

> "...he has remembered me, his lowly servant!"

Youthful servants

Children figure prominently in these ritual-filled days before Christmas. Given Mary's age when she first spoke these amazing words, this strikes me as appropriate. Today's reading forces me to reconsider the connection between wisdom and age.

I usually find it hard to accept such wisdom from "kids," although there are some notable exceptions. Mozart was eight years old when he wrote his first symphony, and fourteen when he began writing string quartets. That's the same age as Joan of Arc when "voices" changed her life, and French history. Here in Canada, Craig Kielburger was only twelve years old when he first established "Free the Children," intended to improve the condition of child workers in the Third World. He's even been nominated for a Nobel Peace Prize.

Youthful, lowly servants, indeed!

Dear God, help me to understand that being older is not linked to being more in tune with you!

The time came for Elizabeth to have her baby, and she gave birth to a son....

When the baby was a week old, they came to circumcise him, and they were going to name him Zechariah, after his father. But his mother said, "No! His name is to be John!" They said to her, "But you don't have any relative with that name!" Then they made signs to his father, asking him what name he would like the boy to have. Zechariah asked for a writing pad and wrote, "His name is John." How surprised they all were! At that moment Zechariah was able to speak again, and he started praising God. The neighbours were all filled with fear, and the news about these things spread through all the hill country of Judea.

Luke 1: 57-66

"His name is to be John."

A God-given name

One of our sons, when quite young, asked us how we knew his name when he was born. He was amazed that we'd gotten it right, given that he'd been unable to tell us himself.

To my son, his name is inseparable from who he is – they are one and the same. And he also felt that he'd been given his name before he was born, just as God told Jeremiah, "Before I formed you in the womb, I knew you."

John the Baptist was named before he was born, and this was seen as a sign of God's favour. Each of us has a unique name spoken by God. We can open ourselves to a life in God if we cherish this God-given name and identity.

**I pray that I will hear you speaking my name, Lord,
at this blessed time, as you have spoken it all my life.**

King David said to the prophet Nathan, "Here I am living in a house built of cedar, but God's Covenant Box is kept in a tent!" That night the Lord said to Nathan, "Go and tell my servant David that I say to him, 'You are not the one to build a temple for me to live in.... When you die and are buried with your ancestors, I will make one of your sons king and will keep his kingdom strong. He will be the one to build a temple for me, and I will make sure that his dynasty continues forever.... You will always have descendants, and I will make your kingdom last forever. Your dynasty will never end.'"

2 Samuel 7: 1-5, 8-12, 16

"Your dynasty will never end."

A living legacy

David wanted to build a monument to himself, and so did I. A friend and I founded a publishing house. When we retired, our former employees took over. The other day, they presented their brand new educational program, called "Seasons of the Spirit."

When we first hired most of these people, they lacked self-confidence. They saw themselves as technicians, doing what they were told. They didn't speak up. They let others make decisions.

Now those same people are running meetings. Making speeches. Interpreting theological concepts. Negotiating contracts involving millions of dollars. After their presentation, I thought, "We must have done something right." Nathan told David his legacy would be a people, not a building. I can understand that now.

Lord, if I enable a few people to become more than they thought they could be, I'll be satisfied.

While they were in Bethlehem, the time came for Mary to have her baby. She gave birth to her first son, wrapped him in cloths and laid him in a manger – there was no room for them to stay in the inn.

There were some shepherds… who were spending the night in the fields, taking care of their flocks. An angel of the Lord appeared to them, and the glory of the Lord shone over them. They were terribly afraid, but the angel said to them, "Don't be afraid! I am here with good news for you, which will bring great joy to all the people. This very day in David's town your Saviour was born – Christ the Lord…."

The shepherds said to one another, "Let's go to Bethlehem and see this thing that has happened." *Luke 2: 1-16*

"Let's go… see this thing that has happened."

Tasting the miracle

My son was born just before Christmas six years ago. In the weeks before his birth, I often thought about Mary. When I registered at the local hospital's birthing centre, I was told that the demand for the two birthing rooms was so high that some women had to be turned away. I was lucky: there was "room at the inn" for me.

A few hours after the birth, a close friend came to visit. As she held my newborn son, her face lit up in wonder. "Now I know how the shepherds felt," she said, tasting the miracle.

Her words have stayed with me. Jesus is there ahead of me, with me, all the time. Will I, like the shepherds, hurry off to find him?

Jesus, you are always here with me. Help me to be open to you even when I feel you are a million miles away.

Hear me! Save me now!
Be my refuge
to protect me;
my defence to save me.
You are my refuge and defence;
guide me and lead me
as you have promised….
I place myself in your care.
You will save me, Lord;
you are a faithful God….
I will be glad and rejoice
because of your constant love.
You see my suffering;
you know my trouble….
I am always in your care;
save me from my enemies,
from those who persecute me.
Look on your servant
with kindness;
save me in your constant love.

Psalm 31: 2-3, 5, 7, 15-16

"I place myself in your care."

Trusting God

I understand worry and fear, and even despair. I have felt them all and know I will feel them again. But I marvel at the other half of today's psalm – the part I'm not very good at – the part that shows a trust in God that is childlike in its unshakable confidence.

When I have fallen into a black emptiness, part of its grip comes from feeling that I'm alone, that there is no one to call to, no one to help me. It's so dark I can barely see my own hand in front of my face, let alone the hand of anyone else.

In today's psalm I'm told if I only put my hand in God's, I will be rescued. Can I do it?

Lord, I'm never alone. Help me see your light in the darkness.

E arly on Sunday morning, Mary Magdalene went to the tomb and saw that the stone had been taken away from the entrance. She went running to Simon Peter and the other disciple, whom Jesus loved, and told them, "They have taken the Lord from the tomb, and we don't know where they have put him!"

Then Peter and the other disciple went to the tomb. The two of them were running, but the other disciple ran faster than Peter and reached the tomb first. He bent over and saw the linen cloths, but he did not go in. Behind him came Simon Peter, and he went straight into the tomb. He saw the linen cloths lying there and the cloth which had been around Jesus' head.... Then the other disciple... also went in; he saw and believed.   *John 20: 1-8*

"The two of them were running..."

God's gift

As I read about people running in the early morning, I am reminded of the way my kids used to thunder down the stairs early on Christmas morning to see what was under the tree. What great and unexpected surprises would they find?

But here, early on Easter morning, it's a different kind of running. Mary Magdalene, Peter and John are running – not with excitement and anticipation – but in horror and fear. They are anxious about what has been taken away from them, not about what they might receive.

But what they find is better than any Christmas present could possibly be! At first only John understands what they have been given: the empty tomb is full to bursting with God's presence.

Lord, this is a time for giving and receiving gifts.
Help me to recognize the gifts I have been given.

It was faith that made Abraham obey when God called him to go out to a country which God had promised to give him. He left his own country without knowing where he was going....

It was faith that made Abraham able to become a father, even though he was too old and Sarah herself could not have children. He trusted God to keep his promise....

It was faith that made Abraham offer his son Isaac as a sacrifice when God put Abraham to the test. Abraham was the one to whom God had made the promise, yet he was ready to offer his only son as a sacrifice. God had said to him, "It is through Isaac that you will have the descendants I promised."

Hebrews 11:8, 11-12, 17-18

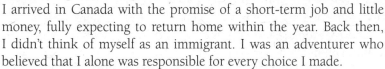

"...without knowing where he was going."

Journey of faith

I said "*Au revoir*" to Britain in 1974 without realizing that I really meant "Goodbye." I arrived in Canada with the promise of a short-term job and little money, fully expecting to return home within the year. Back then, I didn't think of myself as an immigrant. I was an adventurer who believed that I alone was responsible for every choice I made.

Still here more than a quarter of a century later, I now view this experience somewhat differently. My journey continues along an unknown itinerary, but now I realize I have never been travelling alone. I look back in amazement at all the ways God nudged me at a particular fork in the road, though at the time I rarely asked for help.

Dear God, let me discover the ways you continue to make your presence felt in my life.

T he time came for Joseph and Mary to perform the ceremony of purification.... At that time there was a man named Simeon living in Jerusalem. He was a good, God-fearing man.... Led by the Spirit, Simeon went into the Temple. When the parents brought the child Jesus into the Temple to do for him what the Law required, Simeon took the child in his arms and gave thanks to God....

Simeon blessed them and said to Mary, his mother, "This child is chosen by God for the destruction and the salvation of many in Israel. He will be a sign from God which many people will speak against and so reveal their secret thoughts. And sorrow, like a sharp sword, will break your own heart." *Luke 2: 22-35*

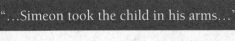

"...Simeon took the child in his arms..."

Symbol of hope

Technically, the purification was Mary's. Jewish law considered a woman unclean for one week after the birth of a son, two weeks for a daughter. One week also coincided with the proper timing for circumcision of a boy.

So they took Jesus to the Temple, and an old man saw them as the fulfillment of his dreams.

Babies have that effect. Shortly after our son died, a young couple brought a baby to church for baptism. I wanted to warn them what grief that child might someday bring them. But I couldn't. To them, to the gathered congregation, the baby was a sign of hope, a symbol of commitment to the future.

Dear God, you entered this world as a helpless infant.
What faith you had in human love!

P raise the Lord, all people on earth;
 praise his glory and might.
 Say to all the nations, "The Lord is king!
The earth is set firmly in place and cannot be moved;
he will judge the peoples with justice."
Be glad, earth and sky!
Roar, sea, and every creature in you;
be glad, fields, and everything in you!
The trees in the woods will shout for joy
when the Lord comes to rule the earth.
He will rule the peoples of the world
with justice and fairness.

Psalm 96: 7-13

> "…he will judge the peoples with justice."

Where is the justice?

Another election over, another one soon to follow. And what has changed? Nothing. During the 1900s the world's population quadrupled. Since the 1700s food production per acre has increased a hundred fold, yet half the world is hungry. War is now a threat or reality everywhere; and this war's friend was last war's enemy. Is there no end to the suffering?

Where is justice found in the strong trampling on the weak? Does one religion have the right to try to obliterate its rival? How can I love my enemy with a knife at my throat?

In today's psalm David celebrates the coming of God's kingdom. His words strengthen my hope that, one day, there will be justice and a return to honour.

Lord, thank you for your promise of a just world.

I n the beginning the Word already existed; the Word was with God, and the Word was God. From the very beginning the Word was with God. Through him God made all things; not one thing in all creation was made without him. The Word was the source of life, and this life brought light to people. The light shines in the darkness, and the darkness has never put it out....

The Word became a human being and, full of grace and truth, lived among us. We saw his glory, the glory which he received as the Father's only Son....

No one has ever seen God. The only Son, who is the same as God and is at the Father's side, he has made him known.   *John 1: 1-18*

"The Word became a human being..."

Word made flesh

Words are easy. It's flesh and blood – being a human being – that are the hard things. What risks must I take, what price must I pay, in order to make my words become flesh and blood?

I have a friend who walks with the shuffling gait of old men. He's a war hero, but those who remember his bravery and his dashing good looks are now dead. He is old before his time: leg blown apart by shrapnel, spirit seared by the horrors he has seen. Like Jesus, he paid the price of making his words become flesh.

And me? How much am I willing to risk? How far will I go to make my words become flesh, in order to become a true human being?

**Dear God, help me have the courage
to become a true human being.**

List of Contributors

Kelly Adams
Tony Adams
Ian Adnams
Dale C. Balkovec
Mary Bastedo
Rosalee Bender
Rick Benson
Louisa Blair
Ina Mae Brooks
Kevin Burns
Alex Campbell
Mary Ellen Chown
Mike Cooke
Regina Coupar
Jim Creskey
Rebecca Cunningham
Helga Doermer

Karen Fee
Patrick Gallagher
George Gilliland
Barbara Green
Caryl Green
Maryanne Hannan
Maura Hanrahan
Charles Harrel
Krystyna Higgins
Karen Johnson
Phil Kelly
Nancy Keyes
Marilyn Kreyer
Bertha Madott
Anne Louise Mahoney
Marguerite McDonald
Jim McSheffrey

John Mihevc
Marilyn Moore
RoseMarie Morris
Rosemary O'Hearn
Michael Reist
Kathy Shaidle
April Strauch
Jim Taylor
Marie-Louise Ternier-
    Gommers
Donald Walker
Pamela Walker
David Weiss
Susie Whelehan
Geoffrey Whitney-
    Brown

Photographs

Photographs are from Photos.com except for the following:

January – 1: Ingram; 9: Novalis; 25: S. Skjold.

February – 4: W.P. Wittman; 8: S. Skjold; 9: Jupiter Images; 14: Ingram; 21: W.P. Wittman.

March – 2: Ingram; 11: J. Boutin; 12: Ingram; 13: Plaisted 16: Novalis (G. Savoie); 25: Jupiter Images.

April – 1: J.L. Frund; 2: H. Remillard; 8: Ingram; 16: Cerac; 20: Jupiter Images; 27: J. Harpell; 30: Jupiter Images.

May – 6: Jupiter Images; 12: W.P. Wittman; 21: G. Larche; 25: W.P. Wittman.

June – 14: Jupiter Images; 20: W.P. Wittman; 27: Ingram.

July – 4: W.P. Wittman; 17: J. Boutin; 26: S. Skjold.

August – 6: Jupiter Images.

September –5: Ingram; 15: S. Skjold; 17: Comstock.

October – 5: Novalis; 8: W.P. Wittman; 10: S. Skjold; 22: W.P. Wittman; 25: Cléo; 28: Ingram.

November – 17: Comstock; 28: Jupiter Images.

December – 10: Ingram; 14: W.P. Wittman; 29: Jupiter Images; 31 W.P. Wittman.